The Supreme Court and
Religion in American Life

_____

NEW FORUM BOOKS

Robert P. George, Series Editor

A list of titles in the series appears at
the back of the book

The Supreme Court and Religion in American Life

VOLUME I
THE ODYSSEY OF
THE RELIGION CLAUSES

James Hitchcock

PRINCETON UNIVERSITY PRESS

PRINCETON AND OXFORD

Library of Congress Cataloging-in-Publication Data
Hitchcock, James.
The Supreme Court and religion in American life / James Hitchcock.
p. cm.
Includes bibliographical references and index.
Contents: 1. The odyssey of the religion clauses
ISBN: 0-691-11696-2 (v. 1 : alk. paper) —
ISBN: 0-691-11923-6 (v. 2 : alk. paper)
1. Church and state — United States — History. 2. Freedom of religion —
United States — History. I. Title.

KF4865.H58 2004
342.7308'52—dc22   2004040722

British Library Cataloging-in-Publication Data is available

This book has been composed in Sabon
Printed on acid-free paper. ∞
pup.princeton.edu
Printed in the United States of America
1 3 5 7 9 10 8 6 4 2

To Consuelo

My Favorite Lawyer

CONTENTS

The Supreme Court and
Religion in American Life

Introduction to Volume 1

THIS VOLUME justifies itself on the grounds that, surprising in view of all the attention lavished on the subject, there are a number of significant religion cases that came before the Supreme Court prior to World War II that have been ignored or whose significance has been slighted. For example, the famous *Dartmouth College* case (1819) is almost always treated exclusively as a landmark in the development of the law of contract, despite significant issues concerning religious liberty. This volume provides the most comprehensive survey of the religion cases that has yet been published and can be used, independent of volume 2, as an overall survey of the historical development of the jurisprudence of the Religion Clauses.

The volume endeavors to show, by close attention to cases, that World War II marked a quite precise watershed in the understanding of the Religion Clauses—after 1940 they were interpreted in increasingly innovative ways. The conclusion seeks to explain that development in terms of constitutional doctrine.

The terms "separationist" and "accommodationist" are used here in a commonsense way—separationists are people who believe that government should give as little support to religion as possible, accommodationists those who argue that it is proper for government to support religion provided it does not do so in ways that infringe religious liberties.

Chapter One

THE KINGDOM OF THIS WORLD

ONE OF THE INHERENT PARADOXES of religion is that most faiths enjoin a spirit of unworldliness, urging believers to look beyond earthly possessions in their search for ultimate reality, while at the same time all religions exist in the temporal order and can only manifest themselves through material realities. Hence organized religions have usually been quick to secure their property rights, justifying this on the grounds that material assets are necessary in order to witness the reality of the spiritual.

Most civil cases in the American judicial system involve disputes over property, and courts have perhaps been most comfortable when adjudicating issues that can be quantified in terms of wealth. It has been the Supreme Court's consistent policy, almost always followed, to ignore what could be called ideological issues in dealing with internal church disputes and to content itself with applying ecclesiastical rules in the ways such rules were apparently intended. Property cases, while perhaps not the most interesting or significant to arise under the Religion Clauses of the Constitution, were the earliest and have been the most persistent. Religious bodies that claim broad autonomy with respect to their beliefs and practices nonetheless submit to the civil law for the final resolution of otherwise irresolvable disagreements over possessions.

Disputes over church property arguably involve both the Religion Clauses, in that religious freedom is potentially threatened if the government is called upon to intervene in religious disputes, and government thereby risks taking upon itself the improper role of favoring one religious group over another. Property cases have come before the Court in almost every era, however, and almost always at the behest of church members themselves.

COLONIAL LAND GRANTS

The first religion cases ever to come before the Court, in 1815, were disputes of this kind, arising out of grants of land made by the English Crown in colonial times.

In *Terrett v. Taylor*[1] the churchwardens of a Virginia Episcopal parish attempted to sell some of the parish land but were opposed by the local overseers of the poor, who contended that the land no longer belonged to the church, under a Virginia statute repealing ecclesiastical land grants made to the Anglican Church by the British Crown.[2]

Justice Joseph Story found that the land in question was in fact not a gift from the Crown but had been purchased by the parish. But even if the Crown had granted it, he continued, the grant could not be revoked unless it was shown that it was originally intended to be revocable.[3]

Later in the same year, the Court heard a case involving a royal grant of land to the Church of England in a town that had been part of the colony of New Hampshire but was now in the state of Vermont.[4]

At the time of the grant (1761) there was no Anglican parish in the town of Pawlet, and not until 1802 did a group of residents organize a parish of the Episcopal Church, which then claimed the land and leased it for the support of the parish. Between 1790 and 1805 the state of Vermont passed and repealed a series of seemingly contradictory laws concerning colonial grants to the Anglican Church, and the latest of these had abolished all claims that churches might make under such grants. The state of Vermont now claimed the land, intending to use the income to support education.[5]

The state argued that, since there was no Anglican church in Pawlet to receive the grant at the time it was made, the grant was void and had reverted to the donor. Since the donor was the English Crown, the land in turn passed to the state of Vermont after the Revolution.

The Church of England as a whole could not receive such grants, Vermont argued, since in English law it was not a corporation but one of the "estates of the realm." Grants to the church could only be made to specific units of the church, such as parishes. Also relevant was the fact that the Church of England was never officially established in the colony of New Hampshire.[6]

Vermont also raised an issue as much ecclesiastical as legal, claiming that, despite "similarities" between the Church of England and the Episcopal Church in the United States, the American church was not identifiable with the English church and could not inherit any rights the Anglican Church might have possessed.[7]

The defense argued that the land in question had been granted to the inhabitants of Pawlet collectively for the support of religion, thus there had been a grantee to receive it. The Crown knew there was no Anglican parish in Pawlet at the time and thus intended the grant to be held in abeyance for future use. The Episcopal Church was the natural recipient of the grant, a fact that for a brief period Vermont law had explicitly recognized.[8]

The case came before the Supreme Court because it involved two separate states—New Hampshire and Vermont—along with the Crown of England. However, Vermont challenged the jurisdiction of the Court, claiming that only one state was involved, since Vermont and New Hampshire had been one at the time of the original grant. Thus the case should simply be tried in Vermont state courts.[9]

Story again rendered the verdict of the Court, quickly disposing of the jurisdictional question by finding that, since Vermont and New Hampshire were now separate states, their previous unity was irrelevant.[10]

The royal grant made clear that the land was to be divided among various individuals and the church land was not to be held in common, Story found. The Church of England was indeed an estate of the realm rather than a corporation, and as such could not receive grants. There was no branch of the Church of England in Pawlet at the time of the grant and for some years afterward.[11]

Based on English law, he defined a parish as "a consecrated place having attached to it rights of burial and the administration of the sacraments." The parson of a parish had the "care of souls" only for the duration of his own life, and any grant made to a parish would thus be held in abeyance if there was no parson. Had there been an Anglican parson in Pawlet at the time of the grant, it would have been made to him and to his successors, but officially there could have been no parson until there was first a parish. The charter of colonial New Hampshire explicitly guaranteed liberty of conscience in matters of religion, and the Church of England was not established there.[12]

Since the grant for the church was made to the inhabitants of the town, such land could be alienated only by the joint action of both the Crown and the citizens, with the rights of the Crown passing to the state after the Revolution.[13]

Story characterized the Episcopal Church established in Pawlet as "a mere voluntary association" and held that it could not claim the rights of the Anglican Church merely "on account of their religious tenets."[14]

Justice William Johnson wrote a concurring opinion complaining that Story relied too much on English law and precedents.[15]

These two pioneer religion cases were decided in the same year but in seemingly opposite ways because the Anglican Church had been officially established in Virginia before the Revolution but not in New Hampshire. Thus the Virginia Episcopal parish could show an unbroken history dating to colonial times, while the New Hampshire parish was treated as a recent creation not in continuity with the prerevolutionary Anglican Church.

In 1823 an English group, the Society for the Propagation of the Gospel in Foreign Parts, sued to regain land that, as in the *Pawlet case*, had been granted in the colony of New Hampshire by King George III in 1761. Also as in the *Pawlet* case, there was an appeal against the postrevolutionary statute by which Vermont claimed the land and authorized leasing it for the support of schools.[16]

The issue took on a complexity beyond the *Pawlet* case when Vermont cited the fact that in England all religious bodies were subject to the Statute of Mortmain and had to be granted an exemption by the king in order to acquire property. Such exemptions were not granted in the colonies, Vermont insisted. The state also asserted that, since the SPGFP's trustees were in England, they could not be made subject to American courts and thus could not be held accountable for the proper use of the land.[17]

Justice Bushrod Washington ruled that the "dismemberment of empire" following the Revolution had not invalidated English land titles in America, the treaty ending the war (1783) specifically protecting such titles. The purposes of the SPGFP were "benevolent and laudable," and the property could not be alienated to a different kind of use.[18] Unlike in the *Pawlet* case, the SPGFP existed as a part of the Church of England in 1761 and was thus qualified to receive the grant.

In 1824 the *Terrett* issue was again before the Court, in the light of its decision in the *Pawlet* case.[19] The appellant had purchased land from the Alexandria parish following the *Terrett* decision. Now, however, he sued to invalidate the transaction, on the grounds that the *Pawlet* ruling had rendered his title suspect.

His contention was that the rights of the parish had to be exercised through its parson, and for a period of time, there had been none. In addition, the prerevolutionary parish had been designated "Fairfax Parish," whereas the putative owner of the disputed land called itself "Christ's Church Parish, Alexandria." As such it constituted merely a part of the original Fairfax parish and could not claim title to the land.[20]

As in 1815, Story found in favor of the parish, holding that according to the polity of the Episcopal Church, the vestry of Christ's Church was the legal successor of the vestry of Fairfax Parish. New Episcopal parishes could only be founded by authority of the diocesan bishop, and no such authorization was either sought or given for Christ's Church, thus demonstrating that it had long existed.[21]

No other land-grant case then came before the Court for almost seventy years.

In 1882 the Court rejected a claim by a Methodist mission society in Oregon.[22] The organization had received land in an Oregon town in 1847, while the territory was under British rule. When it became a territory of the United States the following year, Congress confirmed land grants made to missionary groups. However, because of Indian wars the mission did not occupy the land until 1850, and the mission was later abandoned. In 1850 the U.S. Army purchased part of the land from the mission, and in 1882 the town claimed the remainder on the grounds that the tract had originally been transferred "improvidently." Justice William B. Woods ruled that no land claim before 1850 was secure, and, since the missionary group was not occupying the land in 1848, it could not claim title.

In 1894 the Court heard another case arising out of the same situation.[23] In 1838 a Catholic mission in Oregon had been given the use of a tract of land by the Hudson's Bay Company. In 1849 the company sold most of the tract to the army, but in 1894 the church claimed title to all of the land. Justice David Brewer ruled that it was entitled only to that portion of the tract that was in use as a mission in 1849.

In 1907 the Court decided a case from Puerto Rico challenging the fact that two churches had been built with municipal funds. Chief Justice Melville Fuller again issued the ruling, which found that such grants, made in colonial times, were irrevocable.[24]

CAPACITY TO INHERIT

In 1819 the Court heard a case involving a complex issue of inheritance. In 1790 a Virginia man willed part of his estate to establish a fund for the education of Baptist youth, especially those inclined toward the ministry. Two years later Virginia repealed the English law of charities, hitherto in force in America, and because of this, the executors refused to implement the bequest. Chief Justice John Marshall ruled that the Philadelphia Baptist Association, never having been incorporated, could not receive the bequest as a legal entity, nor could its individual members obtain the money, since it had not been intended for their personal benefit.[25] (The case came before the Court under Article III, Section 2, of the Constitution—"diversity of citizenship"—because the disputants resided in different states.)

In 1866 the Court upheld a 1786 legacy to a Congregational parish in Hartford. The grant had been made "for the maintenance of the ministry of the Gospel," but in 1852 the parish had been granted permission by the Connecticut legislature to sell the property. Descendants of the original donor then sued for ownership of the land on the grounds that the terms of the grant had been violated. Justice Samuel Nelson found for the Court that the legislature had acted within its authority.[26]

In 1872 the Court upheld the right of a missionary group with headquarters in New York to acquire land in Illinois, the acquisition challenged by the heirs of a man who sold the land to the American and Foreign Christian Union. Justice John Marshall Harlan found that Illinois law did not prohibit a "foreign corporation" from acquiring land, nor did it prevent charitable organizations from doing so.[27]

A similar case, also from Illinois, was decided in the same way in 1887. Heirs sought to invalidate the will of a man who had left the residue of his estate to "the board of foreign and the board of home missions."[28]

Harlan saw no difficulty in the fact that the two mission boards were not more precisely identified, since elsewhere in the will the donor made clear that, having been an active Presbyterian all his life, he was referring to the Presbyterian Church in the United States. If the designation were truly unclear, Harlan thought, the legacy would have to be divided equally among all those groups having the same name. He again rejected the claim that the mission boards constituted "foreign bodies" forbidden to own property in Illinois.[29]

The appellants also pointed out that the law allowed only ten acres of land to groups "formed for the purpose of religious worship." However, Harlan ruled that the mission boards were not set up for "worship" but for "the spread of the Gospel."[30]

In 1879 the Court reached a conclusion similar to that in the 1819 Baptist testamentary case. A woman had made a will providing that, if at the time of her death she belonged to some Catholic religious community, all of her assets were to go to Bishop Richard Wheelan (or Whelan) of Wheeling, for the benefit of the community to which she belonged. When she died in 1861 she in fact did belong to the Sisters of St. Joseph, but the terms of her will were not carried out. In 1879 Bishop John J. Kain, Wheelan's successor, sued to gain possession of the estate. (The donor's surviving relatives did not reside in West Virginia, hence there was diversity of citizenship.)[31]

Justice William Strong found that Kain was competent to bring suit, since the bequest had been intended for the diocese of Wheeling, not for Wheelan personally, even though Kain was not a "corporation sole."[32] But the will could not be implemented as written, because of the uncertainty of the identity of the Sisters of St. Joseph. The group was not incorporated, and its membership was fluid, so there was legitimate doubt as to the intended recipients of the gift.[33]

Strong did not think the bequest could be treated as a charity, since the will did not specify that the assets be used for any charitable purpose. Instead, he thought, it seemed to be a "private benevolence," that is, a gift intended for the individuals constituting the Sisters of St. Joseph. They, however, had no corporate identity, hence no ability to inherit.[34]

COMMUNAL PROPERTY

One manifestation of the self-conscious democratic spirit of America in the nineteenth century was the phenomenon of experimental "utopian" communities that, among other things, commonly abolished rights of private property, often for religious reasons, an experiment bound to produce second thoughts on the part of some of those whose right to property had been surrendered. Each of the cases came before the Court because of diversity of citizenship.

In 1852 the heirs of a man who had belonged to a community called the Society of Separatists sued for a share of the group's property on the grounds that their ancestor, who died in 1827, had in effect invested in the community, which in the ensuing quarter century had become quite prosperous.[35]

Justice John McLean found that the ancestor had signed a document surrendering all claims to personal property, and nothing in that contract was against public policy or good morals. On the contrary, it was precisely the religious motivation of the group that had made possible its great prosperity. Although charges were made against the character of the group's leader, John M. Bimeler, the Court found that he performed admirably in a difficult position and that his actions were often misconstrued by "narrow minds."[36]

Over the next half century several cases were brought before the Court involving the Harmony Society, a German group under the leadership of George Rapp, that came to America early in the century and founded communities in Pennsylvania and Indiana. Among other things, the group espoused communal ownership of property and extolled frugality and hard work, so that over the years it became collectively wealthy.[37]

In 1856 a former member claimed that he had been wrongfully excluded from its benefits. Justice John Campbell found, as in the previous case, that the Society had explicitly excluded all claims to private property and that the appellant had signed a document to that effect, in which he acknowledged receiving money from the Society merely as a "donation." Although the appellant made allegations of "extreme tyranny" against the head of the Society, supposedly sufficient to impair its members' freedom, no evidence of this was presented in Court.[38]

In 1887 suit was brought by a man whose parents had joined the Society in Germany and immigrated with Rapp to America. The plaintiff, Elias Speidel, had left the community in 1831 and now claimed a share of the Society's assets as compensation for his and his parents' labor and for the property they had originally given to the Society. Speidel also claimed that Rapp had practiced conscious fraud and had exploited his followers' naïveté about worldly matters.[39]

Justice Horace Gray found that Speidel had no claim in equity because he had allowed more than fifty years to elapse from the time he left the Society. There could be no help for someone who "slept upon his rights." In addition, the terms of the Society's trust explicitly stated that the assets were for the benefit of the community as a whole, not of individuals. A claim concerning a trust was not strictly governed by the statute of limitations, Gray admitted, but a long delay did invalidate a claim in equity.[40]

In 1902 a descendant of deceased members of the Society sued for a share of its assets, on the grounds that in effect the Society had been dissolved. In 1890, according to the claim, one man, John Duss, had gained control of the assets and had "bought out" eighteen members of the Society. The remaining eight members were aged and infirm women with no understanding of business, and the Society could no longer be said to exist. Instead Duss was operating it as a commercial enterprise.[41]

Justice Joseph McKenna found that the Society had not been dissolved and thus the appellant had no claim to its assets. The historical record showed that "the cardinal principle of the Society was self-abnegation," thus members did not expect to be compensated for their labor or to be allowed to claim its property. The Society's rules provided for a "donation" to those who left the community.[42]

Fuller dissented. Although the property was to be held communally, Fuller noted that the title had in fact been vested in "George Rapp and Associates." A board of elders succeeded him at his death in 1847.[43]

Fuller cited a principle of law that, if a trust was "defeated," it ceased to exist and its assets should go to the heirs of those who originally established it, and he accepted the appellants' claim that the original purpose of the Society had ceased. Its membership had declined from over five hundred in 1827 to merely eight, and the fact that Duss paid some members to abandon their membership indicated that he recognized its dissolution. Duss alone was active in the running of the Society, and one man could not constitute a community.[44]

The majority of the Court noted that the members had not formally dissolved the Society. But Fuller doubted that they had the power to do so and thought it necessary for a court of equity to determine if in fact it had been dissolved, which Fuller thought it had. The current operation of the Society was inconsistent with its original purpose of "renunciation of worldly goods."[45]

In the last of these cases, in 1914, the Court ruled in a dispute involving a Catholic monastic order whose individual members had, over a period of more than eight hundred years, been renouncing all rights to personal property.

Augustin Wirth had for over fifty years belonged to the Order of St. Benedict (Benedictines) and had been stationed in various parts of the United States. He was an author whose writings had earned royalties, and at his death in 1904, the administrator of his estate claimed those royalties as Wirth's private property, while the Order claimed the money on the grounds that Wirth had taken a vow of poverty that precluded his owning property and that he had been allowed to keep his royalties only as a "concession," and only for works of charity.[46] (Wirth had belonged to a monastery in New Jersey but had died in Minnesota, hence there was diversity of citizenship.)

Justice Charles Evans Hughes found in favor of the Benedictines. Wirth had indeed taken a vow of poverty that forbade him to own property, and his superiors showed that he had merely been allowed to use his royalties, not to treat them as his property. Although Wirth's administrator objected that it was a violation of freedom to forbid monks to hold property, Hughes held that this renunciation had been voluntary and Wirth possessed the legal right to repudiate it if he chose. Hughes also observed that the commercial value of Wirth's writings probably derived largely from the fact of his being a monk.[47]

INTERNAL CHURCH DISPUTES

Internal religious disputes, usually involving doctrine, have occurred with great regularity in the history of religion and, however much they may turn on seemingly rarified spiritual questions, almost inevitably become disputes over the control of property, hence come before the secular courts.

In 1844, largely because of slavery, the Methodist Episcopal Church split into two parts—north and south—and in 1853 the southern branch brought suit for its share of a fund set up for the relief of needy clergy and their families.[48] The case turned on subtle points of church government and was the first in which the Court was forced to intervene in such a dispute.

The division between the two branches of the church had been authorized by the General Conference, the highest authority within the church. However, the northern church claimed that this approval had been contingent on subsequent approval by "annual conferences" held on a regional basis, and that such approval had been denied. Thus, according to the northern branch of the church, it alone was the true Methodist Episcopal Church and the southern group had seceded without authority. The southern branch alleged that, on the contrary, it had reached an agreement with the northern branch for an amicable separation, in which all assets were to be shared equitably.[49]

Nelson found that, if the 1844 division was unlawful, its unlawfulness affected both sides equally, so that neither could be deemed the official Methodist Episcopal Church. But the constitutions of the church, dating to 1784, showed the General Conference to be its highest governing body. Thus the division was legal, and the agreement to share assets was binding on the northern body.[50]

In a rather bizarre case in 1866 the Court was called upon to adjudicate a dispute over insurance, a dispute that turned on the polity of the Congregational Church.[51] (The case involved diversity of citizenship, the church and the insurance company being in different states.)

The trustees of a parish in Maine had insured its property with themselves as the beneficiaries, an arrangement made by one of the trustees who was an insurance agent. The congregation owed $15,000 to one of the trustees, William Chase, who in turn was indebted to his brother, also a trustee. William Chase used his share of the policy as security for the loan from his brother.[52]

In 1862 the church building burned down, but the insurers refused to pay William Chase's claim on the grounds that, as one of five trustees, he had only a partial claim and that he had no "insurable interest" in the church building.[53] (During the proceedings before the Court no one raised the possibility of arson or insurance fraud.)

Justice David Davis ruled that under Congregational polity the five trustees could designate William Chase to act in their name. The trustees had approved the insurance policy, hence the company was required to pay.[54]

The first Supreme Court case involving a theological dispute was decided in 1861,[55] when Presbyterian groups in New York and elsewhere sued to gain control of the Federal Street Meeting House in Boston. Established in 1735 as "Calvinist and Trinitarian," it had become Unitarian in 1815. Thus, the Presbyterians argued, "the trust is wholly perverted and abused." Justice Robert Grier ruled that the only relevant question was who controlled the property at the time of its civil incorporation in 1805, and he found that the group that did so was in legal continuity with those who adopted Unitarianism a decade later.

As early as the *Mason* case (1824), the Court had begun following the practice of scrutinizing the governing documents of religious groups in order to decide issues of property ownership or other forms of legal control, and in the *Meeting House* case it conspicuously declined an invitation to settle such disputes on theological grounds. Those principles were finally made explicit and general in *Watson v. Jones* (1872).[56]

The Presbyterian Church in the United States enacted a requirement that former slaveholders and former supporters of the Confederacy repudiate those loyalties in order to continue as church members in good standing. A Louisville congregation split over this rule, as did both the Louisville Presbytery and the Kentucky State Synod, thus giving rise to a property dispute. (Since some of the parishioners lived in Indiana, the case involved diversity of citizenship.)

Justice Samuel Miller defined the Court's duty as that of enforcing the established rules of the Presbyterian Church itself, which the bitter internal dispute could not alter, and he laid down a principle that would prove so useful that the Court would employ it ever afterward—it was the Court's duty to scrutinize the established governing documents of a church in order to decide who had final authority to make decisions.[57]

The Court was not to involve itself in religious issues as such, and in an often-quoted epigram, Miller proclaimed that, "The law knows no heresy and is committed to no dogma."[58] In the case at hand the Court found that the national body of the church had authority under established Presbyterian polity.[59]

However, Miller also allowed for an exception by which the courts might inquire into doctrine—in the case of property given to a church for a specific purpose, the courts could decide if it was being used in accord with the donor's specifications. Thus a church building dedicated to "the Holy Trinity" could not later be made into a Unitarian church,[60] a dictum that seemed to go against the Court's decision in the *Meeting House* case eleven years before. Miller's exception was an invitation to the Court to involve itself in theological disputes, an invitation that in fact it would never choose to accept.

In the same year as the *Watson* case, the Court also disposed of a case arising in a Congregationalist church, where two factions clashed over property and one "excommunicated" the other. The Court found that, according to Congregationalist polity, the majority should rule and the excommunication did not affect title to the property, which was still vested in the duly elected trustees.[61]

It was appropriate that the Court's governing principles for internal church disputes should have been formulated in a case involving Presbyterians, since the latter denomination would, over the years, bring the largest number of such disputes to the Court's attention.

In 1911 the Presbyterian Church in the United States sued the Cumberland Presbyterian Church for control of a publishing house.[62] The issue before the Court was the narrow and technical one—whether the trustees of the publishing house should properly be defendants in the suit. Hughes ruled that they should and in effect also ruled for the PCUSA, in finding that the publishing house was "an agent of denominational service." The following year, the Court settled a similarly narrow and technical suit involving the Cumberland Presbyterians and the PCUSA,[63] in which Hughes once again found in favor of PCUSA.

In 1917 the Court settled yet another Presbyterian dispute, this time without scrutinizing the issues.[64] Chief Justice Edward Douglass White merely issued a very brief opinion in favor of the national body of the church, noting that, although not all the justices agreed, the majority thought the dispute was clearly governed by the principles in the *Watson* case.

Two internal Catholic disputes were settled by the Court during the earlier twentieth century.

In 1909 it rejected a property claim by a dissident group in the Philippines, which was then an American protectorate.[65] Justice Oliver Wendell Holmes ruled that the property had been intended for the use of the Roman Catholic Church, whose representatives had been "ejected without right."

In 1929 the Court heard an appeal from a Catholic priest claiming an endowed chaplaincy that had been denied him by the archbishop of Manila.[66] Justice Louis Brandeis ruled against the appellant on the grounds that the archbishop had correctly applied the Canon Law of the Catholic Church, but Brandeis also held that the appeal to civil law was itself valid as a way of ascertaining the provisions of church law,[67] an important principle in that it gave the civil courts entry into religious disputes.

Almost a quarter century then elapsed before the Court heard another church-property dispute, this one raising a unique issue. The Russian Orthodox Church in New York had divided, one group accepting the authority of the mother church in the Soviet Union, the other group remaining faithful to the memory of the czar and rejecting the Moscow church as merely the mouthpiece of the atheistic Soviet government. The former group had made itself independent of Moscow in the years following the 1917 revolution, and in 1945 the State of New York amended its law regulating religious corporations in order to give the anti-Soviet group title to the diocesan cathedral. Their opponents sued on the grounds that the law represented undue interference in the internal affairs of the church.[68]

The Court overturned the New York law and, on the basis of its reading of the Orthodox Church's own polity, awarded the cathedral to the group that retained ties with Moscow, Justice Stanley Reed's majority opinion arguing that the New York law was a violation of the church's autonomy and that the church's own laws were clear as to the proper chain of ecclesiastical authority.[69]

Justice Felix Frankfurter concurred, holding that there was no evidence of political interference by the Soviet Union in the affairs of the church in America and warning that permitting the American government to decide such questions could easily be the entering wedge for governmental control.[70]

Justice Robert H. Jackson dissented, arguing that there was in fact evidence of political interference, since the Soviet government insisted that the Orthodox in the United States refrain from any anti-Soviet activity. New York's laws concerning religious corporations were designed to protect the churches, which were not required to avail themselves of that protection but, if they did, had to adhere to its requirements. Disputes over the real property of churches should not be approached any differently from disputes over bank accounts and other assets, he insisted. In the last of his numerous memorable utterances about religion, Jackson proclaimed, "I do not think that New York State must yield to the authority of a foreign and unfriendly state masquerading as a spiritual institution."[71]

But the issue proved tenacious, and almost a decade later, it was again before the justices, after a New York court ruled that as a matter of fact the Patriarch of Moscow was under the domination of the Soviet government and should thus not be allowed to exercise authority over the church in America. The Supreme Court ruled that this decision repeated the same error as the 1952 case, and it was overturned.[72]

In 1969 two Presbyterian churches in Georgia withdrew from their national body, charging that the national church had departed from historic Presbyterian doctrine. A Georgia law recognized this as a legitimate basis for secession, and a state court authorized the dissenters to retain title to parish property. Justice William Brennan wrote a unanimous opinion overturning the award on the grounds that the state could not attempt to determine correct doctrine and the law was therefore fatally flawed.[73]

The following year the Court ruled similarly in a case involving a group called the Churches of God, holding that property disputes could be disposed of by the courts in various ways, so long as questions of doctrine were not addressed by the judiciary. It was also wrong for the courts to probe too deeply into the exercise of power in a church. Rather the courts should seek to identify the legal governing body in each dispute and defer to it.[74]

A more complex case in 1976 involved the governance of the Serbian Orthodox Church. The mother church in Yugoslavia had deposed an American bishop and divided his diocese into three parts. The deposed bishop and his followers disputed the action, partly on the grounds that the church in Yugoslavia was Communist dominated. The Illinois Supreme Court overturned the Yugoslavian church's proceedings, terming them arbitrary and invalid. The U.S. Supreme Court now overturned that decision, as constituting undue interference in the church's internal governance.[75]

Brennan, writing for a majority, found some apparent contradictions in the governing documents of the church but overturned the Illinois judgment because it failed to respect the decision of the highest governing authority of the church, which was the mother church in Yugoslavia.[76]

No government intervention could be permitted that required excessive inquiries into the operation of the church, he ruled. There was contradictory testimony as to whether proper procedures were followed, and the Illinois court accepted some of this testimony and rejected others. The lower court also overlooked some violations of procedure by the complaining bishop, as well as overlooking the fact that the church in Yugoslavia was the final governing authority.[77]

Following allegedly neutral principles, the Illinois court had substituted its own interpretation of church law for that of the highest ecclesiastical authority, Brennan ruled.[78]

Justice Byron White concurred in the decision, although cautioning that he did not hold that the courts were barred from reaching a judgment as to where and when ecclesiastical authority was properly exercised.[79]

Justice William Rehnquist dissented, observing drily that the case concerned property and asking satirically, "Will the real bishops of the Serbian Eastern Orthodox Church please stand up?" The courts had not involved themselves in doctrine but had merely settled an internal dispute in the same way they might for any voluntary organization. Alternatively, he warned, disputes over property would be settled by brute force. At a minimum, secular courts must get involved, in the sense of accepting one interpretation of church law over another, and he warned that: "If the civil courts are to be bound by any sheet of parchment bearing the ecclesiastical seal and purporting to be a decree of a church court, they can easily be converted into a handmaiden of arbitrary lawlessness."[80]

Rehnquist understood the 1872 *Watson* case as turning not on the Free Exercise Clause but on the more general question of how far the courts could become involved in the internal disputes of private organizations. In the *Kedroff* case the state had thwarted the decision of a particular religious group. Here, however, there was no issue of doctrine, and religious groups should not be exempt from the kinds of legal jurisdiction to which other voluntary groups were required to submit.[81] In some ways Rehnquist seemed prepared to jettison the principle that had governed such cases since the *Watson* decision of 1872.

A 1979 case again involved a Presbyterian congregation in Georgia that had broken away from the national body. The national church determined that the minority in the congregation constituted the true parish, a judgment that was overturned by the Georgia courts on the grounds that legal title to the property was vested in the local congregation, understood as the majority.[82]

Justice Harry Blackmun held for a majority of the Court that the Constitution did not require the state to defer to church bodies on questions of property, so long as disputes over doctrine were not at stake. However, he warned that, in some cases, for the courts even to determine which was the appropriate governing body of the church would itself require impermissible intrusion into the church's internal life.[83]

The Georgia courts assumed that the majority constituted the local congregation, whereas the minority contended that this was a question for church law. The question had not been settled, and the Supreme Court therefore remanded the case to Georgia for rehearing.[84]

Justice Lewis Powell dissented, finding that in effect Georgia had imposed a congregational form of government on a Presbyterian Church, thereby involving itself in a doctrinal dispute over the exact nature of the church. The *Watson* principle required that the polity of each church be accepted on its own terms, and it seemed to Powell that the polity of the Presbyterian Church in the United States clearly favored the minority group within the congregation.[85]

A unique issue was raised before the Court and rejected in 1978, when the Methodist Church in California sought to obtain an injunction forbidding the California courts from proceeding with a case in which Methodist officials were accused of complicity in fraud, in connection with the bankruptcy of a chain of nursing homes.[86]

The church argued that, in determining whether Methodist officials could be held legally responsible, the California court had failed to make use of the church's own constitutional documents, as required by the *Watson* principle, and had instead relied on the testimony of external witnesses to establish responsibility. The church also claimed that it had only an "attenuated" relationship with the state of California and should not be brought to trial there.[87]

Rehnquist, sitting as a "circuit justice," rejected the appeal. Only in rare instances, he thought, should the Supreme Court interfere with state cases still in process. Furthermore, state courts could make an independent judgment about the governing structure of a church, since the requirement to rely on the church's own constitutions applied only to internal disputes. The claim that it applied also to external disputes was, Rehnquist, thought, quite novel. He also found the church's connection to the State of California substantial.[88]

Chapter Two

BELIEF AND ACTION

DURING ITS FIRST century and a half, the Court seldom heard cases involving the Free Exercise Clause and only once found a violation of that clause. However, during every era, the Court has considered cases that substantively involve religious liberty, even if the Free Exercise Clause was not explicitly invoked.

One of the most important of all the Court's early cases—*Dartmouth College v. New Hampshire*[1] (1819)—has always been treated as a landmark in the development of the law of contract. Considered formally, it was precisely that. But in substance it was an important case involving religious freedom.

The case arose from a dispute between John Wheelock, president of the college, and the college trustees. Although his domineering personality was probably the principal source of friction, Wheelock, a Presbyterian, also clashed with the local Congregationalist Church over the appointment of a pastor. In 1815 he was removed by the trustees, and the dispute was soon caught up in the complex religio-political currents of early nineteenth-century New England.[2]

Presbyterians and Congregationalists were both Calvinist in their theology, with Congregationalism the form of church government most widely established in New England. By 1815, however, Calvinist influence was waning and state churches were being disestablished, and Calvinists tended to affiliate with the Federalist Party in politics, regarding the Democratic Republicans as tainted by the "infidelity" of Thomas Jefferson. Conversely, those who opposed the old Calvinist hegemony tended to become Republicans.[3]

Unpredictably, the Federalist Wheelock appealed for help to the Republican governor of New Hampshire, William Plumer, who responded by persuading the state legislature to declare Dartmouth the state university. Plumer then removed the trustees and appointed a board of his own.[4]

Plumer had had a varied religious history. Born and raised a Congregationalist, he had briefly become a Baptist while a young man, even serving as a preacher, before coming under Enlightenment influence and becoming in effect a Deist. Although he occasionally attended a Congregationalist Church, admittedly for political reasons, for the most part he had severed all ties with organized religion.[5]

At first Plumer had little sympathy with either Wheelock or the Dartmouth trustees, but he soon came to see the trustees' action as a conspiracy of "priests" to perpetuate aristocracy and traditional religious and educational institutions. He was opposed to new professorships in divinity and ethics and to the opening of the college chapel to public worship.[6]

Since it had received an official charter and other occasional signs of state approval, Plumer saw Dartmouth as an institution that ought to serve the public good, and he lamented that instead the college "seems more anxious to please the priesthood than to pursue a manly and expedient course to fit men for the business and duties of this world." The school was "medieval" and "dominated by priests," a college for the "rich and idle," offering no practical instruction.[7]

Chief Justice Marshall wrote the majority opinion preserving Dartmouth's character as a private college. His decision followed an exhaustive analysis of the law of contract, finding that under the original charter, from the royal governor of New Hampshire, the trustees constituted a self-perpetuating body who had ultimate authority over the institution.[8]

The college had collected funds, primarily in England, in order to train missionaries to spread Christianity ("our holy religion," Marshall called it) among the Indians and "to uph[o]ld piety and learning in general." Funds given for the purpose of education did not necessarily belong to the state, nor were all teachers to be considered public officers, Marshall ruled.[9]

Justice Story wrote a concurring opinion,[10] as did Justice Washington, who like Marshall noted that the proposed new purposes for the college differed from the original ones.[11] Justice Gabriel Duvall dissented, without written opinion.[12]

The burden of the decision was that the royal charter originally granted to the college constituted a binding contract, which was violated by the removal of the trustees. But part of the breach of contract also lay in the State of New Hampshire's attempt to alter the religious nature of the institution.

An 1829 ecclesiastical land dispute was the second case to involve questions of religious liberty.[13] In Maryland in 1769, in an area that would later become part of the District of Columbia, a German Lutheran congregation had won a plot of land in a lottery conducted by Charles Beatty. The congregation built a church on the site. But the parish was small and poor, and in time, the building fell into ruin, and the parish ended by using the land as its cemetery. More than fifty years after the original conveyance, Beatty's heirs reclaimed the land and began removing grave stones from the cemetery.[14]

Story, ruling for a unanimous Court, acknowledged legal deficiencies in the Lutheran claim—the parish had never actually received title to the land and it was not incorporated, hence was legally incapable of receiving such a grant.[15]

But Maryland law, which governed the district at the time the grant was made, recognized the dedication of land "to public and pious uses," and the congregation had consistently conformed to that. In essence, Story ruled, the issue was not narrowly legal but whether: ". . . the sepulchres of the dead are to be violated; the feelings of religion, and the sentiments of natural affection of the kindred and friends of the deceased, are to be wounded."[16] Thus Story invoked the law of equity to uphold the church's right to the land, in order to "preserve the repose of the ashes of the dead, and the religious sensibilities of the living."[17] The decision was remarkable in terms of the Court's willingness to move beyond strictly legal considerations in order to protect religious values.

In *Worcester v. Georgia*[18] (1832), the Court overturned the conviction of a Methodist minister who defied a Georgia law forbidding white persons from living and working among the Cherokee Indians. The issue of religious liberty was not raised, other than to note that Samuel Worcester was "engaged in preaching the Gospel" and was translating the Bible into the Cherokee language. Marshall found in his favor on the grounds that treaties between the Cherokee and the federal government nullified the Georgia law. Justice Henry Baldwin dissented, finding procedural irregularities in Worcester's appeal.

The law had been enacted as part of a plan by Georgia to remove the Cherokee to the West, a project strongly supported by President Andrew Jackson, and upon hearing of the decision, Jackson was reported, perhaps apocryphally, to have said "John Marshall has made his decision, now let him enforce it." Emboldened by Jackson's support, Georgia ignored the Court's ruling, and Worcester was released from prison only by accepting a pardon and agreeing to leave the state.[19]

In *Permoli v. New Orleans*[20] (1845), the Court erected a major road block to the hearing of religious-freedom cases, ensuring that few such cases would subsequently be brought before it.

The city of New Orleans passed a law forbidding funerals from being conducted in churches, requiring instead that they be held only in cemeteries, a requirement that apparently grew out of factional quarrels within particular Catholic parishes.[21] A priest, Bernard Permoli, defied the statute and was prosecuted.

Permoli claimed that the law was a violation of the Free-Exercise Clause of the Constitution and also of the Northwest Ordinance of 1787, which guaranteed religious liberty to territories not yet part of the Union. When Louisiana was purchased by the United States in 1804, it came under that guarantee. Louisiana's own constitution also provided for religious liberty, and New Orleans was thus in violation of its state constitution as well.

Permoli termed "absurd" the claim that, when Louisiana became a state, it ceased to be bound by an act of Congress, the Northwest Ordinance.[22]

The municipality of New Orleans pointed out that virtually its entire city council was made up of Catholics, who could hardly be thought prejudiced against their own church. The legal issue was precisely what the plaintiff denied—that, when Louisiana became a state in 1812, it ceased to be bound by the Northwest Ordinance. The Free-Exercise Clause was a limit on Congress, not on the states.[23]

Justice John Catron found that New Orleans was constitutionally correct. The Constitution did not protect the religious liberties of citizens with respect to their state governments, nor did it impose obligations on state governments in this regard. The authority of the Northwest Ordinance ceased when Louisiana was admitted to the Union.[24]

Since most violations of religious liberty were likely to occur at the state or local level, this ruling effectively prevented most appeals to the Court under the Free-Exercise Clause, a principle that would be maintained until at least the 1920s.

Almost a generation passed, and a wrenching civil war, before the Court heard its next religious-freedom case—*Cummings v. the State of Missouri*[25] (1866). Missouri, following the Civil War, enacted a new constitution that required a loyalty oath from various classes of citizens, including clergy, an oath designed to exclude Confederate sympathizers from the exercise of citizenship. John A. Cummings, a Catholic priest, refused the oath and was prosecuted.

Cummings's attorney, Reverdy Johnson, did not initially raise the issue of religious freedom. Instead he noted a fundamental ambiguity in the law—it forbade disloyalty to the state of Missouri, yet in the recent war, Missouri itself had been disloyal to the Union.[26]

But the heart of Johnson's argument was that the oath violated the Constitution in being both a bill of attainder—the legislature's classifying of certain people as criminal without recourse to judicial proceedings—and an "ex post facto" ("from after the fact") law—defining as criminal acts that were not criminal when they were performed. In addition, in requiring the oath, the state forced citizens to testify against themselves, contrary to Amendment V of the Constitution.[27]

Missouri replied that the state had never been disloyal to the Union; only its governor had been, and he had fled the state. The case was more than a little ironic, however, in that the Unionist government of Reconstruction Missouri now appealed to states' rights to justify its policies. The state, it was claimed, had the authority to regulate both voting qualifications and the terms under which people could pursue their occupations. The state had not passed a bill of attainder or an ex post facto law, although such were within its reserved powers.[28]

The state itself raised the religious-freedom issue quite bluntly. Freedom of religion, its lawyer argued, was guaranteed by the state constitution only, and the guarantee in the federal Constitution was not binding on the states. If the state "unwisely" authorized an official religion, there was nothing the federal government could do. But, seemingly concerned about public opinion, Missouri's attorney, J. B. Henderson, then made a sweeping assertion:

> The rights of conscience are sacred rights. They are too often confounded, however, with the unrestrained license to corrupt, from the pulpit, the public taste and the public morals. However, this may be, the American people are exceedingly sensitive on the subject of religious freedom; and whenever the people are told, as they have been in this case, that the indefeasible right to worship God according to the dictates of conscience is about to be invaded, the public mind at once arouses itself to repel the invasion. . . .
>
> The Jew, the infidel, and the Christian are equal only in the national councils. The States may make any discrimination in favor of any sect or denomination of Christians or in favor of the infidel and against the Christian.

The state, Henderson insisted, could even regulate the forms of worship.[29]

As to a bill of attainder, Henderson argued that it should be defined only as legislation directed at specific persons or groups, whereas the Missouri oath applied to the entire community. And as to ex post facto laws, the Constitution did not forbid defining as criminal acts that previously had not been criminal but only forbade the punishment of such acts. The acts that the oath sought to uncover were not treated as crimes and were not so punished. The oath looked to the future and punished only those who refused the oath itself.[30]

The only basic rights, according to Henderson, were life, liberty, and property. The right to pursue one's profession was not absolute and could be regulated by the state.[31] Finally, its spokesman asserted, Missouri was justified in enacting the oath because of the terrible sufferings perpetrated there by Confederate sympathizers, including an invasion by a Confederate army supported by treacherous Missourians. Men like Cummings were implicated because "even the minister of heaven, forgetting of what world his master's kingdom was, went forth to perform the part allotted him in the great work of iniquity."[32]

Johnson responded by again insisting that the Constitution forbade states to enact ex post facto laws. Cummings had indeed been punished, since he was forbidden to teach or preach. The oath merely assumed the criminality of past actions and assumed personal guilt solely on the basis of a refusal to swear.[33]

Probably Johnson had not raised the issue of religious liberty because he anticipated the position the state would take. Now he was forced to reply, and he conceded that the Religion Clauses were not binding on the states. Unable to make a legal argument, he offered instead a ringing sermon about the Constitution:

> . . . [I]t announces a great principle of American liberty, a principle deeply seated in the American mind, and now almost in the entire mind of the civilized world, that as between a man and his conscience, as relates to his obligation to God, it is not only tyrannical but un-Christian to interfere with it. It is almost inconceivable in this civilized day that the doctrines contained in the constitution should be considered as within the legitimate sphere of human power.[34]

Thus Cummings's lawyers presented an argument symmetrically ironical to that of the state—the former Confederate sympathizer appealed to the power of the federal government against the tyranny of his state.

Justice Stephen Field wrote for the majority in ruling in Cummings's favor. One defect of the oath, Field held, was that it proscribed things which, far from being illegal, were not even blameworthy. Citizens were required to swear that they had not even extended sympathy to Confederate rebels, and the oath did not distinguish between acts arising from enmity to the federal government and acts arising merely from ties of kinship or personal sympathy.[35]

The oath was indeed retrospective and thus involved an ex post facto law. States' rights were to be respected, Field held, but not against the federal Constitution. Missouri was imposing conditions on clerics and others that bore no relationship to their fitness to discharge their callings, and this was a form of punishment. The oath was in effect a bill of attainder, and the feelings simmering in Missouri after the war, far from being a justification for the state's actions, were precisely reasons for being suspicious of the oath, since the Constitution protected citizens from the consequences of popular prejudice. The oath subverted the citizens' right to be presumed innocent.[36]

Field said nothing about freedom of religion, thus by implication accepting the claims made by Missouri and conceded by Cummings's attorney—that the states were not required by the federal Constitution to respect that freedom, exactly the Court's finding in the *Permoli* case.

Cummings had only a bare majority of the Court on his side, with Chief Justice Salmon P. Chase among the dissenters. Justice Miller wrote the dissenting opinion.

Because of a paucity of cases involving bills of attainder, he noted, the Court relied on various English cases that he thought did not apply in the American situation. No person or class of persons was named in the disputed legislation, and no judicial punishment was inflicted.[37]

Likewise Missouri had not enacted an ex post facto law, because it did not punish past actions but merely the refusal to take the oath itself. Refusal to take the oath showed that a person had "character faults" that disqualified him from full citizenship.[38]

The Court, Miller asserted, exceeded its authority in preventing Missouri from regulating the qualifications of a minister of religion. There was no evidence that the Constitution "interposes any such protection between the States and their own citizens."[39]

Miller pointed out that the majority decision seemed to contradict the findings in the *Permoli* case. In the latter the Court upheld the legislative authority of a mere municipality but was here nullifying that of an entire state.[40]

Apparently Cummings's attorney claimed that Missouri had enacted a bill of attainder and an ex post facto law because he thought those claims made his case stronger, in that both were prohibited within the main body of the Constitution itself, not in the Bill of Rights. Although Missouri claimed, almost in passing, that the state had a right to enact both kinds of laws, it did not press the issue but concentrated on arguing that the test oath did not fit the definition of either.

The *Cummings* case raised fundamental issues of religious liberty, but there was apparent agreement by all parties that the Free-Exercise Clause, and presumably therefore the Bill of Rights as a whole, was not binding on the states. At the end of the war, to preserve the Union, the Court tacitly upheld the doctrine of states' rights as it applied to religion.

The most vexed issue of religious liberty in all of American history was the practice of polygamy by the Church of Jesus Christ of Latter Day Saints (Mormons), a practice toward which the entire federal government, including the Court, was unrelenting in its opposition. The polygamy issue kept reappearing before the Court for over a decade, and in three major cases the practice was absolutely forbidden.

Reynolds v. the United States (1879)[41] upheld the prosecution of George Reynolds, secretary to the Mormon leader Brigham Young. Reynolds was prosecuted under a federal law prohibiting polygamy in the territories. Hoping for a favorable ruling from the Court, the Mormons decided to bring a test case, and Reynolds was designated as the defendant.[42]

Chief Justice Morrison R. Waite affirmed that Congress could not limit religious freedom but ruled that such freedom could be absolute only in matters of belief, not behavior. The law could and must regulate behavior, and polygamy had always been odious to the peoples of "Northern and Western Europe." Emanating from a system of patriarchy, it fettered women in "desperation," and the Court found that the prosecution had acted appropriately in calling to the jury's attention the actual condition of women and children ensnared in the system.[43]

In 1889 the Court heard an appeal from the church after its assets had been seized by the federal government because of the Mormons' refusal to disavow polygamy.[44] Here Justice Joseph Bradley went even further than Waite in denouncing polygamy itself, calling it "abhorrent to the sentiments and feelings of the civilized world .... a barbarous practice."[45] Like Waite, he asked rhetorically whether the Constitution could be said to protect human sacrifice or the Hindu practice of suttee. Thus the federal government was justified in seizing the funds.[46]

In this case, however, three justices—Chief Justice Fuller and Justices Field and Lucius Q. C. Lamar—dissented, on the grounds that the seizure of property was itself an unconstitutional use of Congressional power.[47]

The third major case was heard the next year, when the Court affirmed the conviction for perjury of a Mormon in Idaho who had taken an oath, required of all voters, in which he denied being a member of any group that advocated polygamy, although in fact he was.[48]

Despite having dissented the previous year, Field now delivered the Court's unanimous opinion, again affirming that absolute religious freedom was a matter of belief only, not necessarily of action, if such action injured others. Few practices were as pernicious as polygamy, the First Amendment was never intended to permit "violations of social duties or subversion of good order," and religious freedom had to be subordinated to the criminal law. Both bigamy and polygamy were said to "destroy the purity of the marriage relation, to disturb the peace of families, to degrade women, and to debase men." (Despite the Court's claims about absolute freedom of belief, the appellant had been convicted merely for lying about his membership in a group that advocated polygamy, not for actually practicing it.)[49]

Despite its implacable disapproval of polygamy, the Court was usually scrupulous about correct legal procedures, so that Mormons won some of the minor cases that came before the high tribunal.

The first Mormon case (1872)[50] involved a plaintiff who had invested in a company formed to dig a canal through the Utah desert. The president of the company was Brigham Young, and when the company failed, the plaintiff sued the Mormon Church, claiming that the company was legally part of the church. Justice Davis ruled that, in finding for the plaintiff, the territorial court of Utah had improperly allowed hearsay evidence.

Utah was one of the few states or territories that imposed no limits on the amount of property a religious body might possess. But, despite the fact that Congress in 1862 had nullified Utah's incorporation of the church and had restricted the amount of property it might own, and de-

spite a widespread belief that the church owned too much property, the
Court ruled in favor of the church.[51]

In 1880 the Court overturned the conviction of a Mormon for polygamy, on what were rather subtle legal grounds.[52] The defendant appealed
partly on the grounds that all prospective jurors who admitted a belief
in polygamy had been excluded from service and that this constituted a
violation of religious freedom, since it systematically excluded all Mormons. His second argument was that proof of his bigamy was based on
the testimony of a woman claiming to be his second wife, and that her
testimony should have been excluded, because the law forbade a wife to
testify against her husband in court.

Justice Woods dismissed the first claim easily, noting that the courts
had a right to inquire into possible bias on the part of jurors and that
proper procedure for doing so had been followed. The excluded jurors
did not themselves complain of discrimination, and the defendant could
not complain in their stead.[53] (The issue was a crucial one for the federal
government, in that Mormon juries had for a long time refused to convict
accused polygamists.)[54]

But Woods found the defendant's second claim to have merit. The existence of his first wife was legally established only through the testimony
of his second wife. But until the jury heard and accepted the second wife's
testimony, she was presumptively his legal wife and thus should not have
been permitted to testify.[55] (Since Reynolds's polygamy had been proven
through the testimony of his second wife,[56] the Court's 1880 ruling
seemed logically to have invalidated the *Reynolds* decision retroactively.)

Woods noted that polygamous marriages were reportedly contracted
in Utah in such a way as to make detection difficult, often by means of
perjury. But there was no remedy for this, he thought, short of an act of
Congress requiring wives to testify against their husbands.[57]

In 1884 a collection of cases from Utah argued that citizens had been
denied the right to vote despite having taken the requisite oath swearing
that they were not polygamists.[58] The point proved to be a subtle one,
turning on the definition of polygamy. Justice Stanley Matthews noted
that the law did not punish mere opinion but only action. However, he
found that several of the appellants had merely sworn that they had not
"cohabited" with more than one wife after passage of the law prohibiting
polygamy. Actual polygamous relations may not have been dissolved,
Matthews observed, and cohabitation was not necessary to such a polygamous relationship. However, others of the appellants specifically swore
that they were not involved in polygamous relations, and were thus entitled to be registered as voters.[59]

Matthews, like Waite, discoursed on the moral appropriateness of the
antipolygamy statute. No law, he exclaimed, was "more wholesome and
necessary" than one that sought to establish society on the basis of

the idea of the family, as consisting in and springing from the union for life of one man and one woman in the holy state of matrimony; for the sure foundation of all that is stable in our civilization; the best guarantee of that reverent morality which is the source of all beneficent progress in social and political improvement.[60]

In a related case the same year the Court upheld the denial of voting rights to a Utah resident who admitted to living in the same house with two different families, including two women whom he had married before the enactment of the federal antipolygamy statute. The decision turned on the definition of "cohabitation," with the plaintiff claiming that, after passage of the statute, he had refrained from sexual intercourse with the two women and that cohabitation in a legal sense implied sexual relations. Waite ruled that cohabitation merely meant dwelling in the same house and that the plaintiff was in violation of the law because he had not formally repudiated or terminated his polygamous relationships. Miller wrote a dissenting opinion arguing that in law, cohabitation always implied sexual intercourse.[61]

In 1886 the Court freed a man convicted on three separate counts of polygamy and given three separate sentences.[62] The appellant argued that the crime of polygamy constituted one continuous offense, which justified only one punishment, a contention that Justice Samuel Blatchford accepted on behalf of the Court.

In 1888 Bradley ruled for the Court in overturning the conviction for adultery of a Mormon who had also been convicted of polygamy. The two offenses were the same, and prosecution for the greater crime of polygamy precluded prosecution for the lesser one of adultery, Bradley held.[63]

In 1890 the Court overturned a polygamy conviction based on the testimony of the defendant's lawful wife. Justice Brewer, noting the rule of law that excluded wives from testifying against their husbands except where the husband had threatened his wife with violence, ruled that polygamy did not constitute violence, hence the wife should not have been allowed to testify.[64]

By 1890 the Mormon leadership finally realized that the church could not withstand the power of the federal government, and they circulated a statement calling for an end to polygamy, based on an alleged new revelation from God. Although the change of doctrine was not by any means accepted by all Mormons, the practice began to wane among the faithful and because of this the church was allowed to recover some of its seized property.[65]

In *Church of the Holy Trinity v. United States* (1892), the Court, for the first (and, for decades afterward, the only) time, found a formal violation of religious liberty, in the enforcement of a federal law forbidding the importing of foreign nationals to work in the United States. Somewhat

surprisingly, given the presence in the United States of religions largely
made up of immigrants, the suit was brought by an Episcopal parish in
New York City that had called an English rector.[66]

Brewer offered an ingeniously circular resolution of the case—since the
United States was "a Christian nation," none of its laws could be considered antithetical to religion. Public practice affirmed this religiosity in
countless ways, such as prayers on public occasions and military chaplains.
The Court did not invalidate the federal law but merely ruled that it had
never been the intent of Congress that it should apply in such a way.[67]

In 1899 the Court upheld a Utah practice of impaneling juries of only
eight men, Justice Horace Peckham ruling for the majority that the "Privileges and Immunities" guaranteed citizens under the Constitution (Article
IV, Section 2) did not necessarily include the right to a jury of twelve.[68]
Peckham explicitly rejected the contention that the Fourteenth Amendment made all the provisions of the Bill of Rights into constitutionally
protected privileges and immunities, applicable to the states.[69]

Justice Harlan dissented strongly, asking rhetorically whether a state
could therefore prohibit the free exercise of religion and arguing that, by
the logic of the decision, Utah could legally establish Mormonism as its
official religion.[70] He ignored, if he was aware of it, the fact that the Court
had in effect said precisely that in the *Permoli* case.

Nearly a decade later Harlan had occasion to raise the question again,
when the Court upheld a Kentucky law prohibiting white and black students from being enrolled in the same schools. The appellant was a private
college under Protestant auspices.[71]

The college invoked a recent Court decision nullifying, as an infringement of property rights, state regulation of businesses and also argued that
the law violated the rights of both blacks and whites under the Fourteenth
Amendment.[72] But Brewer ruled that Kentucky had authority under its
state constitution and that limitations that might be unconstitutional if
imposed on private persons could be legal if imposed on corporations.[73]

Harlan dissented vigorously. Noting that the college had been founded
"to promote the cause of Christ," he proclaimed that "the capacity for
instruction is given by the Almighty for beneficent purposes and its use
may not be forbidden or interfered with by the government." Under the
majority ruling, Kentucky could prohibit mixed gatherings in churches
"for the purpose of being instructed in the Word of God" and could prohibit racial mixing "at the communion table." The right to teach was no
less sacred than the right to worship, he insisted.[74]

Harlan termed "absurd" the finding that restrictions could be placed
on corporations that could not be imposed on individuals, and he characterized the Kentucky law as "an arbitrary invasion of the rights of liberty

and property under the Fourteenth Amendment."[75] Justice William R. Day also dissented, but without written opinion.[76]

Once again Harlan appeared not to notice that, given the Court's position that the Free-Exercise Clause did not apply to the states, the infringements of religious liberty against which he warned would presumably be constitutional. He is the only justice of his era known to have believed that the Bill of Rights was applicable to the states.

The transition to Harlan's view of the Fourteenth Amendment began in the 1920s, after his retirement. Particularly relevant to religion was the Court's invalidation of several state laws regulating education, cases that can be seen as presaging its modern concern for civil liberties.

In *Meyer v. State of Nebraska*[77] (1923), the Court overturned the conviction of a teacher in a Lutheran school who had been prosecuted for teaching the German language, in defiance of a state law, passed during the First World War, that forbade teaching modern foreign languages to children in elementary school. Justice James McReynolds found the goal of "a harmonious American people with American ideals" to be "laudable" but found the method of achieving it impermissible, since the state was unable to show any harm arising from the practice.

Several other identical cases were disposed of by the *Meyer* decision.[78] Formally the cases had nothing to with religious liberty. But all the plaintiffs taught in religious schools, a fact of which the Court was undoubtedly cognizant, and the plaintiff in the *Meyer* case claimed that teaching German to Lutheran children was part of their religious education, even though other Lutherans thought it unwise and unnecessary to continue using a foreign language.[79]

Justice Holmes dissented, along with Justice George Sutherland, arguing that the goal of the legislation was reasonable and the law itself a not unreasonable means of attaining the goal permitted under the Constitution.[80]

Pierce v. Society of Sisters (1925)[81] challenged an Oregon law that required all children to attend public schools. The Court, again in the person of McReynolds, upheld the legitimacy of private schools but did not settle the issue on the basis of the Free Exercise Clause. Instead, since a privately owned military academy was party to the suit along with Catholic schools, the Court ruled that the law interfered with property rights. It was a landmark decision because in effect it established the right of religious schools to exist alongside the public schools. However, it did not specifically affirm such a right under the First Amendment. Part of the lasting importance of the case was the often-quoted dictum of McReynolds, "The child is not the mere creature of the state."[82]

A few years later the Court heard a series of cases involving conscientious objection from military service. In one a Hungarian woman belonging to no organized religion was denied citizenship because she refused to swear that she would bear arms in defense of the country.[83] In the second a Canadian Baptist was denied citizenship because he was a "selective" conscientious objector, that is, he did not object morally to all wars, only to some.[84] At the same time the Court decided an almost identical case involving a Canadian woman who had refused to take the oath of citizenship unless she were permitted to insert the phrase "as far as my conscience as a Christian will allow."[85] In the fourth case, several Methodists were denied admission to a state university because they refused to participate in required military exercises.[86] In all four cases the Court ruled that the status of conscientious objection was a privilege, not a right, and could not therefore be demanded under the First Amendment.

In the first of these, *Schwimmer*, Justice Pierce Butler found that the appellant was not in compliance with the legal requirements for citizenship, because of her opposition to all wars. Holmes, the "Great Dissenter," approved her claim but more as a matter of free speech than of religion, although he did recall the historic role of the Quakers in American life and commented acidly, "I had not supposed hitherto that we regretted our inability to expel them because they believe more than some of us do in the teachings of the Sermon on the Mount."[87]

In the second case, *MacIntosh*, Sutherland affirmed religious freedom and the fact that Americans acknowledge the duty of obedience to God, but also asserted that society's duty to defend itself is "not inconsistent with the will of God,"[88] in effect finding that the plaintiff had misconstrued the divine will.

Chief Justice Hughes, with the concurrence of Justices Holmes, Brandeis, and Harlan Fiske Stone, dissented from the majority opinion, asserting that "the essence of religion is belief in a relation to God involving duties superior to those arising from any human relationship." There could be no such thing as religious liberty without assuming "supreme allegiance to the will of God."[89]

In the *Bland* case Sutherland held that for the Court to allow the appellant to amend the required oath would be to usurp the role of Congress, which alone could set conditions for citizenship. Hughes again wrote a brief dissent.[90]

The *Hamilton* decision was unanimous, the Court ruling that since no one had a legal right to attend a state university, no right was violated by excluding those who refused military training.[91] (The case came before the Court because the military training was authorized and paid for by the federal government.)

However, a concurring opinion by Justice Benjamin N. Cardozo was of great importance, since he wrote that "I assume for present purposes that the religious liberty protected by the First Amendment against invasion by the nation is protected by the Fourteenth Amendment against invasion by the states,"[92] the first time any member of the Court had made such a claim with respect to religion. Cardozo's comment signaled a departure from the crucial ruling in the *Permoli* case almost ninety years before.

However, despite this revolutionary idea, Cardozo found no violation of religious liberty in the case, since the government had the right to impose conditions on conscientious objection. Possibly responding to Hughes's earlier statement about the sovereignty of the divine will, Cardozo wrote that to allow religious pacifists to define their own terms

> ... would carry us to lengths that have never yet been dreamed of. The conscientious objector, if his liberties were to be thus extended, might refuse to contribute taxes in furtherance of war ... or any other end condemned by his conscience as irreligious or immoral. The right of private judgment has never yet been so exalted above the powers and compulsions of the agencies of government. One who is a martyr to principle—which may turn out in the end to be a delusion or an error—does not prove by his martyrdom that he has kept within the law.[93]

During the first 150 years of its existence the Court demonstrated only a modest interest in religious liberty, and almost always did so under some rubric other than the Free-Exercise Clause. Cardozo's 1934 opinion bluntly set limits on the claims of religious conscience, even as he urged the extension of the Free-Exercise Clause to the states. It was the latter move that would soon make possible the revolution in the Court's position on religious liberty.

Chapter Three

THE PHANTOM WALL

PRIOR TO 1948 the Court never found a violation of the Establishment Clause and was seldom asked to do so. It did, however, deal with a number of cases that implied the establishment issue.

The most curious of these was *Vidal v. Girard's Executors* (1844),[1] in which the kin of a wealthy philanthropist sought to overturn his will after his death, because he had endowed a boys school with the provision that no clergyman of any denomination should ever teach there. Stephen Girard disavowed any insult to Christianity and said he merely wished to spare "tender minds" the trauma of facing competing theological claims. (The case came before the Court because of diversity of citizenship, some of Girard's relatives being subjects of the king of France.)

The plaintiffs argued that Girard's will was an insult to Christianity and a violation of Pennsylvania's blasphemy statute. Philadelphia city officials, charged with overseeing the school, pleaded that they had unsuccessfully attempted to get the offending clause repealed. Although blasphemy was a crime in Pennsylvania, they argued that Girard's strictures against religious instruction were not blasphemous.[2]

The city also acknowledged the ruling by a state court that Christianity was part of the law of Pennsylvania, but insisted that Christianity must include freedom of conscience. Girard's will did not ban all religious teaching from the school, since religion could be taught by laypeople as well as by clergy.[3]

The plaintiffs were represented by Daniel Webster, whose speech before the Court was an impassioned defense of Christianity and an attack on the provisions of the will. There could be no genuine charity, he asserted, where religion was excluded, and he noted that some religious groups did not permit laypeople to teach religious subjects. The idea that children should choose their religion freely, without indoctrination, was suspect because it came from the writings of Thomas Paine, although Girard had not actually used Paine's offensive word "superstition." Clergy, Webster proclaimed, were "agents of Christ," and when they were excluded, Christ himself was excluded.[4]

There was no historical example of a genuine charity without a Christian foundation, Webster asserted, and he placed particular emphasis on the fact that boys of an impressionable age would be raised without religious instruction, shut up within "high walls" that made the institution as much a prison as a school. The logic of Girard's will would forbid the observance of the sabbath in the school or allowing boys to leave its precincts to attend religious services or instruction elsewhere.[5]

The heart of Webster's argument was his contention that

> however they may be established, there is nothing that we look for with more certainty that than this general principle, that Christianity is part of the law of the land. . . . where there is any religious sentiment amongst men at all, this sentiment incorporates itself with the law. *Every thing declares it. . . . The dead prove it as well as the living.* . . . All, all, proclaim that Christianity, general, tolerant Christianity, Christianity independent of sects and parties, that Christianity to which sword and faggot are unknown, general tolerant Christianity, is the law of the land.[6]

The Court rejected the plaintiffs' claims. Justice Story accepted the defendants' argument that, while Christianity was indeed part of the common law of Pennsylvania, it came with attendant personal liberties. Girard did not intend to insult religion, and no law required that charitable foundations must impart religious instruction.[7]

The case was unique in certain ways. It was perhaps the only Supreme Court case in which a governmental entity (the city of Philadelphia) was sued for affirming liberty rather than for restricting it. In direct contrast to later cases, the issue seemed to be whether there was a constitutional right to establish a secular school, although the Court sidestepped that issue in suggesting that religion could be taught by laypeople. (The modern Court, while permitting Girard to exclude religious instruction from his school, would probably rule that the exclusion of clergy as a group was discriminatory.)

But the deeper implication of the decision was the Court's acceptance of the claim that Christianity was part of Pennsylvania law, that it was in a sense even "established," so that insults to the Christian faith could be punished by law. The decision turned merely on the factual claim that Girard had intended no such insult in drawing up his will. (In 1896 the Court, in passing, reaffirmed that freedom of the press "does not permit blasphemous or indecent articles.")[8]

Ironically, in 1957 the issue of Girard's will was again before the Court, which this time invalidated provisions excluding black people from the school. However, the following year the Court reversed itself, accepting the argument that the school was now private rather than public.[9]

In the *Permoli* case (1844), the Court found that the Free-Exercise Clause did not apply to the states. In the *Girard* case it now found that the Establishment Clause did not apply either. These two decisions, rendered within a year of one another in the mid-1840s, effectively blocked most appeals to the Court involving the Religion Clauses of the Bill of Rights.

In the *Holy Trinity* case (1892), Justice Brewer, writing for a unanimous Court, declared the United States to be a "Christian nation," rehearsing its long history of settlement by religious believers of various kinds. Thus, in an argument strikingly similar to Webster's, he found that Congress could not have intended to inhibit the practice of Christianity by any federal legislation:

> No purpose of action against religion can be imputed to any legislation, state or national, because this is a religious people. . . . From the discovery of the continent to the present hour, there is a single voice making this affirmation.

> These and many other matters which might be noticed add a volume of unofficial declarations to the mass of organic utterances that this is a Christian nation.[10]

Cases with implications for religious establishment sometimes came before the Court in a variety of ways.

LAND GRANTS

All the decisions concerning disputed land claims by churches (chapter 1) in one way or another upheld in principle the legitimacy of land granted by public authorities for religious use, and in the first of these, *Terrett* (1815), the Court even partially reversed the state of Virginia's disestablishment of the Anglican Church, by upholding the validity of land grants made to the church by the British Crown. Story also ruled that Virginia had the right to deprive the Episcopal (formerly Anglican) Church of its exclusive privileges but also had the right to aid all religious groups equally.[11] The Court reached a similar conclusion in the 1823 case brought by the Society for the Propagation of the Gospel in Foreign Parts.

CATHOLIC LAW OF MARRIAGE

In two nineteenth-century cases, the Court recognized limited authority for the Catholic law of marriage in determining the legitimacy of persons in the eyes of the civil law.

In a highly complex dispute over a will in 1850,[12] one of the numerous issues was the contention that one of the claimants, Sidney Collins, was illegitimate, his parents having contracted a civil marriage at a time when

Louisiana was still under Spanish rule. (The Court accepted the case because of diversity of citizenship.)

Justice Grier asked whether such marriages were legal and in answering
the question delved deeply into Catholic law and history, finding that
prior to 1563 the church had recognized marriage by mutual consent but
discountenanced it after that date. However, Spanish colonial law had
been enacted prior to 1563, and had incorporated the earlier code of
Canon Law. Thus it continued to permit marriage by mutual consent.[13]

Another testamentary case turned on the same issue, also in the colonial
territory of Louisiana, also because of diversity of citizenship.[14] In 1848
the Court ruled that Myra Clark Gaines's parents were legally married.[15]
Subsequently, however, papers were discovered showing that a Catholic
priest had declared the marriage bigamous, and in 1852 the Court reversed its earlier judgment.[16]

Thus an 1860 appeal turned on the legal significance of the priest's
finding. Justice James M. Wayne found that Canon Law had been in force
in Louisiana at the time of the marriage of Myra Gaines's parents, and,
like Grier, he delved deeply into Canon Law in terms of the procedures
followed in determining Gaines's illegitimacy.[17]

At the time of the priest's finding, the diocese of Louisiana and the Two
Floridas was without a bishop. Canon Law provided that marital status
could be determined only by a bishop or, in his absence, by the vicar
general of the diocese. But the priest who declared Gaines's father bigamous was merely "presbyter canon of a vacant see" and had falsely styled
himself "Provisory Vicar General and Governor of the Bishopric of the
Province." Therefore he had no authority, Grier concluded.[18] In addition,
Spanish colonial law forbade ecclesiastical investigations into bigamy
without permission of the royal courts, which had not been sought by the
priest in question.[19]

The two cases recognized the legal force of Canon Law only because it
had been so recognized in Spanish colonial law. However, in some minor
way the rulings can be said to have "established" Canon Law because the
Court held that even under American law the church's authority during
the colonial period was in principle still binding.

TAX EXEMPTIONS

Several cases in the nineteenth century defined the status of tax exemptions granted to religious bodies.

In 1860 the Court upheld the city of Philadelphia's partial revocation
of an exemption granted to an Episcopal hospital.[20] The exemption had
been granted in 1833 but was reduced in 1851 when the city found that

some of the property was not being used for its stated purpose. Justice John Campbell ruled that the exemption was a "favor" and a *bene placitum* (literally, "well pleased"—the equivalent of a favor), which could be revoked "at the pleasure of the sovereign."

In 1886 the Court heard an appeal from the Catholic Church over the taxing of some of its property in the District of Columbia.[21] A church building had been demolished and a new one built on the site, the new church placed to one side of the lot and the remainder of the land sold to pay for the new building. District authorities taxed the land that was sold on the grounds that it was not used for a religious purpose. Justice Gray wrote for the unanimous Court in upholding the tax.

In 1902 a Protestant seminary sued to regain a tax exemption on its investment property on the grounds that income from the property was used to support the seminary's work of educating future clergy.[22] Justice Peckham found that there was some ambiguity surrounding the original legal provision of the exemption but that the Illinois court was within its authority in interpreting the exemption narrowly.[23] Justice White, with the concurrence of Justices Holmes and Henry B. Brown, dissented, believing that the original tax exemption constituted a contract that was now being abrogated.[24]

In 1905 the Court again upheld the taxing of church property, in this instance a local Montana tax on cattle owned and sold for profit by the Society of Jesus (Jesuits).[25] The Jesuits conducted schools and other institutions for the benefit of Indian tribes. At one time such institutions had been subsidized by the federal government, but the subsidies had been terminated and the Jesuits began grazing cattle for market as a means of supporting the mission.[26]

The Jesuits contended that since some of the cattle were consumed by Indians, and income from cattle sales was used exclusively for the benefit of the Indian missions, the property should be tax free under a federal law exempting Indian property from state and local taxes.[27]

Peckham ruled against the Jesuits, holding that the cattle were not the property of the Indian tribes and were thus not tax-exempt under federal law. Any such exemption granted for a charitable activity was by state law and was not protected under the Constitution. He rejected the Jesuits' claim that they were acting as agents of the federal government in operating schools for the Indians.[28]

The next year McKenna upheld an Illinois law that granted tax exemptions only to religious or charitable bodies chartered in that state.[29]

By implication the five decisions recognized religious tax exemptions as permissible under the Constitution. However, as Campbell insisted in the first case, they could not be considered a right.

Sabbath Laws

On the eve of the Civil War and again during the 1880s, there were a series of cases involving state laws restricting labor and commerce on Sunday. Although none of the cases challenged the laws on religious grounds, the Court chose in several instances to address that issue anyway.

The first two cases, in 1859, came before the Court as issues in maritime law.

A ship loaded with cotton docked at Boston, and the warehouse to which it had been consigned began unloading it. However, the laborers missed a day of work because of a proclamation by the governor of Massachusetts of a day of "prayer, fasting, and humiliation," and on that day, the remaining cotton on board ship happened to burn.[30]

The shipowners sued the consignees, who responded in part by claiming that they were not obligated to unload the ship on a day of fasting. The shipowners contended that the day of fasting was voluntary in nature and that the warehouse crew could have labored on that day.[31]

Grier essentially upheld the latter contention, finding that people could refrain from work for "caprice or conscientious scruple" but this right could not be exercised at the expense of others. No Massachusetts law forbade labor on any day except Sunday, and Grier offered a historical disquisition on the fact that while there were numerous holidays before the Protestant Reformation, England and America had decided not to observe them. Massachusetts in particular had been settled by people who kept a rigid sabbath but eschewed other religious holidays.[32] Grier's argument seemed almost to imply that the governor had acted improperly in proclaiming the day of a fasting.

In the second case a railroad began construction of a bridge across a river, then abandoned it, leaving piles submerged beneath the surface. A boat was damaged by the piles, and its owners sued the railroad, one of whose defenses was that the ship had sailed on a Sunday, contrary to Maryland law.[33]

Grier ruled that even if the boat-owners were liable to penalties of law for sailing on Sunday, this did not relieve the appellants of their responsibility for the damage. To countenance the loss of the boat would be in effect to impose a second penalty for violation of the sabbath. But there was no sabbath violation, Grier held, because everywhere, boats were classified as "works of necessity" that could be operated on Sundays.[34]

The issue arose again in 1887, when a railroad denied the claim of a man who had been injured in a train accident on the grounds that Massachusetts law allowed travel on "the Lord's Day" only for reasons of "necessity or charity." The plaintiff wished to visit his sister, who was ill, but admitted that his primary purpose was for business. (The case came to the Supreme Court because it involved interstate travel.)[35]

Justice Miller wrote the majority opinion upholding the railroad. Massachusetts law, he noted, explicitly stated that the fact that a plaintiff had violated the Lord's day was not a defense against a claim for injury. However, the state supreme court upheld the railroad's argument, and the high court of the United States ruled that ordinarily state courts ought to be the ultimate interpreters of state law.[36] Justice Harlan dissented.[37]

An 1884 case challenged a San Francisco ordinance closely regulating the activities of laundries, including prohibiting their operation on Sunday. The plaintiff put forward several arguments, including the claim that the law was aimed at Chinese immigrants, but did not argue that it was a violation of the Establishment Clause.[38] (The Chinese appellants were not American citizens, hence the case involved diversity of citizenship.)

In upholding the law, Justice Field observed that sabbath laws were for the purpose of rest, not a use of governmental power to promote religious observances. The Court rejected all the plaintiff's claims, finding that there was no evidence of racial prejudice, and that, even if there were, it would have to be shown that the law was applied by the city in a discriminatory manner.[39]

In 1895 there was a challenge to a Georgia law prohibiting the running of freight trains on Sunday, a statute that the plaintiffs contended violated the Inter-State Commerce Clause of the Constitution.[40] Harlan upheld the law, denying that the Inter-State Commerce Clause was meant to apply in such a case. He went on to say that, even though Sunday was a religious day for some people, this did not prevent the state from choosing it as a day of rest for everyone. If the appropriateness of this was questionable, Harlan ruled, it was not for the courts to decide the issue. Georgia argued properly that many useful moral and religious duties were strengthened by religion, and there was a significant difference between keeping a day holy for religious reasons and merely refraining from labor on such a day.[41] Chief Justice Fuller dissented in the case, holding that the law was indeed a violation of the Inter-State Commerce Clause but saying nothing about religion.[42]

The next year the Court held that the fact that a judge had given a jury instructions on a Sunday did not invalidate a court decision, although no verdict could be received or entered on a Sunday. No federal law declared that Sunday was not a day of business.[43]

In 1899 the Court upheld a Minnesota law permitting "works of charity or necessity" on Sunday but specifically stating that barber shops did not fit that description. Fuller ruled that the law was not discriminatory.[44]

At the very end of the century the Court began to receive cases that explicitly involved the establishment issue.

In *Bradfield v. Roberts* (1899), appellants challenged government support of a District of Columbia hospital that was allegedly Catholic in character.[45] Peckham ruled that the hospital was not officially Catholic, even though it was operated by nuns, then went even further and declared that the institution's constitutional status would not be affected even if the Catholic Church exercised "great control."[46]

In 1905, in a complex case involving a disputed will,[47] the Court clarified the meaning of the *Bradfield* decision through the unusual step of merely adopting as its own the findings of a lower court. Ethelbert Morgan, a resident of the District of Columbia, left a will giving money to Georgetown University, two Catholic orphanages, and an unspecified Catholic parish, with the residue of his estate going to his surviving relatives. His sister contested the charitable bequests on rather subtle legal grounds.

When it was carved out of the state of Maryland, the District of Columbia had enacted the laws of Maryland as binding in the District. The Maryland Bill of Rights (1776) required that if a will was drawn up less than a month before the testator's death, there could be no bequest to a "sectarian institution" without permission of the state legislature. Morgan had in fact died less than a month after the drafting of his will, hence his charitable bequests were said to be invalid. Georgetown was operated by Jesuits, the two orphanages by other Catholic religious orders.[48]

Peckham, without discussing all the arguments in the case, affirmed a decision by the District of Columbia Court of Appeals, accepting the lower court's decision as correct in both law and substance.[49]

Citing the *Bradfield* decision as the basis of its own ruling, the District court[50] had found that the charters of Georgetown and the two orphanages did not restrict them to "the promotion of any religion, creed, or denomination" and that they were open to persons of all creeds. The word "Catholic" did not appear in their charters.

Georgetown had been chartered by act of Congress in 1844, for the purpose of "the instruction of youth in the liberal arts and sciences," without mention of theology. It had also received a papal charter in 1833 that authorized it to offer degrees in theology. However, the school of theology had been separated from the university in 1869, and the university no longer had a theology faculty, nor did it claim to teach the subject. It required no religious test for admission and did not require that students attend lectures on religion.

Since they had charitable purposes apart from religion, the orphanages also did not qualify as "sectarian institutions." Like the District court,

Peckham found that the bequest to the Catholic parish, because its identity was unspecified, was too vague to be carried out.[51]

A minor issue in the case was the fact that Georgetown had been chartered as a "college," and the appellants argued that there was no legal entity called Georgetown University. Peckham, like the lower court, found that the institution was commonly referred to as a university, and its identity was clearly understood.[52]

In 1907 there was a constitutional challenge to the use of federal money to support religious schools for Indians.[53] Fuller merely ruled that the funds belonged to the Indians themselves and that they were free to use them as they saw fit.[54]

Also in 1907 the Court was asked to enforce a contract that required the teaching of certain religious doctrines in a school under the control of the territory of Hawaii.[55] In 1849 a Protestant mission organization had turned one of its schools over to the Kingdom of Hawaii with the provision that the school should never teach anything contrary to the beliefs of the original founders of the school. Should that agreement be violated, Hawaii promised to pay the mission group $15,000 as compensation for the school.[56] The school was later turned into an agricultural college and, after Hawaii had come under American rule, the mission group sued for compensation, the territory of Hawaii denying that the terms of the agreement had been violated.[57]

Justice Joseph McKenna ruled in favor of the mission, construing the original agreement as meaning not only that the school would teach nothing contrary to the beliefs of the founders but that it must also teach those beliefs in a positive way. He found that the 1894 Hawaiian constitution, prohibiting the use of public money for sectarian purposes, did not nullify the agreement.[58]

In 1910 the case returned to the Court, Hawaii arguing once again that there had been no change in the religious teachings of the school, but that if there were, it had occurred in 1877, hence the suit was barred under the statute of limitations. After the 1907 decision the Hawaiian supreme court had reconsidered the case and had taken new evidence.[59]

McKenna again found in favor of the mission body, holding that the new evidence did not alter the facts of the case. The mission had at one time given to Hawaiian officials a statement of its belief, so that Hawaii was aware of what was required to be taught in the school—a Calvinism compatible with the Presbyterian and Congregationalist churches that operated the mission organization. The fact that the school taught nothing contrary to that creed, such as affirming the authority of the pope, did not adequately comply with the terms of the agreement.[60]

In the two cases, the Court found that a contract requiring the teaching of specific religious doctrines in a public school was legally enforceable, and it rejected the claim that the separationist provisions of the Hawaiian constitution nullified such a requirement.

In 1917, as part of a general constitutional challenge to the military-conscription laws, appellants argued that exemptions granted to conscientious objectors violated the Establishment Clause. White, now Chief Justice, dismissed the argument as "too unsound" even to require comment.[61]

In another conscientious-objector case, *MacIntosh* (1931), Justice Sutherland asserted that "We are a Christian people, according to one another the equal right of religious freedom, and acknowledging with reverence the duty of obedience to God."[62] Sutherland could be seen as reaffirming Brewer's claim in the *Holy Trinity* case—that America is a Christian nation—but he found that this did not require the government to accommodate all claims of religious conscience.

In an unusual case in 1924, a meat company sought an injunction against enforcement of a New York law punishing merchants who falsely advertised as "kosher" meat that did not meet the requirements of Jewish rabbinical law, or who failed to post a notice that particular meats were not kosher. The appellants argued that the law placed them in jeopardy, because rabbinical standards were not always clear and a court might at some point declare as nonkosher meat that a merchant offered in good faith.[63]

Sutherland ruled against the plaintiffs. Their claim under the Interstate Commerce Clause was disallowed because the commerce at issue was not interstate, and their argument under the Due-Process Clause of the Fourteenth Amendment was disallowed on the grounds that the law punished only deliberately fraudulent sale of nonkosher meat.[64] An interesting feature of the case is what was not involved—neither the plaintiffs nor the Court itself saw any constitutional significance in the fact that New York state courts were apparently given authority to determine which foods conformed to Jewish dietary laws.

In 1930 the Court heard its first case on a subject that would later become a principal issue in the process of revolutionizing the meaning of the Establishment Clause.[65] Plaintiffs challenged a Louisiana program of providing textbooks to students in both public and private schools on the grounds that the practice violated Louisiana state law; Article IV of the federal Constitution, guaranteeing to every state a "Republican Form of Government"; and the Fourteenth Amendment in that it unlawfully used the plaintiffs' taxes for "private purposes."[66]

Chief Justice Hughes found that the issue of state law had already been determined by the Louisiana Supreme Court. The disputed program benefited all Louisiana children equally and was nondiscriminatory. There was also no issue with respect to Article IV of the federal Constitution.[67] As to the Fourteenth Amendment, Hughes affirmed the finding of the state supreme court that the textbook program involved only secular academic subjects and in no way favored "sectarian schools."[68]

Nothing in the Court's activity prior to World War II gave any sign of the way in which the separationist interpretation of the Establishment Clause would soon become normative.

Chapter Four

CLOUDS OF WITNESSES

THE MODERN Court's concern for civil liberties is conventionally dated from a dictum of Justice Stone in an otherwise rather insignificant 1938 case, *U.S. v. Carolene Products*, one of the series of cases reviewing the economic legislation of President Franklin D. Roosevelt's New Deal. Virtually in passing, in a mere footnote, Stone asked "whether prejudice against discreet and insular minorities may be a special condition, which tends seriously to curtail the operation of those political processes ordinarily to be relied upon to protect minorities, and which may call for correspondingly more searching judicial inquiry."[1] Although the suggestion was made in an exceedingly inconspicuous form, within a few years it would be seen as the first clear enunciation of a new judicial philosophy of individual liberties.

The honor of being by far the most constitutionally important religious group in American history belongs to a small sect ordinarily considered marginal to American life—the Jehovah's Witnesses—to whom also belongs the distinction of being by far the most litigious religious group in the nation's history. Time after time the Witnesses have returned to the courts to argue that their constitutional rights have been violated, and as often as not they have been successful. Their decision to pursue legal remedies, beginning in the late 1930s, coincided with a major philosophical shift within the Court, and the Witnesses' tireless persistence was the vehicle for a complete reconsideration of the meaning of the Free-Exercise Clause.

The sect originated in 1881 with a group called Zion's Watch Tower Tract Society and was officially renamed Jehovah's Witnesses in 1931. They rejected certain traditional Christian teachings such as the Trinity and the divinity of Christ, and often denounced other religions as perversions. Believing that they followed the pure model of Christianity as found in the New Testament, they were pacifists who sometimes also rejected the authority of government as contrary to the laws of God.[2]

During the period of intense litigation by the Witnesses (1938–55), they had a major impact on three important areas of constitutional law—refusal to obey an "unjust" law, public proselytization, and conscientious objection to military service.

During the 1930s local schooldistricts around the country began enacting rules requiring schoolchildren to take the Pledge of Allegiance to the American flag each morning, along with the accompanying salute. The

Witnesses opposed the practice as idolatrous, and many of their children
refused the Pledge and were expelled from school. Witnesses were also
increasingly subjected to mob violence and denounced as unpatriotic, and
as a result, the Witnesses and certain other groups, notably the American
Civil Liberties Union, decided to attempt to bring a case to the high court.[3]

The case that the Court accepted came from Pennsylvania, where the
Gobitis family of Witnesses refused, as a matter of conscience, to make the
Pledge, whereupon their children were expelled from school. The family
claimed both a violation of the First Amendment and monetary damages
because they were now forced to send their children to private schools.[4]

The Court ruled that the law in question was not a violation of the
Constitution. Writing for the majority, Justice Frankfurter raised the question that would continually swirl around the Court in its modern "activ-
ist" period—whether it was proper to invalidate legislation that, while it
might be deemed unwise, was nonetheless the product of the democratic
system. ("We cannot be the school board of the country," Frankfurter
warned.)[5]

In some previous cases (for example, those concerning polygamy) the
Court had ruled that restrictions on religious freedom were legitimate
when acts done in the name of religion were harmful to society. Implicitly
at least, the appellants in 1940 argued that their refusal to salute the flag
harmed no one. Frankfurter, however, thought otherwise, since a duly
elected government deemed such rituals necessary to enkindle patriotism
in the people. ("We live by symbols.")[6]

He acknowledged that the religious conscience was "here put to a se-
vere test" and that only a strong reason could justify that test. But the
encouragement of patriotism was such a reason, and mere religious convictions could not exempt people from general political obligations.
Frankfurter argued that the very religious freedom that the appellants
claimed for themselves actually required some modification of that freedom, since religious liberty rested upon pluralistic principles that of their
nature could not be absolute.[7] (Frankfurter was said to have been initially
torn between "two rights" in the *Gobitis* case,[8] but his resolution subsequently hardened.)

Justice Stone dissented vigorously, although treating the matter more
as a violation of free speech than of religious liberty, since the law sought
to make people utter sentiments that they did not sincerely hold. He rejected Frankfurter's counsel of judicial restraint on the grounds that this
would be a surrender to the popular will and it was precisely the Court's
duty to protect minorities.[9]

But a Court that in 1940 was almost unanimous in denying the Witnesses' claims, dramatically reversed itself in 1943, arguably the single
most important year in the history of the Court so far as religious liberty

is concerned. In *West Virginia State Board of Education v. Barnette*,[10] a majority of the justices held that to force children to salute the flag against their consciences was after all a violation of the First Amendment.

Justice Jackson wrote the majority opinion, interpreting the flag salute as "a form of utterance" and, drawing on Stone's dissent of 1940, arguing that to force citizens to say things they did not believe was as much a violation of liberty as to forbid them to say those they did believe. The issue differed from that of pacifist students denied admission to a state university (the 1934 *Hamilton* case), because enrollment in a university was optional, whereas West Virginia required children to attend school, then expelled those who refused to salute the flag.[11]

The *Gobitis* ruling assumed that saluting the flag was a "need" of the state, which Jackson thought was unproven. The merely symbolic nature of the requirement made it especially flimsy, Jackson insisted, since it could hardly be thought that a healthy democracy required such "barren gestures."[12]

Justices Hugo Black and William O. Douglas had been part of the almost unanimous majority in the *Gobitis* case but now reversed themselves. While religious believers could not be allowed to choose which laws they would obey, Black and Douglas, like Jackson, found that the flag salute was not essential to the well-being of the nation.[13]

Frankfurter, who had written the majority opinion in *Gobitis*, remained unconvinced and issued an aggressive dissent in *Barnette*. Noting wryly that (as a Jew) he belonged to "the most vilified and persecuted minority in history," and thus could hardly be thought insensitive to minority rights, he nonetheless rejected the new "libertarian" views of the Court. As in *Gobitis*, he argued primarily from the inherent limits on the Court's authority and disclaimed any mandate for writing his own opinions (implying that he was sympathetic to the Witnesses) into the Constitution. Citing the *Hamilton* case, he pointed out that the law made no distinction between elementary schools and colleges, thus neither could the Court make one. As an inherently undemocratic body, the Court lacked all legislative powers and should not exercise surreptitiously a power that, if judges were to exercise it, ought to make them subject periodically to the electorate.

Besides the basic question of the Court's competence, Frankfurter also argued that religious liberty was never intended to allow citizens to override laws passed for general purposes without the intention of restricting any particular group.

The constitutional protection of religious liberties terminated disabilities, it did not create new privileges. It gave religions equality, not civil immunity. Its essence is freedom from conformity to religious dogma, not freedom from conformity to law because of religious dogma. Religious loyalties may be exercised without hindrance from the state, not the state may not exercise that which except by leave of religious loyalties is within the domain of temporal power.[14]

As the Court had done consistently, Frankfurter noted that religious liberty involves action as well as belief, and denied that freedom of action could exist in such a way as to "shut out the state." The right to believe does not include the right to invalidate the general laws of society, which often rest on compulsion. Unlike Jackson, Frankfurter argued that "even the most sophisticated live by symbols" and that, if the government believed that such symbolic expression was necessary to the well-being of society, that judgment should be respected, although he also concluded that the West Virginia law might be thought "unwise."[15]

Justices Owen Roberts and Stanley Reed also reaffirmed their positions in the *Gobitis* case, but without written opinions.[16]

Besides Black's and Douglas's reversal of their earlier positions, the case was dramatic for the unparalleled speed with which that decision was overturned, and overturned bluntly, without pretense of consistency with the previous decision. In *Barnette* the Court cooly proclaimed that it had entered a new age of jurisprudence.

This sudden reversal of position occurred not only because of Black's and Douglas's change of opinion but also because of changes in membership during the period 1940–43. Chief Justice Hughes retired in 1941 and was replaced by Stone, the lone dissenter in *Gobitis*, while three additional liberals—Francis P. Murphy, Wiley Rutledge, and Jackson—were also appointed.

Immediately after the *Barnette* case, the Court almost automatically overturned a Mississippi law punishing anyone who "encouraged disloyalty" to the government, which had led to the arrest of several Witnesses who distributed literature urging people not to salute the flag.[17]

While Stone's dictum in the *Carolene* case, followed by his dissent in the *Gobitis* case, marked the beginning of a new era of civil liberties, the *Gobitis* case was not the first time the Witnesses appealed to the Court, and beginning in 1938, the year of the *Carolene* dictum, they brought forward a series of cases that, over the next seventeen years, would lead to a much broader, and much more carefully defined understanding of the rights of religious proselytization. The Witnesses won victories even before the dramatic *Barnette* decision of 1943.

In 1938 the Court invalidated a municipal ordinance in Georgia requiring anyone distributing literature to obtain a license from the city. The law was struck down as an obvious form of censorship that aimed to inhibit the dissemination of ideas, if not their actual publication, the Court treating the issue as one of freedom of the press rather than of religion.[18]

The following year the Court again ruled in the Witnesses' favor, in a New Jersey case in which a city required door-to-door solicitors to obtain a permit from the police, who investigated the applicants and decided on their fitness. The Court ruled that, while the town could legitimately regulate public order and the movement of traffic, the law constituted censorship. Again the issue was more a matter of a free press than of religious freedom.[19]

A few months before the *Gobitis* case in 1940, Witnesses had appeared before the Court because of the arrest of one of their number in Connecticut, for soliciting door-to-door without a license. Newton Cantwell had also been arrested for disturbing the peace, since he carried with him a portable Victrola on which, in a neighborhood that was heavily Catholic, he played a record attacking the Catholic Church.[20]

Two weeks before it handed down the *Gobitis* decision, the Court proved responsive to the Witnesses in the *Cantwell* case. Arguing for the majority, Roberts again noted that freedom of belief was absolute, while freedom of action could not be. In general the government could regulate the time and place of public gatherings, including solicitations. However, the licensing requirement constituted "prior restraint" on the distribution of literature and thus constituted censorship, since Cantwell's behavior did not obviously constitute a breach of the peace. On the whole, Roberts argued, it was better for the sake of liberty to allow "excesses of zeal" than to curtail them.[21]

In 1941 Witnesses were before the Court in connection with their having held a parade in a New Hampshire town without getting a permit. Here the Court found no injury, and Hughes ruled that a well-ordered society could validly regulate the use of sidewalks and other public places. The town had not curtailed the distribution of literature, as in the *Cantwell* case.[22]

In 1942 Witnesses from three states were before the Court challenging city ordinances that imposed licensing fees on the sale of literature.[23] Writing for the majority, Reed summed up, "So the mind and spirit of man remain forever free, while his actions must rest subject to necessary accommodations to the competing needs of his fellows." While ideas could not be curtailed, it was permissible to tax the money-making activities of churches and other groups, just as a tax on newspapers was not a violation of freedom of the press. The sale of literature was a commercial activity.[24]

Stone again dissented vigorously, insisting that this was indeed a tax
on ideas and that the Witnesses' sale of literature was not intended to be
profitable. Again affirming the Court's duty to protect despised minorities, he concluded that "the more humble and needy the cause the more
effective its suppression."[25]

Murphy also wrote a strong dissent, insisting that freedom to believe
also meant freedom to communicate one's beliefs. Thus Witnesses were
taxed on their ideas, as much as if the cities in question imposed taxes on
Sunday sermons.[26] Also writing for the minority on the Court, Black, with
the concurrence of Murphy and Douglas, offered a tantalizing hint of the
future in remarking that, although they had joined in the *Gobitis* decision
of 1940, he and Douglas now believed it had been wrongly decided.[27]

In 1942 the Court also overturned a local Texas law that licensed booksellers, on the grounds that this constituted censorship and a violation of
religious freedom.[28]

In the two years following the *Gobitis* case, the Witnesses also lost
half a dozen appeals by the Supreme Court's simply upholding, without
comment, lower-court decisions.[29] But, although the cases brought by the
Witnesses between 1940 and 1942 had yielded mixed results, even their
defeats could be seen as pyrrhic, in that they laid the groundwork for a
dramatic expansion of the Court's concept of religious liberty.

In 1943, the year of the *Barnette* ruling, the Witnesses also had several
other victories.

The Court overturned the conviction of an Ohio Witness who had ignored a local law imposing a tax on door-to-door solicitation[30] and also
found for the Witnesses in a similar incident in Pennsylvania.[31] The majority opinion in these cases was written by Douglas, who likened the tax to
a levy on sermons and said that there could be no fee imposed on the
exercise of a constitutional right.[32]

Reed, who the year before had written the Court's decision forbidding
the licensing of booksellers, now dissented, arguing that such solicitation
amounted to sales, not a free-will offering, and that there was no evidence
that the law had been enforced in a discriminatory manner. He went on
to suggest that charging a fee for religious goods in any case destroyed
their "sacred character."[33] Frankfurter also dissented, pointing out that
the press was taxed without this being viewed as a violation of the Constitution, and questioning the venerable adage that "the power to tax is the
power to destroy."[34]

In a similar 1943 case the Court upheld a Witness who refused to pay
a booksellers tax, even though he admitted to earning his living by selling
religious publications.[35] Douglas ruled that, since the books were admittedly religious in nature, the defendant had to be assumed to be in good
faith when he claimed that he was "preaching the Gospel." The activities

of preachers of "more orthodox faiths," Douglas pointed out, were not taxed as though they were commercial enterprises, even though those clergy too supported themselves through their callings.[36]

Roberts, supported by Frankfurter and Jackson, dissented. The tax was not discriminatory and in effect amounted to a subsidy of religion, since the Witness resided in the town where he sold books and should be required to contribute to the support of municipal services.[37]

Rhetorically, Roberts asked whether Trinity Church, a famously wealthy New York Episcopal parish, should be exempt from taxes on its income property. The logic of the decision dictated that the government also subsidize the exercise of freedom of speech and the press, and Roberts pointed out that many people, for example, those engaged in healing the sick, might also consider their occupations religious in nature and could therefore demand tax exemptions.[38] Murphy, part of the majority, answered Roberts by insisting that income property owned by religious groups could be taxed.[39]

Another victory for the Witnesses came when the Court invalidated a Dallas ordinance forbidding the distribution of handbills on the streets. Black held for a unanimous Court that the law obviously violated freedom of expression and freedom of religion. The fact that the Witnesses advertised their publications on their handbills did not make those into commercial documents, and they could not be regulated by the city.[40]

But the Witnesses lost a related case that year, when the Court upheld a Pennsylvania town in its collection of a licensing tax on all "merchandise" sold and its arrest of Witnesses who failed to pay the tax.[41] Stone ruled that the Witnesses did not prove that they had suffered any injury other than the incidental ones involved in any "good-faith prosecution" for a crime.[42]

Jackson wrote a longer concurring opinion, arguing that the right to proselytize here came into conflict with "the right to be left alone." The Witnesses had been extraordinarily abrasive and deliberately offensive, in his view, and kept their financial records confidential, so the city could not estimate what kind of burden the tax might place on their resources. While the Constitution aimed to prevent religious persecution, the definition of this could not be left to "the consciences of the minority." If all sects were allowed to do this, chaos would result.[43]

In 1944 the Witnesses lost a case in which a woman had been prosecuted under the child-labor laws for taking her nine-year-old niece with her on an evangelizing mission at night.[44] Rutledge ruled that, even though the child had asked to accompany her aunt, the state's interest in protecting children from exploitation was legitimate. Conceding parental rights to be "paramount," he nonetheless defined, in a phrase with potentially far-reaching implications, the state as *parens patriae* ("parent of the nation"), with ultimate responsibility for child welfare. The dangers of the streets at night, the child's need for sleep, and other factors all rendered the state's interest in the matter legitimate.[45]

Murphy on the other hand saw it precisely as a denial of religious freedom, especially given the fact that in several previous cases the Court found that the Witnesses had a constitutional right to disseminate literature unimpeded. To Murphy the dangers to the child were minimal and the state had failed to prove otherwise.[46]

Jackson also dissented, arguing that if the child-labor laws could be upheld in this instance, they could also be used to prevent children from attending church under certain circumstances. In his characteristically trenchant style, he affirmed that "religious practices ought to be free—as nearly absolutely free as anything can be."[47]

Decided at the same time as the previous case, the Court also upheld the prosecution of a Witness who allegedly cursed a police officer, seeing the incident as merely a routine case of peace disturbance.[48]

As World War II was ending the Witnesses won another victory when the Court overturned the conviction of a Texas Witness who had been arrested, in a village owned by the federal government for the benefit of government employees, for refusing to leave private premises when ordered to do so. Black wrote a majority opinion finding this an obvious violation of religious liberty. Stone, Reed, and Harold Burton dissented without comment.[49]

In a similar case in 1946, a Witness was prevented from distributing literature in an Alabama town that was owned by a private company.[50] Black ruled that this was a violation of religious liberty. If many individuals each owned part of the town, as was true in most places, this would not justify barring the distribution of literature, and the fact that the entire town had only one owner made no difference. The town was open to outsiders who often came there to shop. Even residents of company towns were entitled to "uncensored information," which unsolicited literature attempted to bring them.[51] Frankfurter concurred, arguing that the "technicalities" of local government could not be used to infringe constitutional liberties.[52]

Reed dissented, stating bluntly that the Court had never held First Amendment rights to be "absolute and unlimited" and thought this was the first case to extend religious liberty onto private property without the owner's consent. The Witness could have used a nearby public highway, and access by the public to privately owned territory for limited purposes did not give outsiders the right to go there for unrelated purposes.[53]

In 1948 the Court was again called upon to refine its interpretation of religious liberty with some subtlety, in a case from New York State in which a Witness had been denied a permit to use a public-address system in a public park after the town government said there had been complaints about the practice.[54] Douglas held the town's action to be "prior restraint" on free speech. Among other considerations, the municipal law placed no limits on the police's discretionary power in deciding who should receive a permit. Loud speakers had become a necessary and normal part of modern communications, and their use could not be denied because of possible abuse.[55]

Frankfurter dissented, noting that the park was small and characterizing the Witness's preaching as "aural aggression."[56] Jackson also dissented. The park was indeed small and had been set aside for recreation. The Witness set up his public-address system several feet from his automobile, connected by wires that were dangerous to the public. Jackson thought it "astonishing news" that the Constitution forbade a town from preventing the unauthorized erection of a structure in a public park and called the majority decision "a startling perversion." [57]

The decision went against the recent *McCollum* decision (chapter 6), Jackson argued, since in the latter case the government was forbidden to allow its facilities to be used to propagate religion, whereas here it was actually required to do so. There was no evidence that the Witnesses were discriminated against, or that any other religion used the park to preach.[58] According to Jackson the Witnesses "wanted to throw their message upon people who were in the park for recreation, a type of conduct which involves other persons' privacy and, if it has no other control, may lead to riots and disorders."[59]

In 1951 the Court overturned the conviction of a Witness who conducted Bible-study meetings in a Maryland city park without obtaining a permit. He had requested one but had been refused and was charged with disorderly conduct when he held the session anyway.[60]

Two years later the Court ruled similarly in a Rhode Island case in which a law allowed "religious and political meetings" in public parks but not "sermons or speeches." The Court found that the law was applied to the Witnesses in a discriminatory way.[61]

Chief Justice Fred M. Vinson wrote the majority opinion, noting that the appellant had shown no signs of disorderly conduct and had made an effort to obtain a permit, which in fact was not even required by city law. Treating it essentially as an issue of free speech, Vinson ruled that the requirement of a permit constituted "prior restraint" and that the Witness had been denied permission precisely because city officials disapproved of what he might say.[62] Black and Frankfurter issued a concurring opinion acknowledging the need to balance freedom of expression with the need for "peace and order" but also finding that the Witness had been harassed solely because of his beliefs.[63]

A similar case, dealt with in conjunction with the previous one, involved a Baptist preacher in New York City who had first been granted a permit for street preaching but then saw it revoked after complaints about his "inflammatory" attacks on other religions.[64] Vinson again wrote the majority opinion, holding that city authorities had the right to control disorder but that in revoking the permit they were exercising "prior restraint" on the preacher.[65]

Jackson wrote another of his impassioned dissents, suggesting that the decision might be a "quixotic tilt at windmills which belittles great principles of liberty." The appellant was viciously anti-Catholic and anti-Semitic, in Jackson's view, and posed a real danger to public order because his diatribes might provoke mob violence. Again referring to the *McCollum* case, Jackson wryly noted that three years previously the Court had forbidden the use of public buildings for religious purposes but now seemed to require that New York allow the public streets to be used for those purposes.[66]

In the same year the Witnesses lost a New Hampshire case in which a town required a license before permitting a religious service in a public park. The New Hampshire Supreme Court ruled that the town had made an error in denying a license to the Witnesses but that the law itself was not improper.[67] Reed held that the First Amendment did not mean that "everyone with opinions or beliefs to express may gather around him at any public place and at any time a group for discussion and instruction." The appellant was not justified in ignoring a legal requirement in anticipation of its possible future invalidation.[68]

Frankfurter concurred. The Court had no obligation to concern itself with the case, he insisted, and therefore had an obligation not so to concern itself. The license law was not in itself invalid, and there was thus no constitutional issue.[69]

Black dissented, citing the case as "yet another example" of the restriction of free expression. The license had not been denied to the Witnesses for the normal reasons of public order. Free speech should enjoy special protection.[70] Douglas also dissented, offering the bold opinion that "when a legislature undertakes to proscribe the exercise of a citizen's right to free speech, it acts lawlessly, and the citizen can take matters into his own hands and proceed on the basis that such a law is no law at all."[71] Even "reasonable" impositions on free speech were constitutionally impermissible, Douglas insisted, and he decried what he called a "slowly creeping" judicial doctrine allowing the regulation of speech. The New Hampshire licensing law constituted prior restraint.[72]

Although the rights of religious proselytizers seemed to have been exhaustively litigated by the end of World War II, with the Witnesses the vehicle for an almost revolutionary expansion of those rights, the issue returned, anomalously, shortly after the turn of the next century, in a case not substantially different from those that came before the Court during the 1940s. The 2002 case involved an Ohio village that, for security reasons, required "canvassers" to obtain a permit from the municipality.[73]

Justice John Paul Stevens ruled for the majority that public proselytizing enjoyed the same degree of freedom as worship in a church, and the challenged ordinance restricted a wide range of expression. Some people might, for conscience's sake, refuse to seek a permit to preach the Gospel.[74]

Justice Antonin Scalia concurred in the decision but ridiculed the claim that conscience might forbid a proselytizer from seeking a permit. Such people, he declared, were "crackpots."[75] Chief Justice Rehnquist dissented, holding that the village's concern about possible criminal activity was a justification for requiring the permit.[76]

During World War II the Selective Service Act made provision for those who claimed conscientious-objector status, and local draft boards seem to have routinely granted it to members of the recognized "peace churches," such as the Quakers. The Jehovah's Witnesses were also principled pacifists.

The government also granted a blanket exemption from military service to clergy who, unlike conscientious objectors, were not required to perform alternative kinds of services for the war effort. Officially the Witnesses considered all their members to be ministers of the Gospel, although some were ordained to a higher level.

Local boards determined these classifications, which could only be appealed through the Selective Service Administration itself, during which process the Federal Bureau of Investigation was sometimes asked to review the appellant's history. Congress specifically prohibited draftees from challenging their classifications in the civil courts, fearing that this would clog the courts with appeals that could delay military induction for years. If an individual claimed to have been drafted illegally, he had to rely on applying to a civil court for a writ of habeas corpus claiming that he was being detained unlawfully.[77]

In a 1944 case a Witness had been classified as a conscientious objector but failed to report to the camp to which he was assigned, claiming that he had been denied the opportunity to prove in court that the draft board was prejudiced against him in rejecting his claim to be a minister.[78]

Black merely noted that Congress had not authorized such judicial review and in fact intended a speedy process not delayed by court challenges.[79] Concurring, Rutledge noted that Nick Falbo, the appellant, had not raised the issue of prejudice during his appeal through the Selective Service Administration. Thus if any such prejudice existed at the lower level, it presumably had been corrected by the appeal.[80]

Murphy dissented vigorously. If the claim of prejudice was true, then Falbo did not commit a crime in failing to report. A citizen accused of a crime was entitled to every means of proving his innocence. Basic liberties could not be safely left to the discretion of public officials, and Murphy noted that one draft board member was reported to have said, "I have no damned use for the Jehovah's Witnesses."[81] While Congress did not authorize a civil trial in such cases, it also did not forbid one, Murphy contended. Such a trial would not be a "litigious interruption" of a governmental process but an actual criminal case, since Falbo faced a prison term.[82]

Running through most of the conscription cases was the implicit issue of sincerity, and Murphy addressed that by asserting that the kind of people who would bring such a challenge into court "are invariably those whose conscientious or religious scruples would prevent them reporting for induction regardless."[83] Murphy concluded that "The law knows no finer hour than when it cuts through formal concepts and transitory emotions to protect unpopular citizens against discrimination and persecution. I can perceive no other course for the law to take in this case."[84]

Several conscription cases dragged on beyond the close of the war.

In two 1946 cases, which the Court joined together, Witnesses claiming to be ministers had been classified as eligible for combat. They appealed through Selective Service and lost, then claimed that the local draft board had withheld relevant information from the appeals board.[85]

Douglas found in the appellants' favor. Draft boards could not act in a discriminatory manner, nor could criminal sanctions automatically be attached to every board decision. While Congress had made the decision of the appeal board "final," that decision could be challenged if there was no factual basis for the classification. The appellant in the *Falbo* case had not exhausted all his remedies, whereas those in the pending cases had. Since draftees were allowed to obtain a writ of habeas corpus, it was obvious that Congress did not intend to deny all civil remedies to draftees.[86]

Murphy concurred, repeating his previous contention that citizens could not be punished as criminals without being allowed to mount an adequate defense. The word "final" in the draft law referred only to internal appeals, at the conclusion of which the courts could intervene. He again estimated that few men would abuse the process if it were open to them. (Speaking of "conscientious *or* religious scruples" [emphasis added], at a time when the law recognized only religious motives for pacifism, he anticipated the Court's position of the 1960s.)[87]

The writ of habeas corpus was not sufficient protection, Murphy thought, since the individual lost all civilian rights upon entering the military, and military authorities could thwart the obtaining of the writ, which was in any case of no use to those who were challenging the very conditions of their induction.[88] The entire system involved a denial of due process, something fundamentally contrary to the American system, Murphy contended, and he warned against using the government's war powers to trample individual rights.[89]

Rutledge also concurred. Congress could not make it a crime to violate an administrative order without granting citizens the right to challenge the constitutionality of that order.[90]

Frankfurter began his opinion by pointing out that the decision contradicted the plain words of the congressional act and that words should always be given their "ordinary meaning." As Congress realized, the induction process could not be encumbered by endless jury trials. The writ of habeas corpus offered a swift process that did bring relief to those who used it. Congress had also imposed no conditions on the draft boards' use of their authority.[91]

However, having made this argument, Frankfurter then unpredictably concurred in the majority judgment. The appellants claimed that their right to appeal within the Selective Service system had been thwarted. A crucial disputed point was the government's claim that one of the appellants had failed to report for induction, whereas he claimed that he had been forcibly taken to the induction center. These disputes should be decided by a jury.[92] Burton dissented, finding the earlier part of Frankfurter's opinion more persuasive than his conclusion.[93]

In another case that reached the Court in 1946, a Witness claiming to be a minister had been classified as a conscientious objector and ordered to report to camp, but refused. Another appellant (two cases were again yoked together) made a token appearance at the camp, then departed. In the first case the government now conceded that changes in procedures rendered it unnecessary for an appellant actually to appear at camp in order to begin the appeals process.[94]

Rutledge found in favor of the Witnesses on rather subtle grounds. As the government now conceded, the physical examination to determine an individual's fitness to serve at a camp was made before he appeared at camp. Since there was thus no basis for rejecting him once he had passed the physical examination, the process was "complete," within the meaning of the law, once he had passed, and an objector did not have to appear at the camp in order to lodge an appeal.[95]

The Witness who did appear at the camp did not thereby come under military authority but merely under other kinds of civilian authority. Thus he did not lose his ordinary civil rights. But the writ of habeas corpus was not available in a camp for conscientious objectors, as it was to men in the military. Thus he too was entitled to a civil trial.[96]

In the following year the Court heard three Witnesses' cases joined together. All three appellants claimed to be ministers but had been classified as conscientious objectors and sent to camps. During their trials for leaving the camps without permission, the judge instructed the jury not to consider the question as to whether they had been properly classified by their draft boards. In one case an individual only claimed the ministerial status ten days after being classified as an objector, but the other two had already claimed to be ministers at the time of their applications.[97]

Reed held for the Court that the appellants were not entitled to raise the issue of their classification in a civil trial. At issue was the definition of a minister. Two of the appellants appeared to spend relatively little time in church work, and the draft board thus had a reasonable basis for denying them clerical status. A jury should not be allowed to decide if the draft board's classifications were proper.[98]

Douglas dissented. Congress had mandated clerical exemptions, which were not limited to the "more orthodox or conventional faiths." The fact that some of the appellants were employed in secular occupations did not invalidate their claims, since financial need might dictate this.[99]

Murphy also dissented. He did not think that the courts were required always to sustain the Selective Service classifications. Since the appellants faced the possibility of prison, they should not be required to adhere to high levels of proof in their defense.[100]

Others besides Witnesses occasionally brought forward issues of compulsory military service in wartime.

In 1944 the Court ruled against an Illinois man denied a license to practice law because he would not swear an oath to support a state constitution requiring citizens to serve in the militia. The appellant, without indicating any specific religious affiliation, professed to believe that the teachings of the New Testament prohibited all violent action.[101]

Reed held that the state had not discriminated against the attorney because of his religious beliefs but solely because of his refusal to take the oath. Previous conscientious-objector cases (chapter 2) had established that there was no fundamental right to an exemption from military service, and the fact that the federal government required such an oath from prospective citizens demonstrated that a state could do the same.[102]

Black dissented, holding that the attorney's religious beliefs were the sole reason for his being denied a law license. Black noted that a number of Quakers had submitted briefs in support of the appellant, because under the ruling they too might be barred from the practice of law.[103]

Many people, according to Black, seemed to think that "Christ's Gospel" was not suitable guidance in a harsh world, but the mere profession of such beliefs should not exclude a man from the bar. Besides the Free-Exercise Clause, Black cited Article VI of the Constitution, prohibiting any "religious test" for public office.[104]

The government, Black held, could draft conscientious objectors and punish those who refused service, but it could not impose the oath as a test of citizenship. Black also indicated that he agreed with the dissenters in the conscientious-objector cases decided by the Court around 1930.[105]

Black's position was seemingly adopted by the rest of the Court when, immediately after the war, it granted conscientious-objector status to a Canadian Seventh Day Adventist who had been denied citizenship because of his pacifism, an almost symmetrically opposite decision from the majority ruling in the *MacIntosh* case (1930). Writing now for a unanimous Court, Douglas found that the previous cases had simply been wrongly decided,[106] another blunt reminder that the jurisprudence of the First Amendment had indeed changed.

Shortly after the war the Court heard two cases that resembled those of the Witnesses but instead involved Jews. In both cases the appellant claimed that he was studying for the rabbinate and should therefore be given an exemption from the draft.

In one case a man had been inducted despite his claim to be a theology student, but he gained his release under a writ of habeas corpus. The New York City draft board relied on an unofficial panel of Jews to advise it on such claims, and the panel questioned the appellant's sincerity, pointing out that the seminary in which he was enrolled did not exclusively train men as rabbis.[107]

Douglas ruled against the appellant. The draft board had a difficult task, and it was appropriate to rely on the advice of the panel. No evidence of impropriety had been presented.[108] However, he cautioned, the panel should only give advice on facts about Jewish life, not make a judgment about any applicant's sincerity. Even though the panel in this case exceeded its authority, there was no evidence, Douglas thought, that the draft board's decision was based on that. Douglas himself thought there were indications that the claimant had sought to evade the draft.[109]

In the second case the applicant first told the draft board that he intended to become a social worker, but after receiving an induction notice proceeded to enroll in a theological seminary. Douglas again rendered the unanimous opinion of the Court, holding that there was evidence of lack of sincerity on the part of the appellant and again noting that the school in question was not exclusively for the training of rabbis.[110]

As with the proselytization cases, conscription cases involving Witnesses continued well into the 1950s, given urgency by the Korean War.

In 1953 the Court ruled in favor of a Witness who had been denied status as a minister because he was employed also as a radio repairman. After being classified as eligible for combat, he had become a full-time minister. A basic issue in the case was the claim by the Selective Service

Administration that the courts did not have the authority to overturn its classifications.[111]

Justice Tom C. Clark held that part-time secular work did not preclude a clerical exemption. The draft board apparently doubted the appellant's good faith. While the SSA was correct that the courts could not overturn its decisions, it was still necessary that the draft board show reasons for them.[112]

Jackson dissented. The board, in his opinion, had adequate reasons for being suspicious of the applicant, and it was incumbent on the appellant to show that the board had acted wrongly.[113]

In the same year, two applicants for conscientious-objector status appealed on the grounds that they had not been given copies of their FBI reports. Vinson found for the Court that they had no right to those documents. Frankfurter dissented, believing that religious discrimination might be involved. Douglas warned that such reports might encourage the use of informers, a practice he branded "infamous."[114]

Four such cases were decided by the Court in 1955, the year in which the long series of court challenges brought by Jehovah's Witnesses at last came to an end.

In one case a man first sought an agricultural deferment from military service, claiming that he could contribute to the war effort as a farmer. He stated that he was not a cleric but also submitted an application for conscientious-objector status. The draft board found that he had not given any public witness to his pacifist views. After being denied status as an objector, he claimed to be a full-time Witness minister. Clark found for a unanimous Court that the draft board had adequate reasons to be suspicious of those claims.[115]

In the second case a man who was employed as a chauffeur claimed, three years after he had registered for the draft, to be a conscientious objector, reporting that he had joined the Witnesses a year after registering and had become a minister a year after that. The FBI report allegedly found evidence of character flaws that called the sincerity of his religious conversion into question. The claimant had not been given a copy of the report and said he had only learned of its contents indirectly. Clark held that his conviction should be overturned because, although citizens were not entitled to actual copies of their FBI reports, they were entitled to knowledge of the contents. Thus the appellant had not received a fair hearing. Justice Sherman Minton thought the board had merely made an "honest error," and Reed pointed out that the appellant had not formally requested a copy of the report prior to his appeal hearing.[116]

In the third case a Witness who claimed conscientious-objector status was ordained to the ministry a month after registering for the draft. He too appealed on the grounds that he was not given a copy of the FBI report on his case.[117]

Clark noted that the FBI report allegedly said that the claimant had been a Catholic all his life and had only become a Witness a month after registering for the draft. Had the appellant been been informed of the contents of the report, he might have been able to refute this claim. Reed and Minton held that there was no obligation to furnish him with the report.[118]

A case decided at the same time as the other three, the Witnesses' last appearance before the Court for over forty years, was almost a comic anticlimax. A Witness was denied conscientious-objector status on the grounds that his stance was "selective"—he did not condemn all wars but admitted he would fight at Armaggedon when Jesus would come a second time. Two justices dissented, but the majority of the Court ruled that such a remote prospect, when the fighting would not be with "carnal weapons," was not a disqualification.[119]

Chapter Five

EXPANSION

In 1944, as the Court was negotiating the forest of cases involving Jehovah's Witnesses, it also decided a case, *US v. Ballard*,[1] which brought forward a unique issue that further manifested the new commitment to the rights of minorities.

The I Am Movement took its name from the words of God to Moses in the burning bush (Exod. 3:14). Its leaders were prosecuted by federal authorities for mail fraud, because they solicited funds claiming that they could cure illnesses, had been taken up into heaven, had walked with the angels, and had shaken hands with Jesus. The indictment claimed that Guy Ballard and his associates "well knew" that these claims were false, and they were convicted.

In his instructions to the jury, the judge in the lower court stated that the truth of the I Am claims was not at issue but merely whether their beliefs were sincerely held, an instruction in which the defense acquiesced. On appeal, however, the defense claimed that the judge's instructions improperly altered the charge, since originally the government had raised the credibility issue. The defendants also argued that questions of personal motives should have been excluded, since it infringed religious liberty for the government to make such an inquiry.[2]

Justice Douglas wrote the majority opinion, which affirmed the widest possible leeway for belief and insisted that no one could be required to prove the truth of personal religious convictions. Many familiar Christian beliefs, such as the resurrection of Jesus from the dead, might seem incredible to some people, and it was precisely the nature of religious faith that it was sacred to some, unbelievable to others.[3]

Douglas found that it was practically impossible to separate the issue of sincerity from the issue of truth, hence the sincerity issue should also have been withheld from the jury. No jury had a right to determine the truth of beliefs ("the law knows no heresy," he quoted, from the *Watson* case), but a judgment as to sincerity of belief ultimately depended on a judgment as to inherent credibility.[4] The case was thus remanded to the court of appeals for rehearing.[5]

Dissenting, Chief Justice Stone pointed out that the Constitution did not protect fraud. Some claims, such as the alleged power to cure illness, were susceptible of evidence, and there was in fact evidence that the appellants knew their claims to be false.[6]

Justice Jackson wrote a partially concurring opinion in which he said, relative to the I Am movement, "I see humbug," but refrained from upholding the convictions lest the case become a precedent. It would be impossible for jurors to judge whether Ballard's claims honestly represented his experiences, Jackson thought, or to decide what measure of doubt might be legitimately intermingled with belief. The issue was freedom, and "we must put up with and even pay for a good deal of rubbish" to protect it, he proclaimed. Pungent as always, Jackson concluded his opinion by asserting that "I would dismiss the indictment and have done with this business of judicially examining other people's beliefs."[7]

After the case was returned to the district court, the I Am leaders (Ballard now deceased) were again convicted and in 1946 again appealed to the Supreme Court, this time on the grounds that women had been improperly excluded from the jury that convicted them.[8] Again writing for the majority, Douglas once more upheld the appeal, affirming that it was indeed discriminatory for women to have been excluded from the jury, which was reportedly done because the prosecutors feared that women were by nature more "spiritual" than men, hence more likely to be sympathetic to religious movements.[9] Jackson concurred but went further, holding that the Court's 1944 *Ballard* decision had left no room for the defendants even to be tried a second time.[10]

Justice Frankfurter dissented, arguing that the issue of women on juries had not been the subject of a proper appeal and that the real issue was whether fraudulent solicitation was protected by the First Amendment, an issue the Court was avoiding.[11] Justice Burton also wrote a dissent, arguing that there was no obligation to admit women to juries.[12]

POLYGAMY AGAIN

In 1945, after a lapse of over half a century, the Court heard another Mormon marriage case, this one involving a man charged with having "inveigled, decoyed, and carried away" a fifteen-year-old girl to make her his wife. The appellant was a "fundamentalist" Mormon who continued to believe in polygamy long after the church had officially condemned it.[13]

He was sixty-eight years old and had been the employer of the girl, who was said to be subnormal in intelligence, and had persuaded her that it was necessary to enter into a "celestial marriage" with him in order to save her soul. The seducer was a widower, so that marrying the girl did not make him a polygamist.

When the girl was found to be pregnant, her parents complained to the police, and she was placed under the control of juvenile authorities in Salt Lake City. However, she escaped from custody, received money from her prospective husband's daughters, married him in Mexico, then lived with him in Arizona.

Justice Murphy ruled that the girl had gone with the man voluntarily, thus the charges should be dismissed. There was no kidnapping, physical restraint, or confinement, or any evidence that the girl was incapable of understanding the concept of "celestial marriage." In Utah fifteen was the legal age of consent for girls to marry, so the couple were not in violation of the law.[14]

However, the broadened notion of religious liberty espoused by the Court during World War II did not extend to polygamy itself. In 1946 several Mormons were prosecuted for violating the Mann Act, which forbade the "transportation of a woman across a state line for immoral purposes," in this case for the practice of polygamy.[15]

Again raising the issue the Court had so decisively rejected in 1878, the defendants claimed a violation of religious liberty, complaining that civil officials who were mainstream Mormons tended to prosecute polygamy with particular zeal.[16]

But if they expected the Court to reconsider its decision of 1878, the usually liberal Douglas disabused them of that hope, reaffirming precisely the findings of the earlier Court that polygamy was "immoral" and "a return to barbarism" and, as "criminal action," could not lay claim to constitutional protection.[17] (More than a quarter of a century later Douglas warned that the Court's steady broadening of religious freedom threatened that in time it would overturn its historic condemnation of polygamy.)[18]

Murphy dissented, holding that polygamy was not mere prostitution, hence should not be punished under the Mann Act. Rather it was itself a form of marriage, one that historically had perhaps been even more common than monogamy.[19]

In 1948 the Court modified its position slightly in another polygamy case, in which a man had been convicted under a Utah statute that forbade people "to commit acts injurious to public morals," including polygamy.[20] Jackson questioned whether the law as drawn would permit punishment for any action that a jury might consider damaging to morality, and he ruled that the state court needed to review the law in the light of the Utah constitution and other state laws. He defined the issue narrowly, as the obligation of a state to define authoritatively the meaning of its own laws.[21]

Justice Rutledge dissented, asking whether Utah was not punishing free speech, since the statute included "advising" or "advocating" polygamy as part of a "conspiracy." Acknowledging a distinction between "advocacy" and "incitement," Rutledge argued that even "incitement" should enjoy some constitutional leeway. Rather than remanding the case for reconsideration, he thought the conviction should be overturned because the jury may have had an overly broad understanding of the law.[22]

Except for the occasional Jehovah's Witnesses case (chapter 4), the Court between 1948 and 1961 was inactive with regard to religious liberty, following its sudden burst of interest during World War II. This inactivity may have been due to its preoccupation with momentous cases involving race, cases that overturned long-standing social traditions found to be in conflict with the Constitution.

When the Court returned to the subject of religion, in 1961, it was more vigorous than ever, with three justices who had played crucial roles in the religion cases of the 1940s—Black, Douglas, and Frankfurter—still sitting, while the racial desegregation cases had given it a heightened interest in protecting individual rights. The Court's renewed interest in religion, at the start of a decade of great social and political turmoil, would help to alter the traditional role of religion in American life.

The first of the new cases was *Torcaso v. Watkins* (1961), in which a citizen of Maryland was appointed a notary public, then denied his commission because he would not swear that he believed in God. The Court ruled unanimously in his favor, seeing him as the victim of an obvious violation of religious freedom, but declined to rule on his contention that Article VI of the Constitution, forbidding a religious test for public office, applied to the states. Justice Black wrote the opinion, pointing out that the Maryland law favored those who believed in God, thus discriminating against those who did not.[23]

Conscientious Objection

The principal vehicle by which the definition of religion was expanded by the Court, and the benefits of the Free-Exercise Clause extended much more widely than in the past, was a series of conscientious-objector cases during the 1960s.

In *US v. Seeger* (1965) the Court found in favor of an applicant who had been denied conscientious-objector status because he did not believe in a "Supreme Being." The Selective Service Act, which authorized exemptions, demanded such an affirmation and specified that any religious claim must be based on "duties superior to those arising from any human relation." Seeger on the other hand claimed "belief in and devotion to goodness and truth for their own sake, and a religious faith in a purely ethical creed."[24]

In a related case decided at the same time, another appellant stated that he believed in "Godness" as the "Ultimate Cause for the fact of the being of the Universe," and his claim was also upheld by the Court.[25]

In a third case an appellant declined to affirm belief in a "Supreme Being," since he was uncertain of the meaning of the term, and instead cited a definition of religion as "the consciousness of some power manifest in nature which helps man in the ordering of his life, and in harmony with its demands."[26]

In the majority opinion Justice Clark noted the inadequacy of language to express profound religious ideas. Congress in the Selective Service Act had declared that conscientious objectors had to believe in a "Supreme Being." Clark then proposed as a gloss of the act: "A sincere and meaningful belief which occupies in the life of its possessor a place parallel to that filled by God of those admittedly qualifying for exemption."[27]

Congress, Clark argued, had intended a broad understanding of "Supreme Being," and his proposed formula would relieve the legislature of the suspicion that it was discriminating among different religious beliefs. Government could not inquire into the nature of religious beliefs, merely whether they were sincerely held.[28]

In a concurring opinion Douglas acknowledged that there was some "straining" in the Court's interpretation of congressional intent, because the Court was struggling to "avoid a constitutional crisis" provoked by invalidating an act of Congress. Ingeniously, he found justification for this straining in the fact that, when the Selective Service Act was passed in 1948, Hawaii probably already had a Buddhist majority, and Congress "must certainly" have intended to include them.[29]

In a 1968 case a theological student had been granted an exemption by his draft board but, when he returned his draft card to the board in protest against the Vietnam War, was classified as "delinquent" for not possessing a card and was ordered to be inducted.[30] Douglas ruled simply that the Selective Service Act did not authorize the board's action. Justice John Marshall Harlan III (grandson of the earlier justice of the same name) concurred, holding that the draftee had the right to raise the constitutional issue before he was drafted. Justice Potter Stewart dissented on the grounds that the law permitted review by the courts only in connection with criminal prosecutions, not induction itself.[31]

In 1970 the issue of religious commitment returned in a different form, in *Welsh v. US*, in which an applicant for conscientious-objector status deleted the phrase "my religious tradition" on his application and stated that his beliefs had been formed by the "the study of history and society."[32] Black wrote that the issue presented no real difference from the *Seeger* case. Elliott Welsh's denial that he had a religion should not be taken "too literally," and Douglas found Welsh's letter of application a "thoughtful" exposition of beliefs that were "religious in the ethical sense." The Selective Service Act excluded those with "essentially political, sociological, or philosophical views," but it did not intend to exclude anyone whose views were "strongly held," merely those whose views were not deeply held, or were based on expediency. Welsh said that his principles were not "superior to those arising from every human relationship" but were "essential to every human relationship."[33]

Amplifying the note of cynicism that Black had sounded in the *Seeger* case, Harlan said he had had misgivings in the earlier case that he now found confirmed. He concurred in the *Welsh* decision only in order to avoid having to invalidate parts of the Selective Service Act, and he characterized the Court's reinterpretation of the phrase "Supreme Being" as a "lobotomy of the statute." ("We save the statute by emasculating it," he added in a mixed metaphor.) Congress had obviously intended to distinguish formal church membership from purely personal beliefs or loose associations. Facing the dilemma squarely, Harlan asserted that this discriminated against nonbelievers and was therefore unconstitutional but it could be saved by pretending that it did not mean what it said.[34]

Justice White agreed with Harlan's views but stated one of the consistent positions of "conservative" justices concerning matters of religion—the Court must enforce the will of Congress, not its own will. The Selective Service Act might be unconstitutional, but the Court had no authority to extend its privilege to Welsh in clear violation of congressional intent. Welsh was possibly one of those persons whom Congress had intended should not be entitled to an exemption.[35]

White thought Congress might have had a purely secular purpose in granting such exemptions—possibly the fear that religious objectors would be not be reliable in combat—in which case the exemption was not granted as a religious right. Going directly contrary to what seemed to be the larger import of the case, White stated bluntly that certain rights could be denied to nonbelievers that were allowed to believers.[36]

Also in 1970 the Court upheld an appeal from a Catholic who had left the church but then returned, and who said he had been strongly influenced to become a pacifist through the reading of the works of certain Catholic thinkers. He then applied for conscientious-objector status, but his draft board refused to reopen his case. Stewart found for the Court that the board had acted arbitrarily and was required to examine the evidence.[37]

However, in the same year, the Court, also through Stewart, denied the claim of a plaintiff who sought conscientious-objector status when his decision to become a pacifist "crystallized" between the time he received his induction notice and the time he was scheduled to report for duty, and who had been denied a hearing by his draft board.[38] Stewart found that the board acted within its authority and noted that the military had a policy of not assigning men to combat when claims about conscientious objection were pending.[39]

Douglas dissented. The history of religion, he pointed out, showed many examples of sudden conversions, for example, Saul of Tarsus. Men claiming to be conscientious objectors were often treated harshly while in military service, Douglas claimed, and the plaintiff was entitled to the protection of the law.[40]

The following year the champion boxer Muhammad Ali (formerly Cassius Clay) appealed to the Court after having been denied classification as a conscientious objector. The Department of Justice originally held that he was not entitled to the exemption because he was not sincere, since his objections to war were "selective," that is, the Nation of Islam to which he had converted did not condemn all wars but only forbade its members to fight on behalf of the United States. However, in front of the Supreme Court, the Justice Department conceded that Ali's beliefs were sincere and "religiously based."[41]

The Court found for Ali *per curiam*. Since the government now conceded that he was sincerely motivated, and that members of the Nation of Islam could claim to be conscientious objectors, there were was no evident grounds for denying Ali's application.[42]

But in 1971 the Court did deny conscientious-objector status to an appellant because he was "selective." Justice Thurgood Marshall ruled that the history of the Selective Service Act offered no grounds for selective objection, while the appellant argued that this unfairly favored members of certain religious groups. Like White in the *Welsh* case, Marshall speculated that the government might have purely secular reasons for forbidding selective objection—it would be chaotic to administer. Being denied an exemption from military service in no way interfered with the appellant's personal religious beliefs or practices, Marshall ruled.[43]

Douglas dissented, finding the appellant's "humanist" beliefs "sincere and profound." While in the *Welsh* case White had affirmed the Court's traditional view that conscientious objection was not a right but a privilege conferred by the government, Douglas thought the Court ought to face the question as to whether the government had the right to command a citizen to kill in battle. "I had assumed that the welfare of a single human soul was the ultimate test of the vitality of the First Amendment."[44]

A companion case heard at the same time raised the same issue in a subtler way. A Catholic appellant argued that the Catholic theory of the "just war" was of its very nature a form of selective conscientious objection, since Catholics were taught to evaluate the morality of each particular war. Thus as a Catholic he was being denied his rights. Marshall's opinion in the first case covered the second as well, with little discussion of the issues raised therein.[45] Douglas dissented here as well, finding merit in the appellant's argument.[46]

In 1974 the Court rejected a claim by a conscientious objector who had done "alternative service" that he should share in federal benefits paid to those who had served in the military.[47] Brennan ruled for the majority that nothing in the law required such payment, which was clearly designed to compensate those who had served in the military and to make such service more attractive. The price conscientious objectors paid for exercising their religious freedom—being denied benefits—was not of serious weight.[48] Douglas dissented, holding that the law imposed penalties on those who exercised their religious freedom by refusing to do military service.[49]

A few months later the Court decided a similar case in which the appellant claimed that refusal to pay veterans benefits to former conscientious objectors was a violation of both the First and Fourteenth amendments. Brennan again held that such benefits were in the nature of a "reward" for military service and that those who had not served in the military could not make a claim.[50]

RELIGIOUS LIBERTY AND EMPLOYMENT

In *Sherbert v. Verner*, a pathbreaking case in 1963, a woman who belonged to the Seventh Day Adventist Church was discharged from her job for refusing to work on Saturday, and was then denied unemployment compensation because she had been dismissed "for cause." The Court found in her favor.[51]

Brennan wrote the majority opinion. The claim that unemployment compensation was a privilege rather than a right was irrelevant, he ruled, and the appellant was clearly the victim of discrimination, although Brennan was also careful to warn that the decision did not create a broad claim on behalf of any person who might become unemployed through religious convictions.[52]

Douglas concurred. While religious believers might have to endure many things for the sake of their "scruples," the state of South Carolina here placed an undue burden on the appellant.[53] Stewart also concurred, arguing not only that the appellant's rights were violated but that the government had an obligation to encourage religion. The Court's interpretation of the Establishment Clause was essentially unsound, he insisted, but its finding in the *Sherbert* case was inconsistent even with those erroneous decisions.[54]

Harlan dissented, arguing that unemployment compensation was designed to "help people when work is unavailable, not when they are unavailable for work." The plaintiff was treated no differently from any other employee. While South Carolina could choose to accommodate her religious beliefs, it could not be compelled to do so.[55]

The *Sherbert* case laid the foundation for what would later become the Court's consistent view, although the issue did not arise again for some years.

In 1977 the Court ruled against a man who had been exempted by his employer from Saturday work on religious grounds, until he transferred to a different department, where the seniority rights of other workers precluded his being freed from work on his sabbath. The plaintiff sued both his employer and his labor union, since by its championing of seniority the union had allegedly undermined his religious rights.[56]

This was the first such case heard after the passage of the 1964 Civil Rights Act, which among other things forbade discrimination in employment based on religion. White, writing the majority opinion, thought the intent of Congress was unclear on the question. He judged that the employer had made every effort to accommodate the complainant and that the established seniority system was "neutral and important." To accommodate the appellant would be to penalize other employees.[57]

Marshall dissented, seeing the decision as dealing "a fatal blow even to minor accommodations" of employees' religious rights, forcing employees to make "the cruel choice of surrendering their religion or their jobs." Since believers were sometimes exempt from obligations imposed by the government, they should also be exempt from those imposed by business. "Americans will be a little poorer until today's decision has been erased," Marshall warned.[58]

Also in 1977, Rehnquist, acting as circuit justice, rejected an appeal by a Seventh Day Adventist group in California not to be forced to provide payroll records to the Federal Department of Labor, in connection with an investigation into whether the group discriminated against female employees. The Adventists protested that the principle of equal pay for equal work would violate its religious beliefs.[59] Rehnquist found complex procedural issues that needed to be sorted out in an orderly manner not requiring an emergency intervention by the Court, which would probably be willing to hear an appeal, if at all, only after lower-court remedies had been exhausted.[60]

In 1981 the Court heard yet another case involving a Jehovah's Witness, this time a man who resigned his job in a factory when he was transferred to a department engaged in manufacturing tank turrets for the army. He was denied unemployment compensation on the grounds that he had resigned rather than being dismissed.[61]

Chief Justice Warren E. Burger found in the appellant's favor, on the grounds that even though he resigned, he would have been dismissed for refusing to work in a defense industry, and that he was thus penalized for his beliefs. The state of Indiana's wish to discourage people from leaving their employment "for personal reasons" was not sufficient justification for denial of compensation.[62]

Rehnquist dissented on the grounds that Indiana was being required to accommodate the appellant "on the basis of his beliefs," and the state could not be required to tailor its statutes to such a purpose. Admitting, like Stewart, that he disagreed with many of the Court's interpretations of the Establishment Clause, Rehnquist nonetheless argued that the present decision was a violation even of the principles laid down in earlier cases, since the ruling served only a religious purpose, not a secular one.[63]

However, having generally held that employers have an obligation to accommodate as far as possible the religious beliefs of their employees, the Court in 1984 struck down a Connecticut law specifically requiring this with respect to Sunday work. Such a law singled out particular religious beliefs and gave them privileged status, the Court ruled.[64]

In 1985 the Court ruled that the Fair Labor Standards Act applied to the secular activities of a religious organization.[65]

A 1986 case raised fundamental issues that were disposed of without being reached. A married teacher in an Ohio Protestant school became pregnant and was informed by her principal that, since the school believed that mothers of young children should not hold jobs outside the home, she would not be rehired for the following year. She then threatened to sue the school for discrimination, whereupon the principal immediately dismissed her from her position, because the denomination also forbade its members to take one another to court. She appealed to the Ohio Civil Rights Commission, which found in her favor after the school refused to cooperate in the investigation, viewing it as an infringement of its religious liberty. Rehnquist ruled that the mere investigation of the school by a state agency did not constitute a threat to liberty, and the Court remanded the case to the state for further proceedings.[66]

In the same year the Court decided a case involving subtle distinctions within the overall framework of employees' religious rights. A high school teacher in Connecticut joined the World-Wide Church of God and was in the habit of missing six school days a year in connection with his religious obligations. Teachers were allowed to miss six days per year with pay, but religious holidays could not be counted in that number. The appellant sued to be allowed to treat religious holidays as "personal business," but the school would not permit this. He also offered to pay a substitute teacher on days when he was not in school, but the board also rejected that proposal.[67] Rehnquist ruled for the majority in sending the case back for retrial on the grounds that insufficient information had been presented to the Court.[68]

He nonetheless reached certain preliminary constitutional conclusions, such as that employers were not required to follow any standard plan in seeking to accommodate the religious practices of their employees. They need only offer "reasonable accommodation." It was unclear from the evidence, Rehnquist thought, whether the school board discriminated against religious believers in granting time off from work. Granting religious persons unpaid leave seemed to be a reasonable effort at accommodation.[69]

Marshall dissented, holding that the issue was whether the school board should make further accommodations in order to ease the employee's burden. When an employer's plan did not satisfy the employee, the employer was obligated, Marshall insisted, to explore alternatives. The decision, he thought, was a departure from the Court's ruling in the *Hardison* case.[70]

Justice Stevens dissented from the opposite perspective. The local statute governing the case provided for a series of negotiations, of which the appellant had not availed himself.[71] Since the appellant was not required to be employed by the school system in question, there was no obvious violation of his religious freedom. The school board had a right to exclude religious holidays from "personal business," just as the teacher's own union contract excluded it. The appellant was actually seeking more than other teachers were entitled to.[72]

In 1987 a man brought suit against the Mormon Church because he, as a non-Mormon, had been dismissed from his job in a gymnasium operated by the church. While the Civil Rights Act permitted churches to restrict employment to their own members, the plaintiff argued that his job was secular in nature and should not be part of the exemption.[73] White wrote for the majority that it was difficult to distinguish the religious from the nonreligious activities of churches and that attempts by the government to make such a distinction risked "excessive entanglement" of government and religion.[74]

The same year, the Court heard an appeal from a woman who refused to work on Saturday after being converted to the Seventh Day Adventist Church, to which she had not belonged at the time she was hired. She too was denied unemployment compensation. A unanimous Court held that her claim had been denied because of her religious convictions.[75]

In 1989, in keeping with its expanded understanding of religious freedom as manifest in the *Seeger* and *Welsh* cases, the Court ruled in favor of a woman who had been terminated from her job for refusing to work on Sunday for reasons of conscience, even though she did not belong to a church that required this. White ruled for a unanimous Court that no requirement of church membership could be imposed and that it would be difficult for any government agency to distinguish religious from secular motivation in such matters.[76]

In 1991 the Court held that the Civil Rights Act did not apply to Americans employed by American companies but working overseas. The appellant was born in Lebanon but naturalized as an American citizen, was employed in Saudi Arabia by an American company, and claimed he had been dismissed from his job for religious and ethnic reasons.[77] Rehnquist noted that there was a long-standing assumption that acts of Congress did not apply outside the United States, and there was no evidence that Congress intended otherwise with the Civil Rights Act.[78] Marshall dissented, urging that the law's limits should not be construed from its silence about foreign employment and suggesting that its scope was broad enough to include the case at hand.[79]

The Court also decided several cases claiming violation of the religious freedom of individuals because of state laws forbidding commerce on Sundays, but those cases primarily related to the Establishment Clause (chapter 6).

RELIGIOUS LIBERTY AND ILLEGAL ACTIONS

The first modern cases involving religious activities that were illegal on their face came from the Civil Rights Movement of the early 1960s.

In 1963 the city of Birmingham (Alabama) issued an injunction against a planned civil rights march and picketing after the organizers failed to seek a permit from the city. The appeal by the organizers reached the Court in 1967.[80]

Stewart ruled against the defendants. There might be constitutional problems with the city ordinance, he admitted, but the defendants had not attempted to clarify those prior to defying the injunction. Demonstrations, because of questions of public order and safety, were entitled to less protection under the First Amendment than other forms of expression. The defendants claimed that Birmingham would not have granted them a permit to parade, but they had not in fact sought one.[81]

Dissenting, Chief Justice Earl Warren called attention to the fact that the organizers of the march were ministers of the Gospel and that they intended to invoke the religious symbolism of Good Friday and Easter Sunday by marching on those days. It was obvious to Warren that the city would not have granted a permit, and the defendants had a right to violate an unconstitutional injunction.[82]

Brennan also wrote a dissent, which also called attention to the "world symbolism" of the religious days on which the march was held and to the fact that it originated at a church. Injunctions could not be used to violate First Amendment freedoms, he insisted.[83]

The following year, the Court ruled on an appeal from a minister prosecuted for violating the injunction. In a year's time some of the justices completely reversed themselves on the issue, with Stewart now ruling for a unanimous court (Marshall abstaining) that picketing was a form of speech protected by the First Amendment and that the organizers had been rebuffed in their efforts to get a permit from the city.[84]

In the Mormon polygamy cases the Court had ruled, as almost self-evident, that religious convictions could never justify a violation of the law, a principle also upheld in the *Gobitis* case (1940) requiring Jehovah's Witnesses to salute the flag. However, beginning with some of the later Witnesses cases, the Court in effect granted religious exemptions from certain legal obligations, and those exemptions were considerably broadened beginning in the 1970s.

In some ways the most important of these was *Wisconsin v. Yoder* (1972), involving the prosecution of Amish families in Wisconsin who refused to send their children to high school, in defiance of the state's compulsory school-attendance law. The Amish contended that their way of life, deliberately insulated from the influence of the modern world, did not require a high school education, which was likely to undermine the religious principles their children were taught at home.[85]

Burger wrote a majority opinion supporting the Amish. While the state's interest in the education of the young was "very high," the state had nonetheless not shown that the Yoder children suffered from not attending high school, and the children themselves testified that they did not wish to attend. Merely preserving a historic way of life was not sufficient to invalidate the school laws, but religious freedom was, and the Amish argument was compelling, since exposure to the public high school milieu would very likely undermine the spirit they were struggling to preserve in their communities. In their own terms they were a very successful people—hard-working, self-reliant, law-abiding. Touching what was perhaps the nub of the case, Burger predicted that if the state were allowed to "save" the children from their parents, the state would in effect determine those children's religious future.[86]

Stewart concurred, arguing that the state of Wisconsin had made criminals of the Yoder family merely for exercising their religious rights.[87] In his concurring opinion, White held that parents could not impose their own "idiosyncratic" opinions on their children in defiance of state law. But, in a seemingly paradoxical argument, he concluded that the fact that many Amish children chose to leave their communities as they grew older showed that they were not permanently damaged by their upbringing.[88]

Douglas wrote a dissenting opinion whose implications were far-reaching indeed. He contrasted the interests of the parents with those of the children and argued that the latter had an inherent right to be exposed to "the new and amazing world of diversity we have today." The Court was allowing the parents to "impose" their own religion on their children, and, if the Yoder children indicated their desire to attend high school, the state would have had an obligation to facilitate that. Otherwise the decision might make the lives of Amish children "stunted and deformed."[89]

In 1977 the Court heard yet another case involving a Jehovah's Witness, this time a New Hampshire man jailed for refusing to display his state automobile license plate with the motto "Live Free or Die." His religious beliefs, he said, would not permit him to die for the state, and he valued life above liberty.[90]

Burger held that the right of free speech obviously implied the right not to proclaim particular ideas. The state's claim that the law had the practical purpose of making it easier to identify New Hampshire licenses was not sufficient to override the curtailment of liberty.[91]

White wrote a dissent on procedural grounds, finding that the regular process of criminal appeal had been bypassed.[92] Rehnquist offered a more substantive dissent, arguing that there was no issue of "symbolic speech" involved. The defendant had not been forced to say anything contrary to his conscience and, so long as he displayed the license plate, was free to manifest his disagreement in any way he chose.[93]

In 1981 the Court heard a case brought by the International Society for Krishna Consciousness ("Hare Krishnas"), a branch of the Hindu religion that was controversial in the United States because of what was regarded as its aggressive selling of religious literature in public places. The Minnesota State Fair required that all groups promoting their ideas at the fair rent a booth and confine their activities to it. The Krishnas claimed this was a violation of both free speech and freedom of religion, a case similar in many ways to various Jehovah's Witnesses cases of the 1940s.[94]

White held for the majority that there was no discrimination specifically directed at the Hare Krishnas, since the same rule applied equally to all groups. Space problems made this is a legitimate concern, and if every group claimed unrestricted rights to proselytize it would create "chaos" on the fairgrounds.[95] In a partially concurring opinion, Brennan found that it was permissible to restrict sales to the booths but not the distribution of literature. Everyone had the right to move through the fairgrounds and to speak to people on any subjects they chose.[96]

A case involving religious freedom in the military services was decided in 1986, brought by a Jewish Air Force officer who had been denied the right to wear a yarmulke, a ritual cap worn by Orthodox Jewish men.[97] Rehnquist, now Chief Justice, noted in his majority opinion that the

Court had consistently held that the military services had authority over their members in ways the civil government did not have over citizens. The Air Force's claim that it could not allow deviations from its official uniform should be accepted by the Court, with the Air Force under no obligation to prove that such deviations would undermine discipline.[98] In a concurring opinion, Justice Stevens found the prospect of an exemption for the appellant "attractive" but feared that any such exemption would soon lead to "extreme" demands for other deviations from the official uniform.[99]

Brennan, however, believed that a basic constitutional right was violated. The Air Force offered no argument in support of its claims about discipline, and Brennan found these claims "beyond belief." Allowing the appellant to wear his yarmulké would be a proud symbol of the "diversity" that the service encompassed. Responding to Stevens, he insisted that every case could be judged on its own merits and "extreme" demands thereby rejected. The Air Force's position tended toward the suppression of minority rights.[100]

Justice Blackmun also dissented, asserting that people in the military services did not forfeit their rights as citizens and that sometimes an exemption from "even-handed" laws was necessary to guarantee those rights.[101] Justice Sandra Day O'Connor also dissented, arguing that while the Air Force could restrict the rights of its members, it had to show reasons for doing so.[102]

In the same year the Court heard a case involving a Native American family who refused to make use of a Social Security number assigned to their young daughter, although required to do so because the family was receiving welfare payments. The appellants explained that according to their beliefs, the use of such a number would "represent" the girl and "rob her of her soul" in the same way as a photograph would.[103]

Burger, in one of his last opinions as Chief Justice, again made the venerable distinction between belief and action, and again denied that the government was under any obligation to tailor its laws to the religious actions of the citizens. The requirement of a Social Security number was "wholly neutral" and was a legitimate demand on people who sought benefits from the government, in order to prevent fraud.[104]

Blackmun wrote a partially concurring opinion in which he made a fine distinction, affirming the government's right to issue a Social Security number, but without the recipient's necessarily being required to use it.[105] Stevens thought the appellants' argument inconsistent. They first stated that harm came from the mere issuance of a Social Security card but, when it was revealed that the card had already been issued, shifted their ground to arguing that harm would result only from its use.[106]

O'Connor dissented, arguing that the majority opinion subordinated religious liberty to "mere government policy," whereas past Court decisions demanded "over-riding necessity" before liberty could be restricted. Based on previous Court decisions, she held that welfare was not a privilege but a "statutory entitlement."[107]

Also in 1987 the Court unanimously struck down a regulation by the Los Angeles Airport Commission prohibiting "all First Amendment activities" in the airport. The suit was brought by a group called Jews for Jesus, who were forbidden to proselytize. O'Connor ruled that the regulation was "facially unconstitutional." It was not made for the sake of public order, and it was irrelevant that religious proselytizing was not an "airport-related activity."[108]

In 1990 another case involving Native American religion came before the Court, this time involving actions directly contrary to the criminal law (*Employment Division v. Smith*).[109] Two drug counselors, employees of the State of Oregon, were dismissed when they acknowledged that they were members of a Native American religion that required the ritual use of peyote, an illegal narcotic. They were then denied unemployment compensation because they had been dismissed "for cause."

Justice Scalia wrote the majority opinion denying the appellants' claim on the grounds that a restriction on religious freedom that is "incidental" is not a violation of the Constitution and that it would be "courting anarchy" to hold otherwise. Religious practices did not place people beyond the criminal law. Acknowledging the religious diversity often extolled by liberals, Scalia then argued that such diversity meant that the government could not accommodate all the possible religious practices of its citizens.[110]

O'Connor dissented, finding that the state of Oregon failed to show a "compelling state interest." While the state had a right to prohibit drug use, Oregon in this case had not shown that harm resulted from the ritual use of peyote. The fact that a law was general in nature and not aimed at a particular religion was not in itself sufficient to justify restrictions on religious liberty.[111]

Blackmun noted that not only had Oregon failed to show that the use of peyote had any evil affect, there had been testimony that controlled ritual use of the drug diminished the likelihood of alcoholism. The "unbending" application of the criminal law could not in itself be a "compelling state interest."[112]

In 1993 the Court ruled in favor of a sect, of African and Caribbean origins, that practiced animal sacrifice, after a Florida city had forbidden the practice.[113] Justice Anthony Kennedy ruled for a unanimous Court that the law was overtly discriminatory because directly aimed at the particular religious practice, since the killing of animals in general, such as hunting or the chasing of rabbits by greyhounds, was not forbidden. While animal sacrifice might be "abhorrent to some people," this was not sufficient to curb religious freedom. Although the term "sacrifice" had meanings other than religious, the city of Hialeah deliberately intended to prohibit a specific religious practice.[114]

In the first year of the new millennium the Court decided a case involving the Branch Davidians, a Texas religious group whose members lived in a compound insulated from the outside world, under the dominant leadership of a man who proclaimed Jesus' imminent return to earth and prescribed a detailed code of behavior for his followers. In 1993 the compound was besieged by federal agents acting on reports that the group was molesting children and was engaged in violent and subversive activities against the government. During the raid several federal agents were killed, and the compound burned to the ground, with substantial loss of life by Branch Davidians, some through suicide, others allegedly shot by federal agents. Subsequently Congress authorized an official investigation into the siege.[115]

Several members of the group were convicted of conspiring to murder law-enforcement officers. Ruling on a narrow issue, the Court held that the defendants had been given excessive prison sentences, since they had been prosecuted both for conspiracy and for carrying illegal firearms, whereas the carrying of weapons should have been treated merely as an aggravating circumstance of the crime of conspiracy.[116]

RELIGIOUS RIGHTS OF PRISONERS

In 1972 the Court heard an appeal from a Buddhist incarcerated in a prison, alleging that he had been denied use of the prison chapel, punished for proselytizing his fellow prisoners, not permitted to correspond with Buddhist spiritual advisers, and not provided with religious literature as other prisoners were. A federal district court dismissed the suit, but the Supreme Court ruled per curiam that the allegations should be heard on their merits.[117]

Burger concurred in the ruling but warned that the state could not be expected to provide materials for every religious group.[118] Rehnquist dissented completely, arguing that matters of this kind should be left to the discretion of prison administrators. Obviously, he pointed out, a prisoner could not expect to be as free as other people to practice his religion. The plaintiff had no right to proselytize, and the prison was not obligated to provide equal religious facilities for all groups, so long as the discrimination was not arbitrary or unreasonable. The framers of the Fourteenth

Amendment would be surprised to learn that it extended to prisoners, Rehnquist remarked tartly.[119]

Ever since the Mormon polygamy cases the Court has had occasionally to deal with religious practices strange or repugnant to the majority of the nation, but this was the first case involving beliefs outside the tradition of Judaism and Christianity.

In 1987 a group of Black Muslim prisoners appealed to the Court concerning prison rules regulating worship. Their faith, they claimed, required them to hold services at certain hours and in certain places, which prison authorities had forbidden.[120]

Rehnquist found against the Muslims on the grounds that the rules were not in themselves discriminatory. Prison authorities could not be expected to accommodate all possible claims of conscience and had a right to regulate the daily order of the prison.[121]

Brennan wrote a strong dissent, arguing that the "reasonableness" of the prison rules did not itself constitute justification for restricting the prisoners' liberties. The ceremony of *Jum 'ah*, which was in effect prohibited by the rules, was central to the Black Muslim religion, as the Mass was to Catholics. "To deny the opportunity to affirm membership in a spiritual community, however, may extinguish an inmate's last source of dignity and redemption," said Brennan.[122]

Religious Rights and Educational Institutions

In 1979 teachers in a Chicago Catholic high school sought to form a union and asked the National Labor Relations Board to supervise an election. The Archdiocese of Chicago refused to cooperate with the process, on the grounds that it was not subject to the NLRB because, as a government agency, the NLRB would infringe the freedom of the Catholic schools.[123]

Burger wrote the majority opinion in favor of the archdiocese. Previous Court decisions, he noted, held that Catholic schools were "permeated" by religion, hence were to be considered religious institutions. If the NLRB questioned the sincerity of this claim, it would be necessary to inquire closely into the church's beliefs and this in itself would constitute undue interference. Since Congress, in establishing the NLRB, had granted an exemption to employees who object to union membership on religious grounds, it could also be assumed that Congress intended institutional exemptions as well.[124] Brennan wrote a dissenting opinion, arguing that Congress did not in fact intend such an exemption.[125]

In 1981 the Court decided the case of *Widmar v. Vincent*,[126] in which the University of Missouri denied a student religious group the use of university facilities on the grounds that such use would violate the Establishment Clause. Justice Powell wrote a majority opinion favoring the student group. Any curtailment of religious liberty would have to show a "compelling interest," based on previous Court decisions, and the university's claim that the Establishment Clause itself constituted such an interest was inadequate. Using a test the Court had developed elsewhere, Powell found that providing a forum for diverse student groups was a legitimate secular purpose, so that the exclusion of a religious group would itself be discriminatory. The university recognized over a hundred student groups, and no reasonable person could infer that such recognition conferred approval of each group's purposes or philosophy.[127]

Stevens concurred. Arguing somewhat more narrowly than Powell, he preferred that the university rather than the courts decide the matter, and he thought the university was not obligated to open its facilities equally to all groups. (For example, it might assign a room for a performance of *Hamlet* rather than a showing of *Mickey Mouse*.) However, the university barred the student religious group precisely because of the group's beliefs, which was discriminatory. As formulated by the university, the rule would allow clubs devoted to discussing atheism but not religion.[128]

White reminded his brethren that he believed the Court often interpreted the Establishment Clause too strictly but argued that it was a long step from what was permitted to what was required, and, while the university might tolerate the religious group, it was not obligated to do so. Just as there were incidental benefits to religion from neutral state policies, so there might be incidental burdens.[129]

The issue could not be treated simply as one of freedom of expression, White held, because freedom of worship is necessarily narrower than freedom of speech. Otherwise the Religion Clause would be devoid of all meaning, and religion would simply be treated as speech. White wondered how far such a "right" might extend and asked, "Would a university be forced to accept as a course something called 'Catholic Mass'?" The university's adherence to the Establishment Clause was sufficient reason for not recognizing the organization.[130]

A case extending the *Widmar* principle to public high schools came before the Court in 1986 but was disposed of mainly on procedural grounds. A Pennsylvania school board ruled that a student religious group could not meet in the school building but that students could be released from classes to attend meetings elsewhere. The students sued, and a federal district court held that the school had violated their free speech. All but one member of the school board accepted this ruling, and this sole dissenter appealed the decision.[131]

Stevens ruled that the lone board member lacked "standing to sue," that is, he had no legitimate interest in the case, since the district court's ruling had not been against him as an individual but against the board. The appellant was in principle opposed to prayer in the schools, but he had not demonstrated that he had been injured by the practice.[132] Marshall concurred, noting that the appellant, as a parent of children in the local schools, might have standing to sue but that a claim on that basis would require a new case, not the continuation of the existing one.[133]

Burger dissented, finding that the appellant did have standing as a parent, and urging the Court to consider the case on its merits. He went on to indicate that if that were done, he would rule in favor of the students, based on the *Widmar* decision. The fact that some people might mistake toleration by the school as endorsement of the group's goals was irrelevant, he insisted. Schools should be neutral toward religion, not hostile.[134]

Powell also dissented, addressing the merits of the case but reaching the opposite conclusion from Burger. He thought high school students were more impressionable than college students and thus the school's recognition of a religious group would be more readily seen as endorsement. However, high school students too had rights of free speech.[135]

By declining to consider the case on its merits, the Court allowed the district court's judgment to stand and thus in effect granted the high school religious group the right to meet in the school building. A minority wanted to decide the case on its merits, but the majority chose to settle the issue by default.

But three years later the Court did make the student right explicit, when it decided the case of *Board of Education v. Mergens*.[136] Students at an Omaha public high school formed a religious group. Their principal ruled that all groups must have a faculty sponsor but that assigning a sponsor would constitute endorsement of the group and would thus violate the Establishment Clause.

O'Connor wrote the majority opinion. High school students were mature enough to see that the school's recognition of the group did not constitute an endorsement, she thought. The school was in part funded by the federal government, and Congress had indicated that it was troubled by inhibitions of religious speech in public schools, and had called for a "limited public forum" in those schools. The Court's decision should rest on this congressional intent, not on the Constitution itself, she held.[137]

Kennedy concurred, arguing that the concept of "endorsement" was too broad and that even if recognition did constitute endorsement, this did not affect the merits of the appeal.[138] Marshall also concurred. Unlike Kennedy, he thought the school had to show merely that it tolerated a "range of ideological positions" and that it did not endorse the religious group. The case was different from *Widmar* because the goal of a university is "student autonomy," while that of a high school is "fundamental values." [139]

Stevens called the ruling a "bizarre result" and asked rhetorically whether Congress could really have intended that public schools must endorse religious groups. He thought the immaturity of high school students was a prime consideration. The activities of the religious group were not related to the curriculum of the school, and it was only curriculum-related groups that Congress intended be recognized. The ruling was a "sweeping intrusion" of federal power into local schools.[140]

In 1993 the Court found unanimously that the use of a public school building to show religious films outside regular school hours was not a violation of the Constitution.[141]

In *Rosenberger v. University of Virginia* (1995), the university denied funds to a student Christian publication, even though such funding was provided to other student groups, the university justifying this exclusion on the grounds that it was required by the Constitution.[142]

Kennedy wrote the majority opinion in favor of the student paper on the grounds that their exclusion was clearly the result of discrimination against a particular viewpoint, and he rejected the university's contention that its policy was nondiscriminatory because it excluded all viewpoints about religion, not merely some. The university's policy was so broad that it could exclude any viewpoint that might rest on a belief in God, for example, "hypothetical student contributors named Plato, Spinoza, and Descartes."[143]

O'Connor concurred, arguing that such exclusion demonstrated hostility rather than neutrality toward religion. Subsidies of the Christian paper were part of the general practice of promoting an open forum of ideas, and she noted that the university subsidized a student journal that sometimes satirized Christianity and another that presented a Muslim viewpoint. There was thus little danger that anyone would mistake the subsidy for an endorsement.[144] Justice Clarence Thomas concurred but dissociated himself from Kennedy's reading of the history of the Religion Clauses.[145]

Justice David Souter dissented, noting that, for the first time, the Court upheld direct funding of a religious activity by an arm of the government. Previous cases involving religious organizations in public schools merely rested on the idea of an open forum of opinion, in which the financial subsidy was minimal. Contrary to O'Connor's finding, he accepted the university's claim that all religious beliefs, including Muslim, were excluded, as were atheism or agnosticism. Thus there was no discrimination on the basis of viewpoint.[146]

In 2001, in a case from New York State, the Court again ruled that a student religious group could not be denied the use of public-school facilities that were open to other organizations.[147] Thomas found that denying use of the school building to the Good News Bible Club would be a violation of freedom of speech and could not be justified under the Establishment Clause. The stated purpose of the group—to cultivate morals and good character—was consonant with the school's educational purpose, the club met after regular school hours and was not sponsored by the school, nor was there any danger that students would think that it was. Genuine neutrality required permitting the meetings, and to forbid them would constitute hostility to religion.[148]

Scalia concurred. The possibility that such meetings might subject students to "peer pressure" was, he thought, merely an inevitable consequence of freedom of association. The Good News Club offered religious reasons for its moral teachings, but to deny access on those grounds would constitute "blatant viewpoint discrimination." The claim that because the club used biblical arguments, its activities really constituted "worship" was, Scalia insisted, specious.[149]

Justice Stephen Breyer concurred on narrow grounds, agreeing that the lower courts had erred in granting the school district summary judgment. However, he thought there were substantive issues at stake and that the case should be remanded for retrial.[150]

Stevens dissented. While a school could not prohibit the expression of political ideas, it could prohibit the activities of political groups trying to recruit members. The Good News Club went beyond free speech in seeking, as it acknowledged, "to promote the Gospel."[151]

Souter also dissented, calling the club's activities "an evangelical worship service" and arguing that the majority decision would force public schools to allow their facilities to be used as churches or synagogues. The Good News meetings were scheduled immediately after the end of the school day, during time set aside for extracurricular activities, and could easily be construed by students as official school activities.[152]

RELIGIOUS ORGANIZATIONS AND TAXATION

In 1958 a Unitarian church in Los Angeles lost its municipal tax exemption because it refused to require employees to swear an oath that they did not advocate the violent overthrow of the government.[153] Brennan found it unnecessary even to consider the issue of religious liberty, since the church had been required to prove that it deserved an exemption and due process was thereby violated.[154] Douglas concurred but insisted that the religious issue was relevant. "There is no power in our Government to make one bend his religious scruples to the requirements of this tax law," he proclaimed.[155]

Clark dissented, holding that the church had not shown a violation of religious liberty. The refusal to take the oath could not be characterized as a religious act.[156]

In 1972 the Internal Revenue Service revoked the tax exemption of an evangelistic group alleged to be involved in political activities. The appellants claimed that it was a violation of the Free-Exercise Clause for the government even to inquire as to whether the group was a religion. The Court found per curiam that the Federal District Court was within its authority in overturning the IRS ruling, since this involved not an act of Congress but merely an administrative regulation. There was thus no constitutional issue.[157] In finding none, the Court did not respond to the claim that it was unconstitutional to inquire as to whether a particular group was in fact a religion.

In 1974 the Court heard a complex case involving attempts by Quakers to withhold that part of their federal income tax estimated as budgeted for military purposes. At the request of its employees a Quaker organization withheld only half of the normal amount of income tax. The organization then paid the remainder to the government but sued for a refund. The Court held per curiam that federal law prohibited suits to prevent the collection of taxes. The individuals involved would have to pay the tax, then sue for a refund.[158]

Douglas was the lone dissenter. The Court was inhibiting the free expression of religion, he contended, in that the Quakers had no other way of protesting the payment of taxes for immoral purposes, as their beliefs required them to do. Douglas boasted that he had "not bowed to the majority" in accepting a position, articulated in a number of cases, whereby religious practices could be restricted when there was "compelling state interest." The constitutional phrase "no law respecting an establishment of religion" included every kind of law, he insisted.[159]

In 1981 the Court decided an appeal by a Lutheran Church in South Dakota arguing that it should not be required to pay unemployment taxes for teachers in its school. The church claimed that teachers in religious schools were exempt under federal law and that collection of the tax was a violation of religious freedom. However, the Federal Department of Labor ruled that the exemption was applicable only to "those strictly church duties performed by church employees pursuant to their religious responsibilities." Blackmun found for a unanimous Court that the federal law was intended to exempt such teachers.[160]

But in a similar case the following year the Court rejected a claim by a religious school in California to be exempt from having to pay unemployment tax for its employees, distinguishing the case from the previous one in that the second school was not officially linked to a church.[161]

O'Connor wrote a majority opinion overturning a federal district court decision in favor of the school. The district court, she found, had in effect declared the law in question unconstitutional, but federal courts, in all but the most extreme cases, should not interfere with the collection of state taxes. The school could seek relief in state courts, which would have the authority to make a constitutional judgment.[162]

She also rejected the claim that the requirements of record-keeping and reporting imposed on the school violated religious freedom. The school could be required to submit its records even if its challenge in federal court were upheld, and the issue whether such requirements were unconstitutional itself had to be litigated.[163]

Stevens dissented, finding that the unemployment tax was mandated by the federal government, and the federal courts were thus the appropriate place to mount a challenge.[164]

Also in 1982 the Court ruled against an Amish employer who objected on religious grounds to paying Social Security taxes for his employees. The Amish themselves were exempt from Social Security by act of Congress, because they believed it was a religious obligation to care for the elderly of their own community. But the Court here held that the exemption applied only to self-employed people and that mandatory participation in the program was a legitimate government interest, Burger asserting that some religious practices "must yield to the common good" and that believers could not be shielded from all possible burdens.[165]

Also in 1982 the Court heard an appeal from the Holy Spirit Association for the Unification of World Christianity, commonly called the Unification Church, or "the Moonies," after its founder, Rev. Sun Yung Moon.[166] The state of Minnesota required all charities to register with the state and file an annual report of activities. All churches were originally exempt from the requirement, but later the law was changed to require reports from churches receiving more than half their income from sources other than their own members.[167]

Brennan ruled that the law was discriminatory as applied to the Unification Church. Until the law was amended four years previously, the church had not been required to register, and to be made to do so now was burdensome. The rule concerning a church's income was clearly discriminatory between some churches and others, and the state's claim that churches that were largely self-supporting were more likely to guard against fraud was unproven and probably inaccurate. When the Minnesota legislature debated the statutory change, legislators specifically mentioned the Unification Church and said it was their intention to guard against abuses by religious groups that solicited funds from the public.[168]

White dissented, holding that the law was not overtly discriminatory and that the Court was not competent to judge the factors that caused Minnesota to legislate in the interests of preventing fraud. In a tantalizing statement, White said he thought there was a more legitimate "secular purpose" in the Minnesota requirement about outside income than in the blanket exemption commonly granted to all religious bodies.[169]

Rehnquist also dissented, arguing that the real issue was whether the Unification Church was a religion within the meaning of the law and adding that it should be required to show that it was. As a charitable organization it was already required to register with the state. Even if the Court found the income rule unconstitutional, this did not affect the appellants until such time as they demonstrated that they constituted a religion.[170]

One of the most important case involving religion and taxation came before the Court in 1983—*Bob Jones University v. US*.[171] A nondenominational Protestant institution at first banned all nonwhites from enrolling. Later it admitted them but banned various kinds of socializing between students of different races on the grounds that the Bible forbade the mixing of the races. The Internal Revenue Service not only revoked the school's own tax exemption but ruled that gifts to the college were no longer tax deductible. The case included a similar issue involving a private religious secondary school.[172]

Burger wrote an opinion upholding the actions of the IRS on the grounds that valid charities must have "a public purpose" and must not be "contrary to public policy," which the racist practices of Bob Jones University were. No charity could be "at odds with the common community conscience," and for almost twenty years it had been the official policy of the United States to oppose racial discrimination. Thus the government's interest in the matter was compelling.[173]

Powell concurred. He did not think Congress intended the result that the Court was upholding and, in a rather startling remark, doubted whether most charities could demonstrate that they brought a "public benefit" to society. He accepted the Court's finding but thought the issue should be a matter for Congress, not the IRS.[174] Rehnquist dissented, arguing that the will of Congress in the matter was not clear and that neither the IRS nor the Court could presume to know that will.[175]

The next year the Court heard a case involving the Church of Scientology, a group claiming to enable its followers to rise to higher levels of intellectual and spiritual awareness, without positing a Supreme Being.[176] The Court ruled that money given to the church did not constitute donations but was payment for benefits received, hence not tax-deductible. Marshall, in the majority opinion, noted that there was no evidence that the church forbade its members to pay taxes.[177] O'Connor dissented, warning that never before had the Court taken into account a "spiritual *quid pro quo*" in terms of benefits that churches might bring to their members, such as "stipends" given to Catholic priests for the celebration of mass.[178]

The next year the Court found that a sales tax imposed by the State of California on all merchandise did not violate the religious freedom of a

Protestant evangelist who sold religious goods. There was no advance licensing of sales, thus no "prior restraint" of ideas as in some of the Jehovah's Witnesses cases, nor did the collection of the tax involve any undue entanglement of church and state.[179]

Also in 1990, the Court decided a case involving donations to Mormon missionaries. Young Mormon men were required, at a certain point in their lives, to travel to various parts of the world as missionaries, an activity that was not supported financially by the church. Individuals who contributed to the support of particular missionaries claimed those donations as charitable gifts. The Court ruled, however, that the money was given to individuals, not the church, and thus was not tax-deductible.[180]

MISCELLANEOUS ISSUES

In 1977 the Court heard a unique case, which was virtually the mirror opposite of *Torcaso*, when it overturned a Tennessee law barring clergy from holding public office. A Protestant minister had been elected a delegate to the state constitutional convention, but his election had been successfully challenged on the basis of the old law.[181]

Burger distinguished the case from *Torcaso* in that the latter involved only belief, whereas the definition of "clergy" involved action, which in principle could be regulated by the state. However, Tennessee failed to show that clergy would in any way act improperly, hence the prohibition was invalid.[182]

Marshall concurred, finding the law a patent violation of religious liberty, since it forbade clergy to act in accord with their consciences. Although the Founding Fathers sought to reduce religious strife, this could not be done by barring religion from the arena of public discussion.[183] Stewart also concurred, noting that, like Brennan and Marshall, he did not think Burger's distinction between belief and action relevant to the case.[184]

White too concurred but found not that the appellant's free exercise of religion had been infringed upon but that he had been denied equal protection of the law. The state's goal of preventing "undue interference" by clergy in politics was a valid one, but Tennessee had made it too broad, applying it even to clergy who would not misuse their offices.[185]

A unique issue involving Native American religion was the 1987 case in which Indians opposed the building of a road on government property in California on the grounds that the land to which the road would give access was traditionally sacred to the Indians and that the road, intended to facilitate both logging and recreation, would allow it to be profaned.[186]

O'Connor found for the majority that "the government cannot satisfy every citizen's religious needs and desires" and that, by the logic of their suit, the Indians might try to exclude all human activity from the area, or might claim as sacred "rather spacious tracts of public property" elsewhere. The government had made efforts to accommodate the Indians and it was not necessarily a violation of religious liberty if government action made it more difficult for people to practice their religion, provided they were not required to act contrary to their beliefs.[187]

Brennan wrote a dissenting opinion, arguing that respect for the sacred land was crucial to the Indian religion and that the road, which would bring a great deal of activity to the area, would virtually make it impossible to follow the old Indian customs. Undertaking a detailed summary of Indian beliefs, he found that federal regulations governing land use were "inherently ethnocentric," in that they approached the question in a "traditional Western hierarchical manner."[188]

Also in 1987, White found for a unanimous Court that, although Jews did not constitute a "race" as understood in the Federal Civil Rights Act, they were often thought of as such and thus could bring action under that law against people who had defaced a synagogue with anti-Jewish slogans.[189]

The next year the Court voided a contempt-of-court citation issued against the National Conference of Catholic Bishops for refusing to make available some of its records in a civil suit.[190]

The plaintiffs sought to remove the federal tax exemption from the NCCB and a subsidiary organization on the grounds that, as nonprofit entities, they were engaged in political activity against abortion. Church authorities cited "conscience" as their reason for refusing to make certain documents available, claiming that the suit itself was a violation of the Free-Exercise Clause, and they were then cited for contempt for not complying with the subpoenas.

Kennedy ruled for the majority that the contempt citation was improper, although he did so on narrow technical grounds. The bishops had a right to challenge the jurisdiction of the federal district court in the matter, which they had done. The district court could have issued subpoenas relative to an inquiry into the question of its own jurisdiction, and the bishops would then have been required to comply. Instead the subpoenas were issued relative to the substance of the suit itself, which was precisely the question in dispute.[191] Marshall was the lone dissenter, voting to uphold the lower court's action.[192]

In 1997 a religious issue reached the Court in a unique way, completely outside the established judicial process, when a group of Muslims requested that the Court remove the image of the prophet Muhammad from

the court room, because Islamic law forbade the depiction of human beings, regarding it as a form of idolatry.

Speaking for the Court, Rehnquist refused the request. Muhammad's
image was placed among those of the great lawgivers of history, he
pointed out, and was not intended as idolatry. Federal statute forbade
alteration or removal of art works in government buildings.[193]

A major case the same year was *City of Boerne v. Flores*, an appeal by
a Catholic parish in Texas against a municipal ordinance that denied the
parish permission to expand and remodel its church building, because the
structure had been designated a "historic landmark" by the city government.[194] The appeal was lodged in part under a law of Congress called
the Religious Freedom Restoration Act (1993), which the Court invalidated in disposing of the case.[195]

The Religious Freedom Restoration Act was enacted in large measure
because of congressional dissatisfaction with certain Court decisions on
religious liberty, especially the 1990 *Smith* case permitting the State of Oregon to penalize the use of an illegal drug as part of a religious ceremony.

The decision in the *Boerne* case was highly unusual in that it brought
together a coalition of justices ordinarily on opposite sides in religion
cases—the "conservatives" Rehnquist, Thomas, and Scalia, the "moder-
ates" Kennedy and Stevens, and the "liberal" Breyer.

Kennedy wrote the majority opinion, forthrightly defending the *Smith*
decision. The Court, he insisted, would create an anomalous situation if
it allowed citizens, merely on the basis of their religious scruples, to ignore
valid laws of neutral applicability.[196]

In enacting the RFRA, members of Congress specifically criticized the
Court's decision in the *Smith* case, and the law was enacted on the
grounds that Congress had the authority, under the Fourteenth Amendment, to pass legislation to enforce constitutionally guaranteed rights.[197]

However, Kennedy insisted, there was a crucial distinction between
"enforcing" such rights and "defining" them. Congress possessed the first
power but not the second, and in the RFRA it undertook to define the
meaning of religious liberty as guaranteed by the Constitution.[198] The
Court therefore held that Congress exceeded its constitutional authority
in enacting the legislation, blurring the clear distinction between the legislative and judicial branches of the government.[199]

All congressional action must respect a congruence between means and
ends, Kennedy argued, and in this instance, Congress failed to show that
the dangers to religious freedom in the nation were such as to justify a law
that prohibited all agencies of government, on all levels, from "substantially burdening" the religious practices of citizens, unless it could be shown
that there was a "compelling government interest" in doing so and that the
government used the "least restrictive means" of achieving its purpose.[200]

The act was so broadly drawn as to support a constitutional challenge to almost any legislation, anywhere, by any governing body, Kennedy warned. Among other things it involved a major intrusion by Congress into the activities of the states, whose laws might frequently be overturned under such provisions.[201]

It was in the nature of the modern "regulatory state," Kennedy argued, that it imposed various kinds of burdens on people, many of them merely "incidental" in nature. The fact that some of these fell on religious believers did not mean that such people were suffering religious discrimination.[202]

Supporters of the RFRA could not show that religious persecution was a serious threat in the contemporary United States, nor that legislation to which particular religious believers might object was enacted because of animosity toward their faith, he insisted. Religious persons burdened by state laws were not necessarily burdened more than other classes of people.[203]

In a concurring opinion, Stevens offered the blunt judgment that the act in dispute was precisely a law "respecting an establishment of religion," hence unconstitutional on its face. It embodied discrimination, in that a Catholic Church could seek an exemption that would not be granted, for example, to a museum owned by an atheist.[204]

In his own concurring opinion, Scalia mainly debated with O'Connor the intention of the Founders with respect to religious liberty. He concluded by asserting that matters of this kind should be decided by "the people" through their local government.[205]

In her dissent O'Connor insisted that the *Smith* case had been wrongly decided and that the Court should use the *Boerne* case to overturn it. She agreed that Congress had no power to establish new constitutional rights, but the disputed congressional act was invalid only if the *Smith* decision were a correct reading of the Religion Clause, which it was not.[206]

The Court's error in the *Smith* case, according to O'Connor, was in reading the Free-Exercise Clause as protecting citizens only from laws that were explicitly discriminatory against religion, whereas its true meaning was "an affirmative guarantee of the right to participate in religious practices and conduct without impermissible government intervention, even when such conduct conflicts with a neutral, generally acceptable law." The *Smith* decision had changed this.[207]

In support of her contention, O'Connor offered a detailed account of religious liberty during colonial times and the early years of the Republic.[208] Noting that freedom of religion and freedom of speech were guaranteed in the same section of the Constitution, O'Connor pointed out that free speech had always enjoyed a "central place" in American life and therefore freedom of religion ought to as well.[209]

Souter said he too doubted the soundness of the *Smith* decision but was not yet prepared to either accept or reject it as precedent. The *Boerne* case under consideration did not focus on the proper issues, in his judgment, and the appeal should be dismissed and the case retried at a lower level precisely on the issues raised in the *Smith* decision.[210] Breyer reached a conclusion similar to Souter's.[211]

In the entire history of the country, Boerne was the only religion case in which the Court ever invalidated a federal law.

In 2000 a majority of the Court ruled that the Boy Scouts of America had the right to dismiss an admittedly homosexual scoutmaster, because of the Scouts' professed concept of morality.[212] The Scouts did not raise the issue of religious liberty, but Stevens did so in dissent, pointing out that, although the Scouts professed faith in God, they did not define the meaning of that faith. The organization claimed to be "nonsectarian" and must therefore have been aware of the fact that some religious groups did not regard homosexuality as immoral, Stevens argued. Thus there could be no claim of religious liberty.[213]

In 2002 the Court returned to an issue that had ostensibly been settled nearly sixty years before—whether a village could restrict religious prose-lytizers, once again Jehovah's Witnesses, by requiring them to obtain a permit from the municipality (chapter 4).[214]

Chapter Six

CONTRACTION

DURING THE WORLD WAR II period when the Court was preoccupied with issues of religious freedom arising almost entirely from the beliefs and practices of the Jehovah's Witnesses, it paid no attention to establishment issues. But almost as soon as the War was over, the same factors that made possible the revolution in attitudes toward religious freedom began to shape the Court's understanding of establishment as well.

The legal climate also changed because of the newly aggressive posture of three organizations—the American Civil Liberties Union, the American Jewish Congress, and Protestants and Other Americans United for Separation of Church and State—which, often for somewhat different motives, each espoused a separationist view and mounted systematic legal challenges to existing forms of accommodation.[1]

The seminal case was *Everson v. Board of Education* (1947),[2] challenging a New Jersey law whereby parents sending their children to private schools were reimbursed by local authorities for the cost of bus fare. Justice Black wrote the majority opinion upholding the practice on the grounds that it was a subsidy to parents and students, not to a church. While New Jersey could not single out religious believers for special benefits, equally it could not exclude them from general benefits.[3]

However, just as the *Gobitis* case in 1940 had been merely a temporary defeat for the Witnesses, so *Everson* was a pyrrhic defeat for those who advocated stringent separation of church and state. Black ended his opinion by pronouncing, "The First Amendment has erected a wall between church and state. That wall must be kept high and impregnable. We could not approve the slightest breach. New Jersey has not breached it here."[4] Thus Black revived Jefferson's metaphor after an oblivion of seventy years, a revival that had crucial consequences for the modern understanding of the Establishment Clause.

Justice Jackson pointed out that Black had affirmed the wall, then perversely proceeded to breach it. The acid-tongued dissenter quoted Lord Byron's Julia, who "whispering 'I will ne'er consent,' consented." Jackson found the Court's ruling "utterly discordant" with the principle of the wall.[5]

Students in schools operated for profit were excluded from the reimbursement benefit, Jackson noted, even though they might be needy, and in reality the practice benefited primarily one religion. He went on to give a disquisition on the power of the Catholic Church and argued that the church depended heavily on its schools to secure the loyalty of its members, an effort that New Jersey was now aiding.[6]

Justice Rutledge in his dissent claimed that this was the first case that required the Court to define the meaning of the term "an establishment" in the Bill of Rights, and he thought the phrase was used by the framers of the Constitution to create a complete and permanent separation of the sphere of religion from the activities of the civil authorities, comprehensively forbidding every form of public aid or support for religion.[7]

The word "religion" had the same meaning in both the Religion Clauses, and, if it provided for the broadest possible protection of religious freedom, it applied equally broadly in its prohibition of an establishment, Rutledge argued. Thus all use of public funds for religious purposes was forbidden. The New Jersey program forced taxpayers to subsidize other people's religions, and the argument used to justify bus subsidies could, he believed, be used to finance buildings and other costs of religious schools.[8]

Rutledge candidly acknowledged that the "price of religious freedom is double," in that the same Constitution that guaranteed freedom to the believer forbade any attempt by the government to alleviate the financial burdens of religion. There would necessarily be hardships for those who forwent attending "the common schools," and those who exercised religious freedom most fully must necessarily pay the greatest price.[9]

The *Everson* case was an instance where the specific issue—subsidized bus fares—was a rather minor one, but the case had implications far beyond the issue itself. In winning a small and temporary victory, proponents of religious schools lost the war, because the case gave the Court the opportunity to set forth, for the first time, an understanding of the First Amendment based on the "wall" metaphor, an interpretation that virtually predetermined an increasingly stringent application of the Establishment Clause. Given the drift of later decisions, Jackson's exasperated complaint that Black contravened his own stated principles was justified.

The new jurisprudence won its first victory the next year, in *McCollum v. Board of Education*, when the Court invalidated an Illinois practice whereby students in public schools were permitted to go to different parts of the school building to receive instruction in their particular faiths, those not utilizing the opportunity being excused.[10]

Black held that the practice was clearly a form of governmental support of religion and was thus clearly unconstitutional. Among other things, the various churches were thereby afforded invaluable aid in proselytizing, through Illinois's compulsory school-attendance law. An important aspect of Douglas's ruling was his rejection of the claim that the Illinois practice was constitutional because it was nondiscriminatory in aiding all religions equally.[11]

Justice Frankfurter wrote a concurring opinion in which he chiefly re-
hearsed the history of the "common schools" in the United States, which
he said were intended by popular will to be secular, and of "released time"
programs, of which there were various kinds, some of which might be
constitutional.[12]

Jackson supported the majority decision but warned of certain dangers—the difficulty of determining what was or was not "religious" and
the possibility that the Court would find itself swamped with similar
cases. He also dismissed as irrelevant Vashti McCollum's claim that her
son was embarrassed at not attending classes attended by most of his
classmates. Echoing Frankfurter in the *Gobitis* case, Jackson warned that
the Court could not function as "a super school board for every school
district in the nation."[13]

Justice Reed dissented, arguing among other things that the Court did
not clearly indicate what was unconstitutional in the Illinois practice—
the use of school buildings, the use of school time, or other factors. The
practice did not in any way inhibit religious freedom.[14]

At the beginning of the modern understanding of the Establishment
Clause, Reed made a last effort to uphold the Court's traditional view,
citing the 1930 *Cochran* case as a precedent. Once again raising what had
been a frequent argument against rigorous separation, Reed insisted that
an "establishment of religion" meant merely a state church, not government assistance given fairly to all religions and, as many later commenta-
tors would do, pointed out the anomaly whereby Congress and the various branches of the armed forces employed chaplains, so that religious
services were actually held on government property.[15]

However, in 1952, the Court, in the view of some of its members,
seemed to draw back from its position in *McCollum* when, in *Zorach v.
Clauson*, it upheld a similar "released time" arrangement in New York
State that embodied the crucial difference that religious instruction was
not given on public school property. Instead students left the schools at
certain hours of the day and went to their various churches.[16]

Somewhat surprisingly, Justice Douglas wrote the majority opinion,
dismissing as "obtuse reasoning" the claim that anyone's religious freedom was being violated and insisting, "The First Amendment does not
say that in every and all respects there shall be a separation of church and
state," since that would make church and state alien and hostile to one
another, itself a violation of the Constitution. He too cited the apparent
anomaly of prayers and chaplains for public bodies and noted wryly that
"a fastidious atheist or agnostic" might even object to the fact that the
Court itself opened its sessions by calling upon God. In a sweeping remark
that he may later have regretted, Douglas proclaimed, "We are a religious
people whose institutions presuppose a Supreme Being."[17]

Black now dissented and, with some exasperation, turned the tables and accused the majority of inconsistancy. He thought there was no significant difference from the *McCollum* case and that the main purpose of "released time" was to force "unenthusiastic" children to receive religious instruction. The practice was also objectionable because it treated atheists and other nonbelievers as second-class citizens.[18] Frankfurter also dissented, in part because the schools did not close completely during the hours of religious instruction, thus in effect substituting religious for secular instruction during those particular hours.[19]

Jackson argued similarly in his dissent, claiming that it would have been permissible to shorten the school day but not to use part of that day for religious purposes. Children themselves were in effect deprived of their liberty by being forced to attend church, while the school remained open as a "jail" for those not attending such instructions. An exasperated Jackson complained that the *McCollum* decision "has passed like a storm in a teacup" and accused the Court "almost of cynicism" in the way it had departed from *McCollum*. "Today's decision will be more interesting to students of the psychology of the judicial process than to students of constitutional law," he predicted.[20]

The dissenters in the *Zorach* case, for the first time in the Court's history, also expressed strong opinions about the role of religion in American life and the dangers that religion posed to civil peace, a theme that would become more insistent over time.

For a time, Jackson's fear, expressed in the *McCollum* case, that the Court would be flooded with similar kinds of appeals, turned out to be unfounded, even though his irritated complaint, in *Zorach*, that the principles of the *McCollum* case were being forgotten seemed accurate. After its great burst of revolutionary energy concerning religion in the years 1940-52, the Court seemed to relax, ready to turn its attention to other issues, and for almost a decade after 1952 almost routinely rejected appeals in religion cases, thus avoiding perplexing questions, and allowing lower-court judgments to stand.[21] When once again it renewed its interest in those questions, however, Jackson's dreaded flood did indeed occur, but it moved in the direction charted in *McCollum*, not in *Zorach*.

However, a case of some importance for religious freedom was decided in 1951, when the Court nullified a New York State law against "sacrilege," after the state banned the showing of a film (*The Miracle*) as insulting to religion. The film had been criticized by the Catholic archbishop of New York and others.[22]

Justice Clark held that films were entitled to the same degree of freedom as oral or written expression. Such freedom was not absolute, but he found the statute against sacrilege too broad and confused to be valid. Without explicitly endorsing it, he noted the opinion of a state court that the New York law also involved a violation of the Establishment Clause. It was not the duty of government to protect religions from things that they might find offensive, Clark concluded.[23]

Frankfurter concurred but wrote a much longer and more extensive opinion. Surveying the history of the concept of sacrilege, he found that in English law it meant robbing or damaging a church building, although later it had been used to prosecute people who dissented from religious or political orthodoxies. Historically the law was connected with a state church, and, since the disestablishment of religion, church property was merely entitled to the same protection given by the law to all property. Frankfurter found that the legal meaning of "sacrilege" was not what New York gave it—an act of insult or disrespect against something sacred.[24]

But the nub of the case was the fact that no government could impose censorship on the expression of ideas, could not "put within unascertainable bounds the varieties of religious experience."[25]

The Court's renewed interest in religion, beginning in the early 1960s, continued, after a hiatus of almost a decade, the process of expanding the scope of religious freedom considerably beyond its traditional limits. By contrast, the Court also reconsidered the Establishment Clause and found the Constitution far more restrictive than had been previously thought, as though the Religion Clauses were a balance by which, as one side rose, the other necessarily fell.

The new era began relatively uncontroversially, with the case of *Torcaso v. Maryland* (1961), when a unanimous Court held that Maryland could not deny a commission to a notary public who refused to affirm that he believed in God. (Like many religion cases, the issue was relevant to both the Religion Clauses—Maryland had established a religion, and had thereby infringed the liberty of some of its citizens.)[26]

Black found that the state was placing its authority behind particular religious beliefs, contrary to the American tradition of religious freedom, and that the Maryland law violated both the First Amendment and Article VI of the Constitution, which forbade a "religious test" for holders of public office. The fact that no one is compelled to hold public office in no way justified the requirement.

SABBATH LAWS

The first number of establishment issues to come before the Court in the 1960s were resolved by the older, seemingly more cautious jurisprudence of accommodation, in a number of challenges in 1961 to laws requiring retail businesses to close on Sundays. The Court declined to invalidate existing arrangements, but its caution gave little hint of the kinds of rulings that would begin the very next year.

The principal case, *McGowan v. Maryland*, was brought by retailers who had been arrested for making sales on Sunday and who claimed that their arrests were a violation of the "equal protection" clause of the Constitution.[27]

Chief Justice Earl Warren, who rarely wrote opinions in religion cases, ruled that Maryland had a rational basis for distinguishing between types of retail activity, allowing some (recreational in nature) and prohibiting others. The plaintiffs claimed they had suffered economic hardship through the imposition of the Christian religion. However, since they did not state their own religious beliefs, they could not claim religious discrimination, Warren held.[28]

Making a historical survey of "blue laws," he acknowledged that in their medieval origins they were clearly intended to aid religion. However, beginning in the eighteenth century they also came to have secular purposes and were favored, for example, by many labor unions and trade associations. A law could not be held unconstitutional merely because it happened to coincide with religious beliefs. The law's mention of "profaning the Lord's Day" was not to be taken literally, since the statute permitted many Sunday activities that at one time would have been thought profane. The state merely provided a day of rest for its citizens and chose a particular day of the week for that purpose. It did not directly promote religion.[29]

Frankfurter, consistent with his position in the flag-salute cases, argued that secular laws could be enforced even against those whose religious beliefs were thereby burdened, but only if the law's purpose could be achieved in no other way. The disputed Sunday-closing laws were all of recent enactment and had obvious secular purpose, even if based upon earlier laws that were religious in nature. To allow individuals to choose alternative closing days would require the state to inquire into the religious beliefs of its citizens and would itself therefore be unconstitutional.[30]

Douglas dissented, arguing that the laws were inherently religious and gave a privileged position to the Christian sabbath. It was impermissible to enforce the criminal law against citizens who held minority religious opinions. Whereas the Court deemed polygamy inherently wrong, buying and selling were in themselves legitimate activities that government had no secular purpose for restricting. Religious freedom included "freedom from religion," he asserted.[31]

Decided along with the *McGowan* case was an appeal from Orthodox Jews claiming hardship in being forced to close their shops for two days—their own sabbath and that mandated by Pennsylvania law.[32]

Warren again ruled for the majority, holding that there was no infringement of religious liberty and that the hardship was imposed solely by the consciences of those who believed they had to close on Saturdays.[33]

Justice Brennan dissented in part, denying that the law violated the Establishment Clause but holding that it was an infringement of religious liberty, forcing people to choose between their businesses and their religion. The Court, he warned, seemed to be saying that any encroachment on religious freedom was permissible if the state could claim to have an interest and to be acting neutrally.[34]

Another suit brought by Orthodox Jews was decided in the same way, Warren holding that the religious purposes of the sabbath had long been divorced from the Sunday closing laws and that the phrase "Lord's Day" was "merely a relic." From the nature of the exceptions granted, the law's purpose was clearly recreational, not religious.[35] Another case decided at the same time involved an appeal specifically based on the use of the phrase "Lord's Day" in the Pennsylvania law, Warren holding that this was mere "negligence" on the part of the legislature in allowing an anachronistic phrase to be used.[36]

The next year there was another challenge, which the Court, following the *McGowan* decision, dismissed per curiam for lack of a substantial constitutional issue.[37] Douglas dissented from the consensus. People were denied the right to work, because the law recognized a sabbath day other than their own, as though a Moslem majority might forbid labor on Friday. That the challenged law was essentially religious in nature was shown in the fact that it actually did exempt those who observed a sabbath different from Sunday. "The law is thus plainly in aid of all organized religion, bringing to heel anyone who violates the religious scruples of the majority by seeking his salvation not through organized religion but on his own."[38]

It would be nearly two decades before the Court again addressed the Sunday work issue, this time not as challenges to the laws themselves but as claims about religious liberty and the duty of employers to accommodate their employees' religious scruples (chapter 5). In one such case in 1985 the Court invalidated a Connecticut law that required employers to excuse employees whose religion forbade them to work on Sunday. The statute clearly advanced religion, a unanimous Court held, and did so in a discriminatory way, in that it did not accommodate every personal religious belief of every worker.[39]

RELIGION AND PUBLIC EDUCATION

Perhaps the most controversial aspect of the Court's interpretation of the Establishment Clause has been its consistent finding, beginning in 1962 and based on the *McCollum* precedent, that most religious activity occurring in public schools is a violation of the Constitution.

The first case was *Engel v. Vitali*, in which plaintiffs challenged a New York state directive "recommending" that at the beginning of each school day, a teacher or pupil recite in each classroom the prayer "Almighty God, we acknowledge our dependance upon Thee, and we beg thy blessings upon our parents, our teachers, and our country."[40] Black wrote for the majority, holding that the prayer was "wholly inconsistent" with the First Amendment, not withstanding the fact that such a prayer was intended to be "neutral" among the various religions, and that students were permitted to leave the classroom during the prayer. There was "indirect coercion" stemming from the power and prestige of the government being placed behind the recitation of the prayer. Persecution of religion and government sponsorship "go hand in hand," Black warned.[41]

Douglas concurred. Agreeing that there was no direct coercion, and noting that teachers were forbidden to comment on the prayer, he found the case unlike *McCollum* in that the power of the state was not used to indoctrinate. The issue was rather a narrower one—whether New York was financing a religious exercise. (In a footnote he acknowledged that in fact American public life was "honeycombed" with all kinds of public expenditures in support of religion.)[42]

Before finding against the practice, Douglas seemed to go out of his way to make an argument in its favor, noting an anomaly that critics of the Court would frequently cite—that the public schools were doing no more than the Court itself did when it began each session with the phrase "God save the United States of America and this honorable Court," and no more than Congress did in its own official prayers. Even the financial support given to religion was infinitesimal, Douglas conceded.[43]

However, he also raised an issue that previous cases had only hinted at but that would be increasingly important in the Court's developing view of religion—the "divisiveness" argument, which Black also made. Despite efforts to be nondenominational, the prescribed prayer did not precisely meet the needs of Jews, Unitarians, or members of the Ethical Culture Society, for example, and one of the plaintiffs was an agnostic. Repeating his famous assertion in *Zorach* that "we are a religious people whose institutions presuppose the existence of a Supreme Being," Douglas nonetheless insisted that, according to the *McGowan* decision, religious practice was to be left wholly to the individual. A decision in the pending case would be easy, Douglas thought, had it not been for the *Everson* case, which had been wrongly decided.[44]

Justice Stewart dissented, arguing that no one's free exercise of religion was infringed by the prayer, while prohibiting it denied children the right to participate in the "spiritual heritage of the nation."[45]

In 1964 the Court ruled *per curiam* that the practice of prayer and Bible reading in the Florida schools was unconstitutional.[46] While concurring in the decision, Douglas urged that the Court should have gone further, to consider whether baccalaureate services in connection with public school graduations were permissible. He also questioned the constitutionality of the Florida practice of asking the question "Do you believe in God?" of prospective teachers and allegedly taking the answer into account in determining promotions. The Florida Supreme Court had ruled that taxpayers as such could not bring suit over such matters, but Douglas disagreed.[47]

In between those two cases, while concurring in a decision involving religious freedom and employment rights, Stewart accused the Court of "woodenness" in its interpretation of the Establishment Clause. He thought the Constitution required the government to give positive support to religious belief and urged the majority to amend its "unsound" interpretation. Religious liberty, which was the paramount good the Religion Clauses sought to protect, was being sacrificed to the idea of separation.[48]

In 1952 the Court had been asked to rule on a New Jersey law requiring daily readings from the Old Testament in public school classrooms.[49] Jackson found that the issue was not "ripe." The chief plaintiff was a parent whose child had graduated from the school before the case came to the Court and who did not claim that he personally had been harmed by the Bible reading. But the plaintiffs could not sue merely as taxpayers, Jackson ruled, because they could not show that their taxes were being used to promote religion. In addition, previous Court decisions had found that taxpayer challenges were too remote to give the plaintiff a genuine interest in the case. Here, Jackson speculated, the motives of the plaintiffs were "more religious than mercenary." It was a "feigned interest."[50] Douglas dissented, insisting that the case should be heard, since the plaintiffs might be able to show that the schools were being deflected from their educational purpose.[51]

But in 1963, in *Abington Township School District v. Schempp*, the Court invalidated a Pennsylvania law requiring daily reading from the Bible in each public classroom, with various students assigned to choose and read particular verses. The "King James" (Protestant) Bible was distributed, although students were free to use other translations. Following the reading, the Lord's Prayer was recited in unison. Students could absent themselves from these exercises, and no one was permitted to comment on the biblical texts.[52] Joined with the case was an appeal against a Maryland statute mandating similar practices.[53]

The plaintiffs in the first case were Unitarians who said they feared lest their children's relations with teachers and other students be adversely affected by a refusal to participate. Several Jews testified to the unacceptable character of the King James translation for them, and of any readings from the New Testament, and also testified that Jews attached no importance to Bible reading as such.[54]

The plaintiffs in the Maryland case were Madalyn Murray (later Madalyn Murray O'Hair) and her son William, just beginning their careers as perhaps the most famous American atheists.[55] The State of Pennsylvania defended these practices on the grounds that the Bible was "nonsectarian" and that it would be discriminatory to exclude the New Testament. The Bible was a book of great moral, historical, and literary value and was thus hardly objectionable.[56]

Clark wrote the majority opinion invalidating the practices. He recalled that the Court had rejected the claim that the First Amendment only forbade the establishment of particular sects, and had instead found that the Constitution mandated "a wise neutrality" arising from fear of the combination of government power and religious groups. To withstand scrutiny, such a practice had to show "secular legislative purpose and a primary affect that neither advances nor inhibits religion." While violations of religious freedom always involved coercion, violations of the Establishment Clause often did not.[57]

Bible reading was a religious ceremony, hence prohibited, Clark held, and the Bible was a book used for purposes beyond mere moral inspiration or "secular enlightenment," although it could be taught in the public schools "objectively." In a phrase often later quoted, Clark warned that "Today's trickle may become a raging torrent."[58]

Douglas concurred, noting again that the amount of money involved was insignificant but that the principle was crucial. The churches could not make use of governmental authority to "help themselves gain and keep members."[59]

Justice Brennan's concurrence was the longest and most elaborately argued of the opinions. He too observed that "we are a religious people" but drew from that the significant fact that "feelings run high." It was not easy to separate the religious from the secular, but it was a task to be left to individuals. The public schools were to be neither "theistic nor atheistic but simply civic and patriotic."[60]

Since Pennsylvania compelled students to attend school, it was also compelling them to participate in a religious exercise. Noting the argument that, since the Establishment Clause did not confer a right, it was not incorporated by the Fourteenth Amendment and applied to the states, Brennan replied that the clause was essential for the guarantee of rights.[61]

Bible reading and the recitation of the Lord's Prayer were even more sectarian than the prayer mandated in the *Engle* case, Brennan judged. Conceding that such practices might foster better discipline among students, he nonetheless ruled that religious practices were an impermissible means of achieving that goal and suggested instead readings from great historic speeches. The Bible was inherently sectarian, as the very existence of different translations showed. Excusing children from the exercise did not alleviate the problem, since among other things they might be sub-jected to peer pressure.[62]

With regard to military chaplaincies, prayers in court, and other offi-cially sanctioned religious exercises, the participants were mainly adults and thus much less impressionable, and a refusal to provide chaplains for the military could be interpreted as hostility to religion, Brennan argued. Some practices had lost their religious meaning, while others ("In God we Trust" inscribed on coins) had simply become woven into the fabric of society.[63]

Justice Arthur Goldberg wrote a concurring opinion warning that the Court must not show hostility to religion and noting that a majority of Americans believed in God. However, the specific practices before the Court were impermissible.[64]

As in *Engel*, Stewart dissented, warning that in its ruling the Court did approach hostility to religion. Although he accepted the claim that the Bill of Rights was applicable to the states, he thought the states had more discretion in such matters than the Court allowed.[65]

The core value of the First Amendment was religious freedom, Stewart insisted, and here the Court came close to inhibiting such freedom. Free-dom was not limited to those who could pay for it, and it was unfair to prohibit religious exercises in public schools that students were required to attend. The *Schempp* decision would be perceived as establishing the "religion of secularism," or as government support for those who thought religion was wholly private.[66]

The Pennsylvania practice gave no support to particular religious ten-ets, Stewart argued, and its provisions might be no more than an expres-sion of "community preference." Local variations should be allowed. The schools must protect children from coercion or peer pressure, but the Constitution also required the schools to accommodate religious differ-ences. Allegations that the Engel and Schempp children suffered from ex-clusion were unproven, he judged.[67]

Over a two-year period the *Engel* and *Schempp* cases developed the jurisprudence of the *McCollum* case and formulated the position that thereafter the Court would almost undeviatingly take with respect to cases involving religion in the public schools.

In 1980 the Court struck down, per curiam, a Kentucky law requiring that a copy of the Ten Commandments be posted in every public school classroom. Unusually, the case was considered without formal argument, merely on the basis of the legal briefs submitted by both sides, a procedure indicating that the majority of the Court considered the merits of the case so obvious as to require no oral argument.[68]

In an unsigned opinion the majority found that the Ten Commandments had no demonstrable "secular purpose," despite a notice posted with each copy calling it "the moral basis of Western civilization." The first part of the Commandments explicitly involved duties to God, the Court pointed out, and the entire document was a sacred text. Posting the Commandments would have no value unless students were to read them, meditate upon them, and "perhaps to venerate and obey." The fact that copies of the Commandments were bought by private contributions made no difference, since the authority of the state was still placed behind them.[69]

Rehnquist dissented. The Court, he argued, had not proven that the practice was devoid of secular purpose but merely asserted it. Summary judgment without a hearing was without precedent in cases involving the Establishment Clause, since the Court regularly sought to determine legislative purpose in such cases. The fact that the law's secular purpose overlapped with a religious purpose did not invalidate it. Altogether Rehnquist found the decision a fulfillment of Jackson's warning in *McCollum* that such decisions would in time lead to extreme demands. Now efforts were being made to insulate the public sector from all religious influence.[70] Stewart also issued a dissenting opinion, but without substantial argument.[71]

The modern Court has adjudicated a number of issues that involve both of the Religion Clauses, since an alleged establishment of religion necessarily implies the infringement of the rights of those who are not its adherents. In several cases involving schools a majority of the Court has held that an erroneous application of the Establishment Clause in effect violated the Free-Exercise Clause (chapter 6).

- In *Widmar v. Vincent* (1981), the Court overruled a state university policy of denying the use of its facilities to a student religious group.
- In *Board of Education v. Mergens* (1984), it upheld the right of students in a public high school to form a religious organization and to meet in the school.
- In *Lamb's Chapel v. Center Moriches School District* (1993), it permitted religious films to be shown by a student group, on public school premises, outside regular school hours. In this case Scalia issued one of his scathing criticisms of the Court's prevailing theory of establishment:

Like some ghoul in a late-night horror movie that repeatedly steps out of its grave and shuffles abroad, after being repeatedly killed and buried, *Lemon* stalks over the Establishment Clause jurisprudence once again, frightening the little children and school attorneys of Center Moriches Union Free School District.

It was, he added, a strange notion that the First Amendment, which granted freedom to "religion-in-general," somehow forbade endorsement of "religion-in-general."[72]

- In *Rosenberger v. University of Virginia* (1995), the Court ruled in favor of a Christian student group at a state university that had been denied funding for its publication, even though other student publications were funded.
- In *Good News Bible Club v. Milford Central School* (2001), it again found that a student religious group could not be denied use of public school facilities that were available to other groups.

But the Court was still inclined to interpret the Establishment Clause strictly with regard to primary education, and in 1985 it nullified an Alabama law prescribing a moment of silence at the beginning of each school day. The state first authorized such a practice "for meditation," then amended the statute to say "for meditation or voluntary prayer," then amended it again to authorize teachers to lead "willing students" in a prayer to "Almighty God . . . the Creator and Supreme Judge of the world. . . ." A federal appeals court struck down the two revisions of the law, and what came before the Supreme Court was solely the provision for a moment of silence.[73]

Stevens found that the statute had no secular purpose and that its sponsor said that he intended it to "restore prayer" to the schools. In mandating this, the government was making an endorsement.[74] Powell also relied heavily on the legislative claim that silence was to be a time for prayer, finding that a "mere" moment of silence, divorced from prayer, might be constitutional.[75]

O'Connor offered the most thorough analysis of the issue. Students, she noted, were permitted to pray privately, and a moment of silence might facilitate that. The issue before the Court was whether the state's encouragement of this was valid.[76]

The Court was steadily modifying the Lemon Test (chapter 7) and indeed, she thought, it needed to be refined. State and church existed in a common community, and government actions at various times might incidentally aid or restrict religion. It would be "chaotic" to invalidate laws merely on such a basis. The government was not prohibited from taking religion into account when making law or policy, but it must never convey the impression that a particular religion was preferred.[77]

The moment of silence, she found, was different from the issues brought before the Court in the *Engel* and *Schempp* cases, since it was not necessarily associated with religion. It was difficult, she wryly observed, to discern a threat to religious liberty "in a roomful of silent, thoughtful school children."[78]

But the statute did favor the child who prayed over the one who did not, especially if the teacher urged prayer. The crucial question was whether the state intended to convey a message of endorsement for prayer, and the history of the statute tended to show that it did. No secular purpose had been persuasively demonstrated.[79]

Replying to Rehnquist's dissent (below), O'Connor said that such things as national days of prayer proclaimed by the president were not relevant to the case, since such events involved adults capable of independent judgment.[80] The solution to the dilemma was not "neutrality" but workable limits to the government's encouragement of the free exercise of religion. Alabama had intentionally crossed the line, she concluded.[81]

Burger thought it "bizarre" that the Court should take such a stand, in view of the numerous ways in which public prayer was part of the fabric of American life, observing wryly that since the Court itself prayed, "someone will say that we need divine guidance more than school children do."[82] He found that the decision manifested hostility to religion. Alabama had not intended to endorse religion, and statements to that effect by legislators had all been made after the law was already enacted. The majority decision was discriminatory of religion and bordered on the frivolous. "The mountains have labored and brought forth a mouse," Burger lamented.[83]

White agreed with Burger, wondering whether, if a student asked a teacher for permission to pray, the teacher would be allowed to grant it.[84] Rehnquist's dissent questioned the entire basis on which the Court had been making decisions on church-state matters since 1947, asserting that the majority misinterpreted the Constitution and misunderstood the intentions of the Founding Fathers. He rejected the familiar metaphor of the "wall of separation between church and state," arguing that "The intention of the framers of the Constitution was to prohibit the establishment of a national church or the preferring of one religion over another." The Lemon Test was no longer workable and was a vain attempt to derive order from a false principle.[85]

In 1992 the Court overturned a practice in a public high school whereby invited clergy offered a prayer at the annual graduation ceremony.[86] Kennedy found that, although attendance at the ceremony was supposedly optional, in reality it was mandatory, thus students were coerced into participating in a religious ceremony. Since the principal of the school chose the officiating cleric, in effect the state did so, and some people might be troubled by the choice (in this case a rabbi). The principal had also given the cleric guidelines about the "nonsectarian" prayer, thus redoubling the state's involvement. The Constitution, Kennedy insisted, mandated that the transmission of religious beliefs be entirely through "private speech."[87]

Acknowledging the argument that children were exposed to a variety of offensive and even irreligious ideas in the school, yet were denied the opportunity to pray, Kennedy responded that free speech existed even in cases where government officials might object but that religion was the reverse situation, forbidding the government to "pontificate." The danger was state-sanctioned orthodoxy.[88]

He too cited peer pressure as a danger and observed that the mere action of standing during a prayer would be interpreted as participation, even if the individual did not intend this. It was unfair to put adolescents in a position where they had either to comply or to protest. The legal right to be absent from the ceremony was irrelevant, since high school graduation was an important event in students' lives. The advice that dissenters stay way "turns the Constitution on its head," since it should not be necessary to make sacrifices in order to exercise one's guaranteed rights.[89]

As had been done in other cases, Kennedy drew a firm distinction between religious exercises in schools and such exercises in courts, legislatures, and other public bodies, since in the latter cases people were free to absent themselves without inviting comment.[90]

Blackmun concurred, arguing that when the government placed its approval on formal prayers, it was excluding some people from equal treatment. Democracy's "demand for discussion and dissent" clashed with religious faith's "bowing to higher authority beyond human discussion."[91]

Justice Souter recalled that the Court had consistently struck down government actions that purported to aid all religions equally and that such arrangements were prohibited under the Constitution. However, even the attempt to distinguish between "sectarian" and "nonsectarian" prayers would itself involve the Court in impermissible religious issues. Believers could not say that they were burdened by the prohibition of graduation prayer, since they could still pray privately.[92]

Scalia complained that the Court was "laying waste venerable customs," practices that had a "long and honorable history." The claim that nonbelievers were coerced by being asked to stand respectfully during the prayer was, he insisted, absurd, since people could not be assumed to assent to everything they did not explicitly protest. The desire of some people not to appear to be participating in prayer did not invalidate the government's right to encourage "religion in general." Students stood during the Pledge of Allegiance to the flag, without thereby implying the imposition of a political orthodoxy.[93]

Scalia ridiculed the Court's emphasis on the relative immaturity of high school students, asking whether it would soon also develop "a jurisprudence of mature and immature adults." The concept of coercion had been trivialized to mean something far different than the Founding Fathers intended. The school prayer cases were not applicable in this case, because attendance at school was compulsory and classes were "instructional by nature," whereas graduation prayers should be permitted if the school made clear the fact that standing or sitting during the exercise was not an endorsement.[94]

In 2000 the Court forbade a practice whereby students in a public high school offered public prayers before football games, allegedly without endorsement by the school.[95] Originally a student designated by school authorities offered a prayer over a loud speaker prior to games, and a student was also appointed to lead a prayer at the annual graduation ceremony. Those practices were challenged by, among others, Catholics and Mormons, who complained that the school was biased in favor of the Baptist religion and attempted to pressure others into conforming to Baptist piety.[96]

The school then altered its policy by instructing students to vote on whether or not a student should make a public presentation before each game and, if the vote was favorable, electing a student to make the presentation. But before the new policy could be put into affect, it was challenged on constitutional grounds.[97] Stevens ruled that, despite the claims of the school, the issue was one of establishment, not of religious liberty, asserting that, in any case, religious liberty could not "supersede the fundamental limitations imposed by the Establishment Clause."[98]

Although the school contended that since the decisions concerning prayer were all made by students, the results were not endorsed by the school, Stevens found that the impression of endorsement was unmistakable. Students understood the process as "an invitation to prayer," and the football games themselves were surrounded by signs of official school sponsorship. While attendance at games was not mandatory, most students probably felt a need to attend, with the force of "peer pressure" very strong.[99]

The school's invocation of "free expression" was spurious, Stevens judged, because only one kind of expression—prayer—would result. The election process, far from ensuring fairness, in reality ensured that minorities would always be excluded from presenting a message.[100]

The school stated that the secular purpose of the process was to "solemnize the occasion" of the football games, and in theory the election process might result in something other than a prayer. But Stevens could not conceive what other kind of "solemnization" besides prayer was even possible.[101] As a result of the prayer, some students would be given the message that they were "outsiders" and would be subjected to a "personally offensive religious ritual," he warned.[102]

Rehnquist dissented, charging that the majority decision "bristles with hostility to all things religious in public life," neither its "content nor its tone" in keeping with the true meaning of the Establishment Clause.[103] The very legal basis on which the policy was attacked was improper, Rehnquist argued, because the policy had not yet been put into effect and constitutional challenges could not be mounted against merely hypothetical dangers. The majority of the Court merely assumed that the elections would result in students offering prayers, but some might choose to "solemnize" the games with exhortations to courage and sportsmanship, for example. Solemnization was a legitimate secular purpose that might be fulfilled in a variety of ways. [104]

The policy permitted invocations at public events but did not endorse them and was a sincere attempt to comply with the Court's previous rulings, he argued.[105] Rehnquist warned that the Court had in effect invalidated all student elections, for fear that a student elected as a class officer might, for example, utter religious sentiments that could be construed as endorsed by the school.[106]

THE TEACHING OF EVOLUTION

In 1968 there was a constitutional challenge to an Arkansas law prohibiting the teaching of biological evolution in the public schools, a statute passed in 1928, at the time of the famous Scopes trial in Tennessee. Specifically the Arkansas law forbade teaching that human beings are "descended from lower orders of animals." A Little Rock high school adopted a biology textbook that supported evolution, and a teacher brought suit to resolve an apparent dilemma—if she used the prescribed book she would be in violation of state law.[107]

Justice Abe Fortas, during his brief term on the Court, wrote a unanimous decision striking down the statute. Although judicial intervention in education ought to be sparing, this case justified such action, he found. It was not the schools' obligation to protect religious groups from views they found distasteful, and the Arkansas law had the affect of censoring part of "the general body of knowledge." There was no discernible reason for the state's policy except religious belief, and the law was not neutral—it singled out for exclusion only one of several theories about the origins of the human race.[108]

Black expressed surprise that Arkansas's defense of the law seemed "pallid, unenthusiastic, even apologetic" and called the statute itself "lifeless." The textbook in question was, after all, being used. He was reluctant to see the Court involved in matters of local school curricula.[109]

However, he also thought the statute could be struck down for its vagueness. The state had the authority to exclude from its curriculum matters deemed too controversial, and if evolution were in fact antireligious (a legitimate question, he thought), the state could not constitutionally allow it to be taught. On the whole Black did not think any teacher had the right to teach things that the "school managers" did not want taught, and the theory of evolution could be criticized even on scientific grounds.[110]

Justice Harlan also wrote a perplexed concurring opinion, stating that there was a genuine issue of free speech that the Court had failed to address.[111] Stewart also concurred. The state could, for example, require the teaching only of Spanish in its schools, but it could not forbid mention of other languages. Nor could it forbid mention of evolution. The law was altogether too vague to withstand scrutiny.[112]

But if in 1968 it seemed to some of the Court that Arkansas was making only a "pallid" effort to bar the teaching of evolution, a 1987 case offered a much more serious challenge, when Louisiana mandated that, if either biological evolution or the theory of "creation science" were taught in the schools, both must be taught, creation science being the claim that scientific evidence demonstrated the existence of a Supreme Being who created the universe.[113]

Brennan found for the majority that, under the Lemon Test, the law had no demonstrable secular purpose. Its stated purpose was "academic freedom," but in reality it narrowed the rights of teachers rather than expanding them. Obviously it was drawn in such a way as to give more protection to creation science than to evolution, and the connection between the law and conservative religious groups could not be ignored.[114]

Powell concurred, also finding that the predominant purpose of the law was to alter the public school curriculum in order to make it compatible with religious belief.[115] White also concurred but suggested that the Supreme Court defer to the federal district court, some of whose judges were Louisiana citizens who believed that the law's purpose was religious.[116]

Scalia wrote another of his biting dissents. The Court, he charged, claimed to know what motivated the Louisiana legislators, when in fact such motives might be be quite diverse, mixed, and difficult to discover.[117] The law stated that creation science was based on scientific evidence, and expert witnesses had testified to this. It was therefore presumptuous of the Court to insist that the law's basis was really theology. The law was not invalid merely because it coincided with the beliefs of some religious groups, Scalia insisted.[118]

He also questioned the factual assumptions on which the decision was based. Only a small minority of Louisiana residents belonged to what could be termed "fundamentalist" denominations, and the legislature had shown caution, even reluctance, in passing the law. Its sponsor denied that his purpose was to teach religion.[119]

The Court had heard no evidence that creation science was based on anything other than scientific reasoning. To posit a creator of the universe was not the same as positing "a god who is the object of worship," or even Aristotle's Unmoved Mover, Scalia thought.[120]

The law's seeming bias in favor of creation science came from the fact that legislators were informed that teachers of creation science were dis-

criminated against in the schools and were in need of protection. The
theory of evolution was not so firmly established as to exclude any contradictory opinion, Scalia argued.[121] He concluded by urging that the Lemon
Test be abandoned. It was not useful and was having the affect of ex-
acerbating the tension between the two Religion Clauses.[122]

In another Louisiana case, the Supreme Court in 2000 let stand a lower-
court decision prohibiting a school board from issuing a disclaimer in
connection with the teaching of evolution.[123] The school board mandated
that whenever the theory of evolution was taught, students were to be
shown an official statement indicating that evolution was a scientific theory only and was not intended to exclude other theories about the origins
of the universe, such as the biblical account of creation. They were also
to be told that the theory of evolution was not intended to undermine the
beliefs of their parents and that they themselves were encouraged to
"think for themselves" on the question. The lower court, applying the
Lemon Test, found that the rule had no secular purpose and was a mere
ploy to support the biblical account of creation.[124]

Scalia, one of three justices who wanted to hear the school board's appeal, wrote a dissent. Acknowledging his disagreement with the Lemon
Test, he nonetheless argued that here it was being misapplied. The stated
secular purpose of the law—to encourage students to form their own opinions—was valid, and the biblical account of creation was cited only as an
example of an alternative point of view, not as the preferred theory.[125]

Religion and Public Institutions

The principles laid down with regard to public education also have pre-
sumptive application to other kinds of public institutions.

A 1983 case, *Marsh v. Chambers*, mounted a constitutional challenge
to a custom whereby the Nebraska legislature had a paid chaplain.[126]
Burger wrote a majority opinion upholding the practice. While acknowledging that history alone could not settle the issue, he stressed that it was
a venerable tradition dating from the time of the Founders.[127] Building on
an argument often used with respect to religion in the schools, he pointed
out that everyone involved in the chaplaincy issue was an adult and thus
presumably "not easily subject to indoctrination."[128]

The fact that a Presbyterian minister had held the chaplaincy for sixteen
years did not prove favoritism toward one group, because clerics of other
denominations were also authorized to lead prayers in the legislature.
Salary was no issue, since Congress also paid its chaplains.[129]

Brennan dissented, confessing that while in the *Engel* case he had approved the practice of legislative chaplains, he now realized that he had

been wrong. The prayer clearly violated the Lemon Test, in that prayer had no secular purpose at all. The Court was thus granting an exemption from the Establishment Clause.[130]

Here the power and prestige of the state were put behind praying, and this caused rancor and division within the legislature, with some members' rights of conscience violated, Brennan warned. It was not necessary to go so far as to expunge the "religious words" from the Lincoln Memorial, he conceded, but legislative prayer was not a mere acknowledgement of religion; it was actual worship.[131]

So important was religious liberty, Brennan argued, that it gave rise to rights of conscience that other freedoms did not. In that sense the Constitution was not neutral.[132] Acknowledging Burger's point about the long precedents involved, he nevertheless found them not compelling and suggested that the Founding Fathers and others might simply have been mistaken in authorizing such practices.[133] But even Brennan was unwilling to go so far as to prohibit the Court's own prayers, justifying them on the grounds that the phrase "God save this honorable Court" had "lost all religious meaning."[134]

Stevens also dissented, finding that the legislative arrangement favored one religion at the expense of others, as the minister's sixteen-year tenure demonstrated.[135]

In 1983 the Court heard a challenge, *Lynch v. Donnelly*, to a practice whereby at Christmastime every year a Rhode Island city government set up a Nativity scene in a public park, with secular symbols alongside depiction of the birth of Jesus.[136] Burger found the practice constitutionally permissible. Absolute separation of church and state was not possible, he thought, and that fact should be balanced against the demands of the Establishment Clause. The government's attitude to religion should not be "callous indifference." There were religious paintings in public museums, for example, and an absolute prohibition would be "simplistic." Burger, the author of the Lemon Test, thought that test inapplicable in this case.[137]

The Nativity scene had a secular purpose in that it recalled the historical origins of the Christmas holiday, he continued. There was no direct benefit to religion, and the incidental benefits were no greater than the very name of the holiday—"Christ's Mass"—provided. Because it was merely seasonal, there was no continuing involvement of the government and religion because of the creche.[138]

Burger modified the "divisiveness" doctrine cited in other cases by observing that over a forty-year period, the only apparent strife generated by the creche was by the plaintiffs themselves, and it was not permissible to create the appearance of division merely by filing suit. The scene "displays a friendly community spirit of good will in keeping with the season," and it would be ironic, Burger thought, if "one symbol of twenty centuries' standing" could taint such an exhibit.[139]

O'Connor concurred. She especially rejected the divisiveness argument as irrelevant, proposing that the sole issue was the use of government money, not the public's possible reaction to it. The city of Pawtucket did not intend to convey a message of approval of Christianity, as the creche's presence among other, more secular symbols showed.[140]

Brennan dissented. He found no secular purpose and thought the Court had been swayed by the "familiarity and comfort of the feast," which could in any case be appropriately celebrated by secular symbols. The city fathers themselves acknowledged the religious significance of the creche when they testified that to exclude it would in effect be antireligious.[141]

"Divisiveness" could be presumed, since the presence of a Christian symbol conveyed to non-Christians the message that their beliefs were not worthy of similar respect. Soon the government would be forced to become involved with other religious groups demanding equal status for their symbols. The filing of the suit unleashed a "powerful emotional conflict" in Pawtucket, thus proving the fact of division.[142]

The Court ignored the clear religious meaning of the scene, Brennan argued, along with the fact that it was placed in a very prominent place. Christmas had both secular and religious meanings, and the government could embrace the former but not the latter. The creche inspired "awe and wonder" over a "mystical event" and was not the mere commemoration of a historical event. It could not be studied for purely aesthetic reasons, as could a Gothic cathedral or a religious poem.[143] As with prayers in the Supreme Court, Brennan conceded, it was permissible to place the phrase "In God We Trust" on coins because the practice had lost its religious meaning, and it merely served the secular purpose of "solemnizing public occasions" and "expressing inspiration."[144]

A long history could not justify an unconstitutional practice, and even the historicity of the creche was exaggerated, since it was not used in America until the nineteenth century, at which time it aroused religious controversy. The task of preserving America's religious heritage was given exclusively to the churches, not to the government.[145]

Blackmun also dissented, noting that the mayor of Pawtucket had spoken of "keeping Christ in Christmas." Somewhat contradictorily, Blackmun also thought that the city had reduced the symbol to a mere ploy for attracting shoppers, and he refused to join in this "desacralization" of the symbol.[146]

In 1989 the issue returned in a Pennsylvania case. A Catholic group donated a creche that was displayed each Christmas in the county courthouse. On the adjoining grounds was a Christmas tree and an eighteen-foot menorah donated by a Jewish group.[147]

Blackmun wrote a majority opinion disallowing the custom. On the face of it the decision was a direct reversal of the *Lynch* case, and Blackmun found the majority's reasoning in *Lynch* to be "fuzzy." While some Christians and Jews celebrated the holidays as secular, inherently they were religious in nature, he asserted.[148]

After reviewing the history of Christmas celebrations at some length, he concluded that the Constitution's concern with "religious diversity" was undermined by the practice. While at one time freedom of religion might have been thought to extend only to Christians, that was no longer the case, and non-Christians were rightly offended by the Christmas display.[149]

A relevant factor detracting from the fairness of the display was the fact that the creche was in the courthouse itself, situated in a place where no one could overlook it, while the menorah was outside. The phrase "Glory to God in the Highest" written over the creche was a quote from the New Testament and an obviously sectarian statement. There were no mitigating secular symbols next to the creche, as there had been in the *Lynch* case.[150]

Blackmun reacted sharply to Kennedy's dissent (below), finding Kennedy's claim that the Court was hostile to religion "absurd and offensive." The Court was motivated merely by "respect for pluralism," and those who objected were "would-be theocrats audacious enough to claim that they were being discriminated against."[151]

Display of the menorah was permissible, Blackmun concluded, because it was situated alongside a Christmas tree, with an accompanying sign that the city "salutes liberty." In addition, the creche was inherently more religious than the menorah. Both Christmas and the Jewish feast of *Chanukah* could be celebrated as secular feasts.[152]

O'Connor now appeared to depart from her position in *Lynch*, finding that the Nativity scene conveyed to non-Christians the sense that they were "outsiders in the political community." In the *Lynch* case the creche was in a public park, which made it much less official than in a courthouse.[153]

She rejected Blackmun's claim that Chanukah could be a secular holiday but nonetheless found the display of the menorah permissible, because it was modified by the secular symbol of the Christmas tree. It was also impossible to think that the city was endorsing Judaism, since Judaism was a minority religion.[154]

Brennan agreed with the main thrust of the majority argument but thought that the menorah also violated the Establishment Clause. He considered it dubious that even the Christmas tree could be viewed as a secular symbol, given its historical connections. The menorah did not speak of pluralism but only of the religion of Judaism, and even if Chanukah could be shown to have some secular meaning, that would not alter the basic reality. Indeed, the meaning of Chanukah itself may well have been "distorted" because of its proximity to the Christian feast of Christmas. Finally, Brennan raised, without attempting to resolve it, the fascinating possibility that a "message of pluralism" might itself be offensive to some people on religious grounds.[155]

Stevens thought there should be a strong presumption against religious symbols on public property, which among other things had the effect of emphasizing "sincere and deeply felt differences" that the government ought not to exacerbate.[156]

Kennedy offered a ringing dissent, beginning with the claim that offended Blackmun—that the majority of the Court showed "an unqualified hostility toward religion." Taken to its logical extreme, some of the majority language would require a "relentless extirpation" of all contact between government and religion. But that was not the history and purpose of the Establishment Clause. Government policies of acknowledgment, accommodation, and support for religion were an accepted part of the nation's political and cultural heritage, he insisted. Given the expansion of the "modern administrative state," it was difficult to argue that the failure of the government to help religion would be viewed as neutrality.[157]

A large cross on the front of the courthouse would violate the Constitution because of its "intrusive permanency," and it would risk being coercive. But the creche did no more than celebrate the season. If the government acknowledged only the secular meaning of Christmas, it would show "callous indifference" toward religious faith and would discriminate against believers. The *Lynch* decision did not hold that secular symbols somehow "subdued" religious symbols, merely that the various symbols together did not threaten the Constitution.[158]

Some Court decisions (*Widmar*) found that the government was required to allow its property to be used for religious purposes, and the "endorsement" test only began with O'Connor's concurring opinion in *Lynch*, Kennedy pointed out. The *Marsh* case concerning legislative chaplaincies ruled that the endorsement test could not invalidate long-standing traditions. Thus the Court should not be asked to regulate the "minutiae" of holiday displays, he argued.[159]

The present case, Kennedy warned, created categories of religions based on the number of their adherents (O'Connor's reference to Jews as only a minority). The corollary was that "Those religions enjoying the largest following must be consigned to the status of least favored faiths, so as to avoid any possible risk of offending members of minority religions." This, he concluded, was an "Orwellian rewriting of history." The Court was undertaking to define the meaning of particular religious symbols, thereby becoming a "national theology board."[160]

In 1995 the heard Court heard another case concerning religious symbolism, *Capitol Square v. Pinette*,[161] a case whose implications were complex and subtle. For some years the government of Ohio had allowed the square in front of the capitol building in Columbus to be used by the public for speeches, demonstrations, and exhibits. In 1993 both a Christmas tree and a menorah had been authorized. However, when the Ku Klux Klan applied to erect a cross in the square, its application was denied on the explicit grounds that such an exhibit would violate the Establishment Clause.

A federal district court overturned the ban, ruling that the Klan could erect a cross provided it included a sign disclaiming any sponsorship by the state of Ohio. Once the Klan's cross was erected, several churches received permission to erect their own crosses, in order to dilute the force of Klan sponsorship.[162]

Although the Klan asked the Court to hear the case as an issue of freedom of expression, Scalia in his majority opinion noted that that issue had not been raised in the lower court, thus the case had to be decided on the basis of the Establishment Clause. He ruled in favor of the Klan on the grounds that the square was open to the public in general and this eliminated any possibility that the cross would be thought to be endorsed by the state.[163]

However, he also noted that free speech and freedom of religion were often related in that historically the suppression of free speech had often been the suppression of religious speech. "[I]n Anglo-American history, at least, government suppression of speech has so commonly been directed precisely at religious speech that a free speech clause without religion would be Hamlet without a prince."[164]

The question, according to Scalia, was whether the capitol square had been used as a "public forum," which it had. Previous cases (*Lamb's Chapel* and *Widmar*) held that access to public forums could not be denied to groups on the basis of religion.[165]

The *Lynch* case raised the question as to whether an exhibit on public property could be construed as an endorsement by the state of particular religious beliefs. But in the previous cases the public forum had not been open to all groups equally, whereas in Ohio it was, and the display of the cross was privately sponsored.[166]

Scalia thought it irrelevant whether some people might erroneously conclude that the cross was endorsed by the state. The government need only consider what a "reasonable person" might conclude and was not required to "guess" every possible reaction. Guessing wrongly about such reactions could cause the state to be in violation of either of the Religion Clauses, depending on its policies.[167]

Scalia made a direct attack on the opinion of the dissenting Justice Stevens (below), charging that Stevens's opinion . . .

> exiles private religious speech to a realm of less-protected expression heretofore inhabited only by sexually explicit displays and commercial speech. . . .
> It will be a sad day when this Court casts piety with pornography and finds the First Amendment more hospitable to private expletives . . . than to private prayers.

Such a position, he charged, was "outright perverse."[168]

In fact, Scalia argued, the First Amendment required that religious expression be given preferential treatment. Restrictions were meant to apply only to government action.[169] The state could require all displays to be clearly marked as under private sponsorship, but this would give rise to "ridiculous" arguments about the size such signs must be and the distance from which they were capable of being seen.[170]

Justice Thomas concurred, observing that the issue was not purely religious but also political in nature. The Klan's objective was "racist white government," and it used the cross only in connection with its "negative ritual" of cross burning, primarily a nonreligious purpose.[171]

Thus, Thomas argued, the use of the cross was "a symbol of hate," not a religious symbol, so the case might not turn on the Establishment Clause at all: "There may be much less here than meets the eye."[172] Like Scalia, Thomas implied that the case was really one of free expression, even though the Court had excluded that issue from its deliberations.

O'Connor also concurred, mainly differing from Scalia in her understanding of "endorsement." She thought there was no need for Scalia's criticisms of the endorsement test, since in the case at hand there was little danger that such endorsement would be inferred. For her the public disclaimer, as ordered by the district court, was crucial.[173]

She also disagreed with Scalia's view that it was irrelevant whether the public inferred such endorsement, and she charged that he took "an exceedingly narrow view of the Establishment Clause," which she thought "forbids a state from hiding behind the application of formally neutral criteria and remaining studiously oblivious to the effects of its actions." The intention of the state was not conclusive, but the affects of its actions were.[174]

She disagreed with Stevens's dissent because a "reasonable person" was someone who had a better understanding of the situation than Stevens's "casual passerby." Under the dissenting opinion, all public religious displays would be invalid, because anyone might erroneously believe that they were officially endorsed.[175]

The "reasonable observer" had to be familiar with the history and context of the display and should realize that the square was a public forum for speakers of various kinds. Stevens overlooked the function of the square as a public forum and treated it merely as public property.[176]

Souter also concurred, seeing the public disclaimer as important, because a person need not be a "dimwit" to think there was a state endorsement; a "reasonable person" might do so. Government ownership of the display was not required to make it unconstitutional, so that each case had to be decided on its merits.[177]

Scalia was in error, Souter asserted, in thinking that the government must intend to make an endorsement in order for there to be a constitutional issue. Otherwise, Souter warned, the government could "contract out" religious displays and recruit private groups to do what it could not do itself.[178]

Much of the time the Klan cross was the only display in the square. The state's ban was in error because, short of rejecting the display, Ohio had other available options, such as requiring the disclaimer mandated by the district court.[179]

Stevens's dissent stressed the possibility that even intelligent and informed observers might believe that the state had endorsed the exhibit. O'Connor's position, he thought, required some "ideal standard" of knowledge that deprived "ordinary people" of protection against such things.[180]

Public demonstrations by citizens were understood as not being sponsored by the government, but silent symbols might not be understood, and the state had the right to forbid exhibits "with which it does not wish to be identified—erotic exhibits, commercial advertising, and perhaps campaign posters." It might be expected that many people would not see the disclaimer, nor could the public be expected to know the history of the square and its traditional availability to citizens, nor to understand the Court's concept of a "public forum."[181]

Stevens believed the Klan had erected the cross because Jews had erected a menorah. Thus, he argued, the cross was intended either as an affirmation of Christianity or as an attack on Judaism and either way was unconstitutional, because the state could not allow its facilities to be used either to advance or to oppose religion. The state should also have disallowed the menorah. In effect it ended by endorsing two religions instead of one.[182]

The case showed "the power of symbolism," Stevens observed—Jews erected a menorah, the Klan reacted with its cross, then other Christian groups erected crosses to counteract the Klan's. Thus even members of the same religion were sometimes offended by its symbols.[183]

Justice Ruth Bader Ginsburg also dissented, largely because of what she considered the inadequacy of the required disclaimer, which did not mention the Klan by name, was not physically sturdy, did not deny unequivocally that the state endorsed the cross, and was not legible from a distance. She explicitly left open the question as to whether an adequate disclaimer would remove the constitutional difficulties.[184]

The following year Rehnquist, with the concurrence of Scalia and Thomas, dissented from the Court's refusal to hear an appeal from a city ordered by a lower court to eliminate the figure of the cross from its official seal. Those bringing the suit had claimed no injury, Rehnquist argued, except in the fact that they were not Christians.[185]

In a similar case in 2001, Rehnquist issued a written opinion objecting to the fact that the Court had refused to hear an appeal from an Indiana city ordered by a lower court to remove a monument to the Ten Commandments from the grounds of its municipal building.[186] Rehnquist believed that the lower court had decided the constitutional issue wrongly. The city council declared that the monument merely "reflected the moral and spiritual heritage of the city." The *Stone* decision forbade the posting of the Ten Commandments in public school classrooms because students were invited to meditate on them, which was not true in the Elkhart case. The Elkhart monument was on a lawn alongside other monuments, and the city government was not restricted to conveying only secular messages to the public, he argued.[187]

Stevens questioned the appropriateness of dissenting opinions in cases where the Court had merely refused to hear an appeal from a lower-court judgment. Usually only dissenters issued such opinions, and their statements often gave a one-sided account of the issues, he warned. In the case at hand the words "The Ten Commandments—'I Am the Lord Thy God' "—appeared on the monument in larger letters than the other commandments, and the monument also included Jewish and Christian religious symbols.[188]

Religion and Public Policy

An area in which there has been little substantive litigation, but which is potentially significant in its implications, is the relationship between the teachings of particular churches and official public policy.

An unusual issue of this kind came before the Court in 1982, on an appeal by a Massachusetts restaurant that had been denied a liquor license under a state law banning the sale of alcohol near houses of worship.[189]

Burger found for the majority that in general, laws restricting the sale of liquor near churches were reasonable. But in the case at hand Massachusetts had in effect delegated the licensing power to each church, by allowing each church a veto over the sale of alcohol in its vicinity. Ironically, a total ban on the sale of alcohol near churches would be constitutional, but placing discretionary power in the hands of the churches was not. The existing law gave the churches power without restraint. They could, for example, use that power to give licenses to their own members and deny them to others. The law certainly involved "excessive entanglement" between government and religion.[190]

Rehnquist dissented. Observing acidly that "silly cases make bad law," he pointed out that by giving the churches discretionary power the state was merely trying to make the law more flexible. The matter in question could not be religiously neutral, since the only way to determine whether the sale of liquor interfered with houses of worship was to ask the worshipers themselves. The government could protect churches from the affects of liquor just as it protected them from fire.[191]

After the Court in 1973 found abortion to be a constitutional right,[192] efforts by antiabortion groups succeeded in prohibiting most federal funding of the practice. Suit was brought contending that the bans were discriminatory, among other claims that they were a violation of the Establishment Clause because motivated by religious belief.[193]

By a narrow vote the Court upheld the prohibition on federal funding. Writing for the majority, Stewart observed that the provisions of a law might coincide with the teachings of a religion but did not thereby contravene the First Amendment. The plaintiffs, he ruled, lacked standing to claim that their religious liberty was being violated.[194]

Brennan, Marshall, Blackmun, and Stevens each dissented separately, arguing that the ban was invalid because it restricted the constitutional right to abortion. However, none of the four reached a conclusion as to whether it violated the Establishment Clause.[195]

In 1984, Rehnquist, acting as circuit justice in California, refused to intervene in the case of a Catholic organization that had been prevented from conducting a funeral service for sixteen thousand aborted fetuses that had been discarded. A state court, claiming a violation of the separation of church and state, reversed a decision by local authorities giving the group custody of the fetuses.[196]

Rehnquist ruled that the appellants had suffered no infringement of their freedom of religion or speech, since they could conduct a service without the fetuses. Because the lower court's decision was based on state law, there was no federal issue.

In 1987 there was a constitutional challenge to a federal program authorizing sex education programs that emphasized premarital chastity as a solution to the problem of adolescent pregnancies.[197] Rehnquist found in favor of the program, stating that there might be disagreement about sexual behavior along religious lines, as there might be on many issues, but that this was not sufficient to make the "chastity program" a sectarian issue.[198] Kennedy went further, holding that even a showing that the program was "passively sectarian" would not invalidate it.[199]

Blackmun wrote a dissent. Even when values like chastity had a secular purpose, they took on religious meaning when advocated in public by religious figures. Reasons offered in opposition to abortion and contraception, for example, would be different coming from a believer than from a nonbeliever.[200]

In 1985 the Court invalidated a Pennsylvania law imposing certain restrictions on access to abortion.[201] In a concurring opinion, Stevens conceded that "a somewhat theological argument" could be made on behalf of the law, but he insisted that the Court was obligated to decide only on the basis of secular criteria. He made an analogy with the rite of baptism, which Christians might believe was essential for children but which could not be required by law.[202]

Speaking of a pregnant woman, he found abortion "a difficult choice having serious and personal consequences of major importance to her own future—perhaps to the salvation of her own immortal soul—[she] remains free to seek and to obtain sympathetic guidance from those who share her own value preferences."[203]

Dissenting, White insisted that his own position was not more theological than Stevens's. The fact that a law coincided with the beliefs of a particular religion, for example, forbidding murder, did not make the law itself religious in nature. Whatever position the state took on such issues was bound to coincide with some religious tenets.[204]

In the same year, the Court, upholding a raid on a private apartment where the presence of drugs was suspected, in effect also upheld the State of Georgia's antisodomy law, since those in the apartment at the time, while not found to be in possession of drugs, were arrested for being engaged in homosexual acts.[205]

Dissenting from the decision, Blackmun saw the sodomy law as unconstitutional, because it seemed to have been inspired by religious beliefs. The State of Georgia partially relied on theological arguments in defending the law, and Blackmun insisted that "private behavior" could not be punished because of "religious intolerance." Historically, the prosecution of sodomy was connected with heresy, and not all religions condemned it.[206]

In 1996 the Court invalidated an amendment to the constitution of the State of Colorado, enacted by a popular referendum, forbidding all laws explicitly giving homosexuals protection against discrimination.[207] Kennedy found that the amendment did not merely place homosexuals in the same category as other citizens but denied them the protection given to all citizens. Noting that one argument in favor of the amendment was that it protected the rights of persons with principled religious objections, for example, landlords unwilling to rent to homosexual tenants, Kennedy found that the amendment went "far beyond" that purpose.[208]

Dissenting strongly, Scalia charged that the Court was treating principled opposition to homosexuality as though it were like racial or religious prejudice. The Constitution offered no guidance on the matter, and he noted that historically the Constitution had always allowed the prohibition of certain private acts, notably polygamy.[209]

TAXATION AND THE CHURCHES

In 1966 there was a court challenge to a tax exemption granted in Miami to a Baptist Church for a parking lot owned by the church but used partly for commercial purposes.[210] The Court found per curiam that, although under a previous Miami law the parking lot was not entitled to an exemption, the law had since been changed, making the case a dead issue.[211] Douglas dissented, finding a substantial constitutional question. The law might be unconstitutional, in which case, he pointed out, the church would owe back taxes.[212]

One of the most fundamental religious questions ever to come before the Court was a 1970 case, *Walz v. Tax Commission of the City of New York*, which challenged, on the grounds that these constituted a public subsidy of religion, the constitutional basis of the exemptions from property taxes given to religious bodies.[213]

Burger wrote a majority opinion upholding the exemptions. He warned against overly sweeping applications of the First Amendment and suggested that, if they were taken to extremes, the two Religion Clauses would clash with each other. There was a tightrope between hostility and neutrality, which hitherto the Court had successfully negotiated.[214]

Churches could receive tax exemptions in the same way as other nonprofit institutions, such as art museums, received them. The secular purpose of such exemptions was to ensure that institutions that exist "in harmonious relationship with the community at large," and foster its "mental improvement," not be impeded. The state considered them "beneficial and stabilizing influences" on community life.[215]

The exemptions also reflected the government's historic intention not to hinder religion in any way. It was not necessary, Burger thought, to evaluate the churches on the basis of whatever good works they might perform for the community, since to do so would itself constitute the entanglement of government and religion. Religious bodies varied greatly with respect to such community services. Taxing the churches would itself constitute government involvement with religion, of a more serious kind than exemptions did. Granting tax exemptions to museums did not make them arms of the state, he noted.[216]

However, Burger seemed to feel a nagging doubt about the logic of his argument and cited Justice Holmes's famous dictum that "a page of history is worth a volume of logic," warning that an overly rigid application of the Establishment Clause would have the affect of inhibiting religion. No one acquired the right to violate the Constitution merely through long usage, but the history of tax exemptions could not be set aside. The plaintiff had not shown that exemptions constituted an establishment of religion, and if, as Black predicted in his dissent, this was the first step, "the second step is long in coming," Burger countered. Justice Cardozo had once noted the tendency of every principle to expand to the limits of its logic, and it was imperative that the Court interpret these principles by reference to their historic purpose.[217]

Brennan concurred, also arguing that history, while not determinative, was nonetheless relevant. Rarely had the Court considered a practice for which the historical support was so overwhelming. From the beginning, numerous states had exempted church property from taxation, and there was no evidence that any of the Founding Fathers opposed the practice.[218]

Religious groups provided many benefits to the community, performing tasks that otherwise might be left undone. The plaintiff had sued to remove exemptions from property used solely for religious, as distinct from charitable, purposes, but Brennan thought this simplistic. Activities of public welfare and religious activities were often conducted in the same building, and churches used their resources for both purposes. For example, Boy Scout troops might meet on such property, and churches were used for musical concerts. Even during worship itself churches often collected funds for community purposes. [219]

The government also granted tax exemptions because the churches contributed uniquely to the "pluralism" of society. "Diversity of associational viewpoint and enterprise are essential to a vigorous pluralistic society," he proclaimed.[220]

The State of New York exempted a wide range of activities from taxes, with religion given no special help. Exemptions were different from subsidies because they involved no transfer of funds from government to church. Removal of exemptions would not lessen church-state involvement but would actually deepen it, since an extensive state investigation would be necessary to distinguish purely religious practices from activities of community betterment. It would also require that church property be assessed, and perhaps foreclosed, if taxes were not paid.[221]

Taxing the churches would impose heavy burdens on those religious groups least able to pay, and the churches, in order to survive, would have to curtail their community activities, the resulting burden then falling on the government.[222]

Brennan concluded that the government did not "champion religion per se, but it valued religion among a variety of non-profit enterprises which contributed to the diversity of the Nation." There is no "non-religious substitute for religion."[223]

Harlan also concurred, warning that the Court needed to avoid issues likely to lead to religious strife.[224]

In his dissent Douglas argued that the issue was whether nonbelievers were to be taxed at the normal rate, while organized groups of religious believers were exempt. He did not think that New York extended such exemptions to nonreligious groups, hence the state practiced discrimination. Exemptions did constitute a governmental subsidy.[225]

The historical argument was inherently suspect, Douglas thought, since exemptions dated from the early days of the country when churches were often the arm of the state. Confessing that he now doubted the wisdom of his vote upholding the *Everson* decision, he argued that religious schools at least performed a secular function in a way churches as such did not.[226]

The constitutional right to freedom of worship did not imply a tax exemption, any more than freedom of the press required an exemption for newspapers. Churches might perform socially useful tasks, but their creeds often made them unacceptable to many people, and their welfare activities might merely be "a phase of its sectarian activity."[227]

The Constitution required that all people and groups be treated equally, yet tax exemptions inherently did not do so, because of the great variety of activities engaged in by religious groups. Thus some sponsored a large number of schools, while others had none at all. Some churches possessed vast amounts of property, and Black found alarming the degree to which they were "feeding at the public trough."[228]

In 1988 the Court struck down a Texas law granting tax exemptions to religious publications, Brennan writing the majority opinion, which held that such exemptions unfairly discriminated between religious and nonreligious publishers.[229]

Scalia wrote a dissent, again arguing that the ruling was inconsistent with numerous practices by which the government favored religion, such as the official proclamation of Thanksgiving Day. The real issue, he asserted, was whether such an exemption was actually required in order to avoid interference with religious proselytization, an issue raised in some of the Jehovah's Witnesses cases. It was absurd that the state had the authority to prohibit "unwholesome" literature but could not support the dissemination of "stories contained in the sacred writings." The Court's opinion reached "a new strain of irrationality," Scalia charged.[230]

Chapter Seven

RELIGIOUS EDUCATION AND PUBLIC SUPPORT

THE PARADOXICAL *Everson* decision of 1947, upholding indirect state aid to religious schools while laying down the very principles that militated against such aid, was a time bomb that did not begin detonating until over twenty years later.

In *Board of Education v. Allen* (1968), the Court heard the first of a long series of modern cases turning on the question of whether, and in what way, government might assist private religious schools. The Court upheld a New York State practice whereby secular textbooks were lent by the state to students in religious schools.

Justice White wrote the majority opinion, drawing on *Everson*. Admitting that the line between support and neutrality was not easily drawn, he found the New York practice constitutional. Books were lent, not given, to students and their parents, and not to the schools themselves.[1]

Beginning with the *Pierce* case there had been a series of decisions affirming that the government had an interest in educational standards, and the lending of books was one way of maintaining those standards, White suggested. Private schools played an important role in the total educational system, White maintained, and no evidence had been offered that the schools in question were in any way acting improperly.[2]

Justice Harlan concurred, holding that to forbid the loan of books would violate the state's neutrality and pointing out that religious schools were not the only ones receiving assistance.[3]

Justice Black dissented vehemently, calling the practice "a flagrant, open violation" of the First Amendment. The state was using taxpayers' money to support the religious activities of those groups strong enough to influence the state legislature. This was a "great stride," he warned, toward "a state religion."[4]

Reminding the Court that he had himself written the *Everson* decision cited by White as a precedent, Black distinguished the two cases by arguing that the earlier case merely conferred a general benefit—bus transportation—on all children, while the lending of textbooks was a specific benefit to religious schools. He warned that the principle would in time be used to pay teachers' salaries and give other kinds of direct financial support to religious schools. Any government giving such aid would be "to that extent a tyranny."[5]

Justice Douglas also dissented vigorously, focusing his argument on the sectarian character of the schools receiving aid. Teachers in religious schools chose the textbooks, and religious influence was pervasive in such schools, even in secular subjects.[6]

Expounding the paradox inherent in the "divisiveness" argument, he pointed out that, if school boards "supinely" acquiesced in the private schools' requests for aid, the Constitution was being breached, while, if they resisted, religious conflict was engendered.[7]

There was nothing "ideological" about a bus, as there was about textbooks. Thus Douglas wondered whether it would be permissible to lend a book that spoke both of God and of evolution, or which history books would be acceptable in Catholic schools. There would be a continuing battle to control textbooks, which made the stakes "very high."[8]

Justice Fortas also dissented. He thought the New York arrangement camouflaged the fact that teachers in religious schools chose their own textbooks. This was not a general program for the benefit of everyone but was tailored to specific kinds of schools.[9]

In the same year, in *Flast v. Cohen*, the Court granted "standing to sue" to plaintiffs objecting to a federal program that included religious schools. Reversing earlier decisions that mere status as a taxpayer did not qualify a citizen to challenge a law on constitutional grounds, the Court now found that it did. The decision directly made possible a number of the later establishment cases brought before the Court.[10] (It is not clear, however, how plaintiffs had standing to sue in the *Bradfield*, *Cochran*, or *Everson* cases.) Chief Justice Warren ruled that one of the principal purposes of the Establishment Clause was to prevent the use of taxpayers' money to favor a particular religion and that taxpayers could bring suit to show that this was being done in violation of the Constitution.[11]

Douglas concurred, warning that "the mounting federal aid to sectarian schools is notorious and the subterfuges numerous." Those who objected to such aid often could obtain little help, if they were not members of powerful churches, and it was necessary for the Court to assist them.[12]

Justice Stewart concurred, arguing, however, that the special status of the Establishment Clause governed the case. Taxpayers' standing to sue was not necessarily applicable to other kinds of issues.[13] Fortas concurred, also arguing that the specific provisions of the Establishment Clause gave taxpayers standing to sue in ways they did not have in other cases. Few issues were as basic and pervasive in the lives of the citizens.[14]

Harlan dissented. He thought that the interests of the taxpayers as such were primarily "personal and proprietary" and only secondarily representative of the whole citizenry. The plaintiffs could not show financial loss, their claim to the contrary an "obvious fiction." The government was not the mere trustee of the taxpayers' money, and expenditures were limited only by "the common rights of all citizens."[15]

Harlan could not understand why the standing of taxpayers to sue could vary according to the issue. He charged that somehow the Court now saw the Establishment Clause as conferring unique rights. The historical meaning of the clause was unclear and gave no basis for special rights.[16]

The Establishment Clause imposed no specific limits on spending beyond those imposed by any other provision of the Constitution. The issue in question did not involve a tax in support of religion. All taxes were absorbed into the general fund, and no taxpayer was entitled to a refund on the basis of how the money was spent, Harlan argued.[17]

He cited Justice Holmes's reminder that, besides the courts, the other two branches of government were also defenders of the people's rights. The recent history of the Court, Harlan warned, showed that the religious issues were difficult to resolve even without the added complication of taxpayers' suits.[18]

The pivotal case in the new jurisprudence concerning religious schools was *Lemon v. Kurtzman* (1971), involving two state programs, one in which Pennsylvania purchased books for students in private schools and paid teachers' salaries, another in which Rhode island supplemented teachers' salaries in private schools. In both cases this was done only for secular subjects, not for the teaching of religion.[19]

Burger wrote a majority opinion invalidating the practices. Admitting that interpreting the Establishment Clause was difficult and its meaning "opaque," he nonetheless attempted to synthesize the principles that the Court had used in previous cases over the years, yielding a three-part standard that came to be called the Lemon Test and was intended to be a universal formula applicable in all such cases:

1. Each program must have a "secular legislative purpose."
2. Its principal effect "neither advances nor inhibits religion."
3. It must not foster "excessive government entanglement" with religion.[20]

In the case at hand Burger found that there was clearly a secular purpose, which was the improvement of academic quality. Acknowledging the difficulty of making clear judgments on such matters, he nevertheless found what seemed like an inherent contradiction in such arrangements— the state had set up machinery to ensure that no money was used to teach religion, but in the very process of so doing, it violated the third clause of the test he had formulated.[21]

The religious character of the schools in question was obvious, and, although some teachers testified that they would not inject religion into the secular curriculum, Burger thought it would be difficult to avoid doing so, given the fact that the churches controlled the schools. But for the state to guard against this would create "excessive and enduring entanglements."[22]

In a state where religious schools were numerous, this would lead to considerable political agitation for or against aid, with voters lining up according to their faith. Other vital public issues would be obscured because of the urgency of the religious question, Burger predicted.[23]

Alluding to the spate of religion cases that had come before the Court in the previous decade, he expressed impatience. The Court had other issues to consider and should not allow religion to occupy so much of its time. Aid programs like those under review would be enacted continually, and would be continually subject to controversy. Such aid also gave maximum opportunity for a gradual breach of the wall of separation of church and state.[24]

The chief justice conceded that church schools had been important in national life and that their existence had saved the taxpayers vast sums of money. However, lines had to be drawn.[25]

Douglas concurred. Given the zeal of religious groups, all such programs would require a close watch. The free exercise of religion was infringed by using taxes to support religious activities. The pressure of finance had seemingly brought to an end the idea of a purely private religious school, Douglas judged.[26]

Douglas thought it dubious that teachers in religious schools could teach secular subjects as well as teachers in public schools. While public schools ran the danger of molding all students according to some kind of public orthodoxy, religious schools allowed deviations from that orthodoxy only in accordance with their respective creeds.[27]

Thus the case at hand would require, for the first time, massive state surveillance of private schools. It would be necessary to scrutinize the teaching of Shakespeare, and even of mathematics, to see if religious dogma was injected. Douglas cited a Jesuit sociologist to the effect that religion was pervasive in parochial schools.[28]

Such aid would also raise the issue of the hiring and firing of teachers who, because of the schools' religious nature, had no recourse to the courts. The Catholic laity were given no voice in running their schools, he charged.[29]

Brennan also concurred, finding all subsidies of religious schools controversial. One bad result of the program would be that teachers would engage in self-censorship in order to qualify for public money. Parochial schools had not considered the possible implications of such aid, he warned. Once they received public money, would they be permitted to restrict their enrollments, for example?[30]

The state had an interest in prescribing minimum educational standards but not in dictating their precise form, which it would have to do if it subsidized private schools. He too thought that secular education in religious schools went "hand in hand" with their religious mission. The practices under review were in violation of the *Engel* and *Schempp* decisions because they employed religious means to a supposedly secular goal.[31]

White concurred in some of the Court's findings concerning the constitutionality of the disputed programs, but expressed dissent from some of its reasoning. Parochial schools did have secular functions, and the state was merely funding those, and the Free-Exercise Clause created a presumption against denying aid to religious schools.[32]

White thought the majority's position concerning entanglement was "curious and mysterious." There was no proof that teachers, some of whom were not even Catholic, were teaching religion in the guise of secular subjects. The Court had created an insoluble paradox whereby teachers were not allowed to teach religion but attempts to ensure that they did not were deemed "excessive entanglement." [33]

The *Lemon* decision spawned a further case the next year,[34] when Burger found for the majority that Pennsylvania was permitted to reimburse private schools for costs incurred before such reimbursement had been declared unconstitutional. Court decisions were not retroactive, Burger held, and citizens could reasonably rely on state law even while it was being challenged in the courts. Reimbursing such costs did not create the kind of entanglement that violated the Lemon Test.[35] Douglas dissented, insisting that the constitutional rule forbidding all such subsidies was absolute, and that the citizens had had "clear warning" of that fact.[36]

At the same time as the 1971 *Lemon* case, the Court handed down its decision in another appeal, *Tilton v. Richardson*, which took the the application of the Establishment Clause in an entirely different direction. A federal program authorized the subsidizing of buildings and other facilities of religiously affiliated colleges, provided that none of the facilities were used for religious instruction. The Court upheld the program but struck down a provision that for twenty years the government should oversee use of the facilities, to guard against violations of the rule. This, the Court found, was not sufficient, and the period of governmental oversight should be indefinite.[37]

Burger again wrote the majority opinion. Congress intended that church schools be included in the program, he found. Backing away somewhat from the Lemon Test, which he expounded for the first time on the same occasion, he advised that the test not be applied mechanically and that its three points provided "guidelines" only.[38]

The secular purpose of the law was to ensure the safety and security of the nation through education. Referring back to the *Bradfield* case (1899), he found that the Court had never held that all public assistance to religious institutions was unconstitutional, grants to hospitals being one example. Fear of fraud was not itself sufficient to invalidate the act, and none of the four colleges benefiting from the program were charged with violation of its provisions. There were no religious symbols in the buildings financed by federal money, for example.[39]

The plaintiffs argued that religion so permeated denominational colleges that it affected secular education, but Congress itself had debated that question and found it unpersuasive, Burger recalled. The schools imposed no restrictions on the books acquired for their libraries, and there was no evidence of attempts at indoctrinating their students. The four schools all subscribed to the statement on academic freedom of the American Association of University Professors.[40]

The plaintiffs cited a "composite portrait" of a sectarian college in which students were required to attend religious services and to enroll in particular theology courses, but the four Connecticut recipients did not fit that mode, Burger noted, and some schools that did not fit had been denied access to the grants. Should any recipient be found in violation, the government had developed a formula whereby the violators would have to repay some of the money.[41]

Such grants involved much less entanglement between the government and religion than did some other programs, Burger estimated, because of the difference between higher and lower education. College students were much less susceptible to indoctrination than were children, and the "internal discipline" of college courses inhibited attempts at such indoctrination.[42]

Many church-related colleges provided a high degree of academic freedom and sought to encourage critical thinking in their students, according to Burger. Catholic colleges included non-Catholic students and faculty, there were no compulsory religious services, and, although theology courses were required, they were taught "professionally." In fact a broad range of religious traditions were represented, including a rabbi on the faculty of one institution. Thus the need for government oversight was minimal, Burger judged.[43]

Paying teachers' salaries, which the Court disallowed the same day, was more dangerous than constructing buildings, in part because salaries were a continuing process, while buildings involved a single grant. The plaintiffs objected that they were being forced to pay for religious instruction, but they were unable to show any specific burdens imposed on them, or any coercion, Burger found.[44]

Douglas dissented. He doubted the significance of the difference between higher and lower education, finding that religiously affiliated colleges were no less sectarian. The "more sophisticated" institutions admitted students of other faiths but without changing the schools' dominant character.[45]

It was "sophistry," he thought, to prefer a single grant to a continuing series of grants. Religion permeated the recipient schools, thus precisely requiring the kind of close scrutiny that the majority of the Court denied was necessary. Even though no money was given for religious purposes, grants for one purpose obviously freed money for other purposes.[46]

Government requirements for receiving aid, such as the prohibition on holding religious observances in publicly financed buildings, themselves constituted an offense to religious believers, Douglas thought. The state would have to inquire as to whether particular courses were biased in favor of religion, for example, with respect to the Reformation.[47]

The churches were said to be in financial need, but Douglas cited the contrary opinion of the national head of the United Presbyterian Church, who claimed that the wealth of the churches allowed them to finance their own schools. This wealth made especially objectionable their "incessant demands on the public treasury," according to Douglas.[48]

The *Tilton* decision manifested two recurring tendencies in the Court's understanding of the Establishment Clause—its reluctance to invalidate an act of Congress and its willingness to grant much more leeway to higher education than to elementary and secondary schools.

In *Committee of Public Education v. Nyquist* (1973), the Court invalidated a New York program reimbursing private schools for the repair and maintenance of buildings and safety equipment, along with tuition reimbursement for parents with an annual income of under $5,000.[49] Justice Powell wrote the majority opinion. Applying the Lemon Test, he found the secular purpose of the law—supporting and encouraging education, especially for poor children—adequate. The law's stated purpose of wanting to promote "pluralism" in education was also adequate, as was the stated purpose of relieving the burdens of overcrowded public schools. But money given to religious schools for one purpose (maintenance) could be used for other purposes. There was no need to consider whether this required excessive entanglement, because the grants were wrong in themselves.[50]

Reimbursing bus fares and buying books were subject to restrictions by the state that were not present here, and "ingenious plans" to get state aid for parochial schools showed the wisdom of Black's dissent in *Allen*, Powell said. Such grants were inducements to attend religious schools, and while the Court was sympathetic to efforts at helping poor children obtain an education, it could not overturn the Constitution. There was no historical precedent for such an arrangement.[51]

Tax exemptions for various purposes minimized the entanglement of religion and government, but this was a special tax benefit that violated neutrality, Powell ruled. Thus it also increased entanglement, and it carried with it the danger of political strife over such aid.[52]

Burger, two years after he had formulated the Lemon Test, now dissented in part, voting against the reimbursement for repairs and maintenance but in favor of tuition reimbursement. In earlier cases, he argued, the Court had regarded as irrelevant the fact that certain arrangements (e.g., bus fares) might encourage children to attend religious schools, and in the *Quick Bear* case (1907) had justified paying for American Indians to attend religious schools. The tuition-reimbursement plan involved aid to individual students and was entirely different from aid to schools themselves.[53]

Obviously the government could not pay people to attend church. But education had an equally obvious secular purpose. In the past the Court had always tipped the balance in the direction of religious freedom where aid to individuals was concerned. The only difference from the *Everson* and *Allen* cases was in the manner of reimbursement, which in the earlier cases had been given to all parents, not merely to those with children in private schools. That, however, was not the issue. The law merely sought to equalize benefits for all children. The Court, Burger argued, was deciding the issue on the basis of the percentage of recipients attending religious schools, which ought to make no difference.[54]

Justice Rehnquist's dissent argued that the benefits given taxpayers by the statute were substantially less than those the Court had upheld in the *Walz* case, and the fact that general tax exemptions for churches were an ancient tradition had no bearing on the case. There was no evidence that a slightly lower tax bill would encourage parents to send their children to private schools. The purpose of the law was merely to equalize the financial burdens between public and private education.[55]

White also dissented. The *Pierce* case of 1925 found that religious schools were competent to educate, and here the state was merely reimbursing parents for the costs of services that the public schools consequently did not have to provide. Because of increasing costs, enrollment in private schools was declining, as public school enrollment was increasing, thus putting pressures on the public schools. The Court ought not to make private education more difficult to obtain than it already was.[56]

White thought the Free-Exercise Clause dictated approval of the New York law, and he rejected the Lemon Test as too rigid. The "sparse language" of the First Amendment made its interpretation unclear. The Court should decide such cases on the basis of desirable national policy, and the prospect of excessive entanglement was here remote. The Court appeared to assume a certain kind of sectarian religious school, White thought, whereas there might be other kinds as well. While indicating that he would prefer to uphold both parts of the New York law, he voted with the minority to uphold only the reimbursement of teachers' salaries.[57]

Handed down along with this decision was a judgment invalidating aid by the state of South Carolina to a Baptist college. Powell found that, since the college was overtly religious, scrutinizing the use of the money would involve excessive entanglement.[58]

Also decided along with the *Nyquist* case was an appeal concerning a Pennsylvania statute enacted in an effort to avoid the Court's strictures in the *Lemon* case. After the latter had invalidated a program of state aid, Pennsylvania offered to reimburse parents for tuition payments to private schools. To avoid "entanglement," the law forbade the state to exercise any control over those schools.[59]

Powell wrote the majority decision invalidating the program, on the grounds that it was not substantively different from that invalidated by the *Nyquist* decision. The program involved public support of religion, and Powell rejected as "spurious" the claim that since the state was reimbursing parents who sent their children to private secular schools, the "equal protection" clause of the Constitution (Amendment 14) required the same for religious schools. The "equal protection" clause could not be used as a "bludgeon" against other parts of the Constitution, Powell concluded.[60]

Burger and White dissented, merely referring to their opinions in the *Nyquist* case.[61]

In the same year, the Court also struck down a New York program whereby the state reimbursed private schools for the cost of testing their students as required by the state. Burger applied the same reasoning as in *Nyquist*.[62]

Also in 1973 the Court outlawed the lending of textbooks to private schools by the state of Mississippi, because the state paid no attention to whether those schools were racially segregated.[63] Burger noted the rapid growth of private schools in the state, following official desegregation almost twenty years before. The state pointed out that the textbook program long predated the end of segregation, but Burger found that this was not a conclusive argument.[64]

The *Pierce* decision, which generally governed the constitutional status of private schools, did not exempt them from all forms of governmental oversight, Burger held, and had established no right for private schools to share equally with public schools in the public bounty. Thus a state could decide to give no aid to any religious schools. The Constitution permitted racial discrimination in private institutions but did not compel states to give it financial support, Burger concluded.[65]

He also rejected the state's argument that various precedents upheld the right of students in private schools to "indirect aid." Unlike water or electricity, textbooks were a form of "direct aid" intimately related to the school's educational mission.[66] Private schools performed a useful educational function, Burger acknowledged, but that purpose could not be isolated from the practice of segregation.[67]

The same year, the Court summarily rejected an appeal that in effect attempted to stand the prevailing jurisprudence of the Establishment Clause on its head, by claiming that the *Everson* case, which had upheld the reimbursement of bus fares to students in religious schools, created a constitutional right to such assistance. The state of Missouri was thus accused of denying that right to some of its students, a claim the Court rejected.[68]

White was the sole dissenter, arguing that the *Everson* decision had separated things like bus transportation from religion and had defined them as benefits given to all students. Such assistance could not be denied to some students on the basis of their religious affiliation. Missouri's denial of this aid raised suspicions of antireligious bias, he charged.[69]

The following year the Court heard an appeal urging that the public schools of Kansas City administering federal funds appropriated for "remedial" programs be required also to support such programs conducted by religious schools during regular school hours.[70] The case was unusual in that, instead of a program of public aid to private schools being challenged as unconstitutional, the private schools contended that it was unconstitutional to exclude them from the program.

Blackmun found for the majority that the city was not required to include them under the terms of the federal law. While the services provided by religious schools might be inferior if denied public support, the intent of Congress on the matter was not unclear. "Comparable" programs, as specified by Congress, did not need to be identical in all institutions. Blackmun ruled that the matter should be left to the discretion of the state, explicitly noting that the Court was not ruling on the constitutionality of the program itself.[71]

White concurred, remarking that he was "pleasantly surprised" that the Court seemed to think the city could fund such a program if it chose.[72] Douglas dissented, finding the program, and the law of Congress enacting it, both unconstitutional.[73]

In *Meek v. Pittenger* (1975) the Court reached mixed findings relative to a Pennsylvania program for providing textbooks and "auxiliary services" to students in private schools. The lending of textbooks directly to students was permitted, while the lending of equipment to the schools themselves, along with state payment for testing, counseling, and other functions, was forbidden.[74]

Stewart found for the majority that the former practice was constitutional because it benefited students directly, while the latter was not, because it supported the activity of religious institutions. It was impossible to clearly separate the secular and religious functions of such schools.[75]

Providing testing and other services on private school property would obviously require close scrutiny by the state and would therefore be excessive entanglement, while guidance counseling, for example, was an activity with possibilities for religious indoctrination. The program also contained the potential for divisiveness in the form of an annual battle in the legislature over the appropriation of funds.[76]

Brennan wrote an opinion concurring in the prohibition of services but holding that the loan of textbooks was also unconstitutional. As with the provision of services, he thought the loan of textbooks was likely to stimulate divisive conflicts, and he noted that the textbook program upheld in the *Allen* case had been approved by the Court before it had formulated the Lemon Test.[77]

It was "pure fantasy," he charged, to treat the loan of textbooks as benefiting only the students, not the schools. The latter made a collective request for books, which were stored in the schools and concerning which students and parents had no voice. Unlike the *Allen* case, this program did not include public schools. Sophisticated attempts to evade the demands of the Constitution were as invalid as simple-minded ones, Brennan concluded.[78]

Burger in general sided with the majority but criticized what he regarded as the extravagant rhetoric of the arguments. The dangers of entanglement were not as great as the Court feared, and the decision went beyond *Lemon* and *Nyquist*. It penalized children whose only error was that their parents chose to send them to religious schools. It was a "melancholy choice" to force parents to choose between help for their children's educations and exercise of their religious freedom, a choice affluent parents did not have to make, he lamented.[79]

Rehnquist also supported the majority finding, but went beyond Burger in his criticisms of the Court's reasoning. He found the "primary effect" clause of the Lemon Test not very useful. The fact, cited by the Court, that three quarters of all private schools were religious was not relevant, especially given the fact that religious schools were only a small percentage of all schools.[80]

The problem did not lie in the type of material loaned by the state, since the Court admitted that some of it, for example, maps, were immune from sectarian misuse. The loan of textbooks did not differ from the arrangements upheld by the Court in the *Allen* case. If there was an allegation of impropriety on the part of private schools, the burden of proof should lie with the plaintiffs, but the Court here merely assumed that, for example, guidance counselors and others might misuse their positions.[81]

The decision, Rehnquist warned, showed that any hope of ever satisfying the demands of the "entanglement clause" of the Lemon Test was illusory. The Court appeared to be siding with those who believed that society should be wholly secular.[82]

The next year, the Court gave full expression to its previous judgments that higher and lower education were to be treated quite differently, when it upheld a Maryland program making grants to private colleges willing to certify that they would not use the money for "sectarian purposes."[83] Indicative of the Court's accommodationist position with respect to higher education was the fact that the decision was written by Blackmun, who was ordinarily inclined to be a separationist.

A government whose activities had become as pervasive as that of modern America could hardly expect that at no point would its paths cross with the churches, and the two could not be kept hermetically sealed, Blackmun argued. He too cited the *Bradfield* case as showing that not all aid to religious institutions was forbidden, and he pointed out that the government was perfectly free to provide fire and police protection to churches, for example.[84]

The Maryland program passed the first part of the Lemon Test in that it had an obvious secular purpose, which was the training of an educated citizenry. Recipients of the grants were also found not to be pervasively sectarian, in that they:

a. were not under church control;
b. made religion exercises optional; viewed the spiritual development of the students as secondary to academic matters; did not seek to indoctrinate their students;
c. offered theology courses taught in a broadly professional manner; subscribed to the statement on academic freedom of the American Association of University Professors;
d. left classroom prayer or the wearing of religious dress to the discretion of individual teachers;
e. except in theology departments, did not practice religious bias in hiring;
f. did not discriminate in the admission of students.[85]

Maryland had monitored the program in question and had found no evidence of misuse of funds. The issues were not substantially different from those in the *Tilton* case, and it had never been the Court's practice to invalidate programs merely on the basis of possible future abuses.[86]

Addressing the "excessive entanglement" issue, Blackmun thought the need for surveillance was greatly reduced because of the "pervasively secular" character of the institutions receiving the grants. The danger of divisiveness was likewise reduced by the fact that the state gave aid to private colleges in general, most of which were secular in character.[87]

White concurred but took the occasion once again to register his disagreement with the Lemon Test. There was no constitutional basis at all for the "excessive entanglement" doctrine, he argued, and he thought that in this case, the Court used the fact that the program under challenge had a secular purpose in order to argue illogically that it was therefore not in need of supervision.[88]

Brennan dissented, finding the program to involve general subsidies to religious institutions. Such subsidies had historically been the focus of bitter disputes.[89]

Stewart also dissented, finding the case different from *Tilton* because the defendants had not been able to show that theology was taught in a "professional" way. In addition, religious affiliation was admittedly a criterion for hiring theology professors, many of whom were clergy.[90]

Stevens also dissented, proclaiming that "I deplore the pernicious tendency of state money to tempt religious institutions to compromise their principles."[91]

In 1977 the Court considered its most comprehensive case involving public aid to religious schools, scrutinizing an Ohio statute that provided a variety of services to private education. In *Wolman v. Wolter*[92] the Court sorted out its own principles when faced with a panoply of public programs, upholding some and forbidding others.

Blackmun wrote the majority opinion, ruling that:

a. All the programs had a secular legislative purpose, which was the improvement of education.
b. The lending of textbooks directly to students was constitutional.
c. Testing services provided to private schools were constitutional because they were administered directly by the state, thus avoiding any suspicion of religious control.
d. The state also controlled diagnostic and therapeutic services provided to students, again avoiding religious control. These service were not provided on private school premises.
e. Besides textbooks, other instructional materials, such as maps and film projectors, were also lent, supposedly to parents. However, this program in fact constituted direct support for religious schools and was therefore unconstitutional.
f. State payment for student field trips was also unconstitutional, because the private schools themselves controlled the use of the money, unlike the bus fares reimbursed in *Everson*, and there was a danger that teachers would intrude religion into those trips. Enforcing secular use of the money would then lead to excessive entanglement.[93]

Rehnquist and White, without writing formal opinions, announced that they dissented and that they would uphold the constitutionality of all parts of the disputed statute.[94] Brennan dissented, holding that the entire statute was unconstitutional, nothing less than "sophisticated evasion" of the Court's past strictures.[95]

Justice Marshall also dissented. He saw no real difference between lending books to children and lending them to schools, regarding this as an evasion. He urged the Court to overturn its *Allen* decision and to draw a line between educational programs as such and programs of general benefit to children carried out in the schools. The latter could be allowed, the former could not be.[96]

Diagnostic and therapeutic programs relating to the health of students were thus constitutional, while guidance counseling and remedial academic programs were not, because the latter directly supported the mission of the schools. Testing would be permissible if used by the state to measure the effectiveness of the private schools, but in this case, tests were used by the private schools for their own purposes.[97]

Powell wrote an opinion whose conclusions almost seemed to deny its premises. He considered private religious schools to be of high academic quality. They provided "wholesome competition" for the public schools and saved the taxpayers a significant amount of money. The state might legitimately aid them because the state had an interest in higher educational standards for all children.[98] He also thought that there was no longer a danger of sectarian control of American institutions, as there had been when the First Amendment was enacted, thus the Court need not apply the Constitution rigidly, even if this meant "loss of analytical tidiness."[99]

But, despite these remarks, he found that the lending of textbooks by the state was "obvious fiction," and in reality they were lent to the schools. A program of genuine loans would be acceptable. He favored support for field trips, since the state paid only for transportation, not for the salaries of the teachers.[100]

Stevens also dissented, holding that there was no meaningful distinction between direct and indirect aid to religious schools, Black's opinion in the *Everson* case being a correct analysis of the issue. He thought diagnostic and therapeutic services might be permissible.[101]

In the same year, the Court ruled against a religious school in New York that was seeking state aid.[102] White dissented, charging that "the Court continues to misconstrue the First Amendment in a manner that discriminates against religion and is contrary to the fundamental educational needs of the country."[103]

In 1980 the Court upheld a New York program whereby private schools were reimbursed for the cost of tests required by the state. Originally there was no provision for state oversight, but this had been changed in accord with a previous Court decision.[104]

White wrote the majority opinion. He found almost no danger that the test could be used for sectarian purposes, since the state provided the tests and merely reimbursed the schools for the cost of grading them. He was satisfied that the Court was avoiding an "extreme view," even at the sacrifice of complete clarity.[105]

Blackmun saw the decision as a "long step backwards" from *Meek* and *Wolman*. Admittedly, he conceded, the line of separation was not altogether straight, but he was disappointed that some justices who had voted correctly on earlier cases now seemed to have "defected," and he said he could only attribute this to the force of "emotional issues."[106]

The arrangement permitted by the Court allowed substantial direct payments to religious institutions, unlike the *Wolman* case, which actually forbade such payments. Testing and record-keeping would be carried out even if the state did not pay for them, and there was no way of distinguishing whether these activities were used in conjunction with religious or secular classes. Monitoring the processes would require excessive entanglement.[107]

Stevens also dissented, warning that the decision could be extended to include, for example, reimbursement for time spent in fire drills. He called for an end to all subsidies to private schools.[108]

In 1982 plaintiffs challenged the gift, by the army, of a disused military hospital, the recipient being an avowedly Christian college. The gift was made under a regulation authorizing the army to make such donations where a "public benefit" would occur. The suit was brought by an organization called Americans United for Separation of Church and State, and a large part of the issue was whether that group had standing to sue.[109]

Rehnquist, writing for the majority, upheld the gift, dismissing the plaintiffs as without standing because they could not show an "injury in fact." Citing previous cases, he pointed out that the Court had consistently held that citizens could not sue the government over general constitutional issues but only when they could show direct applicability to themselves. The case at hand was different from *Flast* in that the latter involved the power of taxation directly, while the current case merely turned on a general act of Congress regulating the disposal of surplus military property.[110]

Brennan, writing for the dissenters, decried what he called an "unfortunate" tendency to decide cases on "threshold" issues (for example, standing to sue) rather than substantive ones. Here the Court failed even to ascertain whether the plaintiffs had suffered injury.[111]

The *Everson* case (1947) had established that there were restrictions on government expenditures where religion was involved, and one of the principal purposes of the Establishment Clause was to prohibit such expenditures. Indeed the only strictly constitutional limit on government spending was precisely for matters of religion, and the majority decision was "pernicious to our constitutional heritage and hostile to the Framers' intent." Here the Court contradicted the *Flast* decision, Brennan contended.[112] Stevens also wrote a dissent, finding that the case involved "urgent necessities," in that there were few matters about which the citizens had greater legitimate interest than the spending of their taxes.[113]

In *Mueller v. Allen* (1983), the Court upheld a Minnesota program permitting parents to claim a tax deduction for certain expenses connected with sending their children either to public or private schools.[114] Rehnquist found for the majority that there was the obvious secular purpose of strengthening education, along with the fact that private schools saved the taxpayers significant amounts of money. In principle this was no different from a number of other deductions, such as medicine, and it was available to families with children in public schools as well, which distinguished the case from *Nyquist*.[115]

It was significant also, he ruled, that this aid went directly to the parents, not to the schools, thus there was not the remotest danger that it could be used for sectarian purposes. The fact that the principal beneficiaries were families with children in religious schools was irrelevant. Such families could hardly be penalized for wanting to be relieved of financial burdens that brought benefits to the state. The only possible point of entanglement was the obligation of the state to ensure that parents did not claim deductions for the purchase of religious books.[116]

Marshall saw no difference from the *Nyquist* case and insisted that all tax benefits for private schools were forbidden. While there was a secular purpose, the primary affect of the law might well be religious, encouraging parents to send their children to religious schools. In reality only an insignificant percentage of tax deductions would accrue to parents with children in public schools.[117]

The educational materials that the deduction subsidized could clearly be used to inculcate religious beliefs, and the decision was obviously inconsistent with earlier rulings that had forbidden the subsidizing of various kinds of instructional material. Here the deduction subsidized books and other materials chosen by the schools themselves, not by the state. Brennan regretted that for the first time, the Court was allowing a subsidy quite capable of being used directly for religious purposes.[118]

In *Aguilar v. Felton* in 1985, the Court invoked the prohibition against excessive entanglement in order to invalidate a New York program whereby the state gave money to private educational institutions to hold special classes for "disadvantaged" children. Teachers from the public schools taught the classes, and they were enjoined to minimize their contact with the regular faculty. There were to be no religious symbols in the classrooms, and periodic unannounced supervisory visits were made to ensure that the conditions of the grant were being complied with.[119]

Brennan held for the majority that the giving of money to a religious institution infringed the liberty of nonmembers of that church, but in this case it also infringed the liberty of members, who were forced by the state to modify the conduct of their schools in order to qualify for grants. Unlike the *Roemer* case dealing with higher education, many of these institutions were pervasively sectarian.[120]

Powell concurred. He saw no danger of a state religion or that any church would control public education. However, in a time of diminishing financial resources for education, it was likely that such a program would generate political strife. The program also failed the Lemon Test in that it involved direct aid to religion.[121]

Burger wrote a sharp dissent, charging that "under the guise of protecting the United States from the evils of eighteenth-century establishments, thousands of children are being deprived of desperately needed services." The Court had made no attempt to demonstrate that there was actually an infringement of religious liberty. This fear, he charged, "border[ed] on paranoia" and showed not neutrality but hostility toward religion.[122] Rehnquist also dissented, dismissing what he called the Court's "gossamer abstractions."[123]

Justice O'Connor, as part of the gradual process by which members of the Court were moving away from the Lemon Test, found that the arrangements in question did not involve excessive entanglement, but she went further and argued that entanglement itself should not be a test of constitutionality. The Court had made only a perfunctory examination of the clear secular purpose of the law in this case, and the majority's abstract theories of how the program violated the Constitution dissolved upon close inspection.[124]

The subsidies did not free funds that the schools might then use for religious purposes, because they funded services that would otherwise not be available. It was difficult to see, she thought, how such programs on private school premises posed a greater danger than those conducted elsewhere.[125]

While the Court often expressed fear as to the conduct of teachers in religious schools, no evidence had ever been presented to show that such fears were justified. Indeed, taken seriously, such fears would force even the closing of the public schools, out of concern for how public school teachers might misuse their positions.[126]

There were many anomalies in the Court's decisions, due to the dubious "entanglement" test, O'Connor judged. There was no evidence that the program in question was the cause of divisiveness. The true losers in the case were the children who would not be able to receive the same services elsewhere. It was a tragedy, she regretted, that they would be deprived of the chance for "success in life."[127]

Along with the previous case, the Court rendered a verdict (*Grand Rapids v. Ball*) on a related kind of program in Michigan, where a public school district offered students in private schools basic courses in secular subjects, in classrooms leased from private schools during regular school hours, taught by teachers from the public schools. The district also offered evening classes for both children and adults, once again using private school classrooms but with most of the teachers from private schools. The Court nullified both arrangements.[128]

Brennan wrote the majority opinion, finding that, while the program obviously had a secular purpose, it involved the potential for abuse. Teachers from religious schools might use the classroom to proselytize, and the government's very act of leasing space might be seen as promoting religious schools. How, he wondered, could the same teachers teach from a religious standpoint during the day and a secular standpoint in the evening?[129]

The school district escaped excessive entanglement only by failing to monitor the program, and there was a real possibility that it could be abused. The fact that there had been no complaints was not definitive, because students might not realize that they were being indoctrinated. The symbolic union of church and state was especially crucial for impressionable children, who would have little ability to distinguish two different kinds of classes in the same school.[130]

The claim of benefits given directly to the students was "transparent fiction," he charged, quoting his own opinion in *Meek*, and any aid to religious schools was indistinguishable from subsidizing their purpose. If the Court upheld the controversial arrangement, it would "let the genie out of the bottle" and begin a development whereby private schools could gradually abandon many of their secular functions and allow the state to undertake them.[131]

Burger and O'Connor wrote partial dissents, finding that the use of the classrooms during the day was permissible, but the evening classes were not.[132] White dissented from the entire decision, affirming the constitutionality of both provisions of the program and reminding the Court that he rejected the Lemon Test and the *Nyquist* decision.[133] Rehnquist also dissented, charging that the Court allowed itself to be blinded by the faulty metaphor of the "wall of separation between church and state," which ignored 150 years of history. He thought the Court gratuitously questioned the integrity of teachers employed in the program.[134]

In *Witters v. Washington* the following year, the Court ruled unanimously in favor of a state grant to a college student who, in the process of becoming blind, applied for assistance as a handicapped person. The state denied his request because he intended to use the grant to attend a Protestant Bible college.[135]

Marshall wrote the principal opinion, in which he found that the grant in question was given to the student directly, for his own educational purposes, and was not indirect aid to a religious school. The state of Washington claimed that its own constitution forbade such a grant, but the Supreme Court, Marshall ruled, would not anticipate that issue.[136] White concurred, noting that he believed that actual aid to religious schools was permissible but that the grant in question met even the Court's much stricter standards.[137]

Powell also concurred, but took pains to emphasize his belief that the case was governed by the *Allen* decision, which had forbidden any subsidy to a religious schools. No such subsidy was involved here.[138] O'Connor also concurred, arguing that since it was the student's own choice to attend a religious school, no reasonable person could infer that this was an attempt by the state to subsidize a religious institution.[139] (The plaintiff did not, however, receive the benefits to which the Court decreed he was entitled. The Washington State Supreme Court ruled that the grant violated the state constitution, and the federal Supreme Court declined to hear an appeal.)[140]

After the *Witters* case there was an unusual hiatus of seven years before the Court again considered an issue involving public aid to religious schools, and the next case—*Zobrest v. Catalina School District* (1993)— also involved assistance to a handicapped student. A public school district in Arizona refused to provide a sign-language interpreter for a deaf student enrolled in a Catholic school, but the Court ruled in favor of the student.[141]

Rehnquist wrote the majority opinion. The Court had often held, he recalled, that religious institutions may share in government benefits that are broadly distributed. There was no evidence that the sign-language interpreter would do anything more than interpret the teachers' words, and it was an "antiquated" notion that somehow a "taint" arose from the religious nature of the school.[142]

Blackmun dissented. In effect, he argued, the Court was requiring a public employee to participate directly in a religious activity. Religion was pervasive at the Catholic school, and the interpreter would thus convey a message of state approval. The state was actually furnishing a medium for the communication of a religious message. Potentially the religious liberty of the interpreter might even be infringed, since a Hindu school might require certain dress or a Jewish school certain kinds of food.[143]

In 1995 the Court heard a case (*Kiryas Joel School District v. Grumet*) so unusual as to have no likely sequels, when it ordered the dissolution of a public school district in New York State. A group of Orthodox Jews called the Satmar Hasidim had settled as a community in a small town. After disputes with the town government over zoning, they made use of a New York law permitting a minimum number of households to constitute themselves legally as a village, drawing the boundaries so as to encompass only members of their group.

Most of the children in the village attended private religious schools, the sole exceptions being a small number of handicapped children for whom at first the neighboring town provided special classes within the village, an arrangement that was terminated following the Court's decisions in *Aguilar* and *Grand Rapids*.

The children then attended "special" schools in the town, but in time, the Satmars found that it was traumatic for the children to go outside the community and mingle with nonmembers of the group, and they obtained from the state legislature permission to constitute the village as a school district, the district's only activity being the operation of a school for the handicapped. The Court ruled that the establishment of the school district was a violation of the Establishment Clause.[144]

Justice Souter wrote the majority opinion, finding it anomalous that the state had passed a statute solely for the benefit of one religious community, the uniqueness of the arrangement making it impossible for the Court to judge whether the state would act with impartiality toward all religious groups. Thus, as it stood, the statute was special legislation on behalf of a particular religious body. Political power had been allocated for religious purposes. The fact that authority in the school district was not explicitly given to the Satmar leaders was irrelevant, since it had been given exclusively to their members.[145]

Admittedly the authority had been granted on the basis of territory rather than religion, but it was necessary, Souter held, to look beyond the form of the statute, which had clearly been drafted in such a way as to exclude all but the Satmars from belonging to the school district.[146]

In the kind of personal exchange that had become not uncommon in religion cases during the 1990s, Souter accused Justice Scalia (below) of making "thrusts at lions of his own imagining" and charged that he would reduce the Establishment Clause to "a few simple rules."[147] Blackmun concurred and went out of his way to record his view that the decision was consistent with the Lemon Test, which some justices now wished to discard.[148]

Stevens also concurred, finding that the purpose of the law was to cement Satmar children's adherence to their faith. He thought it significant that two-thirds of the children enrolled in the special school were Hasidim from outside the village.[149]

O'Connor also concurred, finding that the state could accommodate the needs of particular groups but could not discriminate, which it had done by passing a law especially for the Satmars' benefit. There was no assurance that another group seeking the same benefit would likewise be accommodated, although in principle the state could permit every village to constitute itself a school district. Unlike Blackmun, she did not find the Lemon Test helpful in the case.[150]

Justice Kennedy also concurred. He too thought accommodation by the state permissible, and the law placed no burdens on nonmembers of the sect. In his view there was no proof that the legislature would act in a discriminatory way in other cases; it had merely responded to a unique situation.[151]

The issue, however, was whether the state could use religion as a criterion for drawing political boundaries. The original establishment of the village was constitutional, because it merely followed existing law, but the school district was consciously established for religious purposes. There was, he insisted, more than a fine line between communities that, by voluntary association, had come to be comprised mainly of people of the same faith, and boundaries drawn explicitly to ensure that result. He thought the situation unfortunate and speculated that it possibly came about because of the Court's erroneous decisions in the *Aguilar* and *Grand Rapids* cases.[152]

Scalia wrote a characteristically biting dissent, charging that the Court had construed as a form of establishment a law designed to ensure religious liberty.[153] The case involved public, not private, schools. The principal and teachers were not Satmars and did not live in the village. There were no religious symbols in the school building, and, contrary to the usual principles of the group, girls and boys sat in the same classes together. Nothing prohibited all the students in a public school from being of the same religion.[154] The case differed from the *Larkin* case concerning liquor licenses because there the state had delegated authority directly to a church, and Scalia found it "astounding" that the majority could not recognize the difference.[155]

The history of the United States showed numerous examples of communities all of whose members were of one religion, Scalia citing certain counties in Utah and New Mexico as contemporary examples. By the Court's reasoning the governments of those communities were inherently suspect.[156]

As to the charge that the statute was religiously motivated, Scalia replied that "in the Land of the Free, democratically adopted laws are not so easily impeached by unelected judges." The arrangement had the clear secular purpose of relieving handicapped children of the trauma of going to school in an unfamiliar and threatening environment.[157]

New York had a record of authorizing the establishment of numerous small school districts, and special legislation did not necessarily demonstrate religious favoritism. The identity of the district was not religious but cultural, based on dress, language, and other factors, and Scalia suggested that Souter would actually praise such an arrangement if it benefited, for example, American Indians or Gypsies.[158]

The law did not discriminate against anyone, he contended, the school boundaries merely following those of the village. Nonmembers of the group had been excluded from the village not because of religion but because of the Satmars' preference for high-density zoning, which allowed multifamily dwellings and certain nonresidential uses of land.[159]

Even if the act did directly aid religion, Scalia argued, it would still be permissible, and, if the state sanctioned similar arrangements for other religious groups, he predicted, the majority of the Court would strike those down as well. Recourse to the courts would be a guarantee of governmental impartiality in case such discrimination did occur. Making law one case at a time violated no principle, and its prohibition was "unheard of." Scalia found Kennedy's point illogical, since it was the village itself whose boundaries had been drawn on religious lines, not the school district.[160]

Scalia again found the Lemon Test not useful but said the Court could not devise an alternative because it had no consistent principles. The case at hand manifested a "recent tendency of the Court to turn the Establishment Clause into a repealer of our Nation's tradition of religious toleration."[161]

If in the *Zobrest* case the Court had shown signs of mitigating its rigid prohibition of public funding of religious education, this shift was made explicit in the 1997 case of *Agostini v. Felton*,[162] a request to the Court to reconsider its 1985 *Aguilar* decision, in which it had ruled against public funding of "remedial" programs in religious schools.

New York State, endeavoring to comply with the restrictions of the latter case, first transported students from private to public schools for this instruction. When this proved both relatively unsuccessful and quite expensive, instruction in the private schools after regular school hours was attempted, which also failed to reach many potential beneficiaries.

The state then began providing those services on private school premises during regular school hours, using only public school teachers who were carefully instructed as to their conduct, so as to avoid any impression that they represented the private school itself.

Writing for the majority, O'Connor upheld the program. Two claims—that its high expense constituted "new facts" requiring a new hearing and that the majority of the Court had, in the *Kiryas Joel* case, indicated their dissatisfaction with the *Aguilar* decision—were rejected as irrelevant. However, the claim that the Court itself, in decisions subsequent to the *Aguilar* case, had repudiated the principles of the latter, was found to be correct.[163]

In earlier cases the Court had ruled that the mere presence of public employees in a religious school tended toward "state-sponsored indoctrination" or "symbolic union between government and religion." But the *Zobrest* case had rejected both assumptions, O'Connor found.[164] She thought that there was no significant difference between providing a sign-language interpreter and providing various kinds of remedial education, since an interpreter also had the opportunity for "religious indoctrination."[165]

In the *Witters* case, the Court had repudiated its earlier position that all aid to religious schools, of whatever kind, was automatically invalid.[166] O'Connor denied that a teacher entering a religious school would be likely to engage in religious indoctrination. The impression of a "symbolic union of church and state" was in any case not lessened by having such instruction carried on in a van parked outside a religious school, which New York had also attempted for a time.[167]

While funds for remedial education were not given directly to parents or students, they were also not given directly to the religious schools. Instead they were given to public agencies to distribute as they saw fit. The claim that by funding such programs, the government permitted religious schools to reduce their overall costs was not relevant.[168]

The fact that cooperation between public and private schools was necessary to the program did not itself invalidate it, O'Connor held. "Excessive entanglement" was no longer a danger, once the Court had ceased to assume, in the *Zobrest* case, that the conduct of public employees in private schools was inherently suspect. Close scrutiny was therefore not necessary.[169]

The *Agostini* decision was unusual in being an explicit repudiation of earlier Court decisions, and O'Connor also addressed that issue. The principle of "stare decisis" ("to stand by the things decided") was not absolute and had to accommodate itself to changing views of the law. In matters pertaining to the Constitution, to follow precedent rigidly would mean that the law could change only through constitutional amendment.[170]

Souter dissented, affirming his adherence to the *Aguilar* decision. The Constitution banned all forms of aid to religion, he insisted, and "hard lessons" had taught that religions supported by the government were eventually compromised by the government. But citizens tended to forget this, and the Court had the duty of "stopping the corrosion before it starts."[171]

The fact that certain classes were designated as "remedial" did not make them essentially different from regular classes conducted in religious schools. Among other things, such a program merely allowed religious schools to shift funds from one purpose to another and was thus a subsidy. If support for remedial programs was constitutional, support for the entire educational mission of the school would be also.[172]

Conducting such courses away from private school premises made it less likely that the private schools would try to save money by ceasing to offer those courses themselves. Holding classes away from the school also substantially reduced the danger of their being perceived as governmental endorsement of religion.[173]

Although Souter had dissented in the *Zobrest* case, he now sought to distinguish it from the case at hand. A sign-language interpreter functioned "more like a hearing aid than teacher," he claimed, and the *Zobrest* decision did not overturn the assumption that bringing public school teachers into private schools carried the danger of endorsement of religion by the government.[174]

In the *Zobrest* and *Witters* cases, aid did not come directly to the school but was given to the student. In neither case was the religious school relieved of a financial burden that it would otherwise have to bear.[175]

Souter also castigated the Court for departing from its earlier precedents. The principles enunciated in the *Aguilar* case had not been overturned in any subsequent cases, and there was no basis for doing so now.[176]

Souter concluded by acknowledging that the disputed program was "worthy" and that there were major difficulties in complying with the Court's earlier strictures. "But constitutional lines have to be drawn, and on one side of every one of them is an otherwise sympathetic case that provokes impatience with the Constitution and with the line. But constitutional lines are the price of constitutional government."[177]

Justice Ginsburg wrote a dissenting opinion arguing that the legal requirements for rehearing the issue had not been met.[178]

In *Mitchell v. Helms* (2000), the Court again seemed to move away from its long commitment to the separationist position, when it upheld a Louisiana program using federal money to provide private schools with computers and other equipment.[179]

Writing the majority opinion, Thomas indicated a willingness to repudiate some of the Court's key decisions on the subject of aid to religious schools.[180] In recent cases the Court had not held that direct aid to religious schools was forbidden by the Constitution but merely that any such aid must be "neutral," in the sense of being distributed equitably to all, Thomas asserted. In addition, the Court need no longer concern itself with whether aid supposedly given for the support of secular subjects might be "diverted" to religious uses, nor need it concern itself with whether a particular school was "pervasively sectarian" or whether an aid program tended to incite "divisiveness."[181]

The Court in its past decisions had been illogical, upholding the providing of books to religious schools in the *Allen* case, forbidding the providing of other educational materials in the *Meek* case.[182]

The *Agostini* case abandoned the requirement that religious schools be watched carefully to ensure compliance and, if the *Meek* and *Wolman* rulings were also abandoned, such scrutiny would no longer be necessary, hence there would be no "excessive entanglement" in granting aid.[183] The program under challenge was unquestionably neutral and did not fund the religious mission of the schools, hence was constitutional.[184]

Recalling that legislation forbidding aid to religious schools originated during a time of intense anti-Catholic prejudice in the United States, Thomas asserted that the term "pervasively sectarian" was a product of that anti-Catholicism, which he called "a shameful pedigree which we do not hesitate to disavow." [185]

O'Connor voted with the majority but wrote a concurring opinion warning that Thomas's opinion was too sweeping in its implications.[186] She too admitted that the *Allen* and *Meek* decisions were incompatible. Computers were now as necessary to education as were books and thus should be provided by government programs. However, she did not believe that "neutrality" was a sufficient criterion for determining the constitutionality of such grants.[187]

In principle it was still necessary to inquire as to whether funds given for one purpose might be diverted to other uses, O'Connor thought. However, the Court's traditional distinction between books and other materials was untenable. For example, even governmentally funded meals might be "abused" if teachers urged students to say a blessing on their food.[188]

But at the same time O'Connor also thought it unnecessary to inquire closely into this possibility. No evidence had been presented that teachers in religious schools abused their positions, and one admitted violation—the use of federal money to buy religious books for a school—had been detected and corrected, thereby demonstrating the effectiveness of the program's safeguards.[189]

Souter dissented, attempting to uphold the classical separationist position, which he claimed was the clear intention of the framers of the Constitution.[190] The term "neutrality" was inadequate, since it merely implied "evenhandedness," without regard for whether aid was constitutional at all.[191]

Since Catholic schools were "pervasively sectarian," it was necessary to inquire into how public funds were spent, Souter insisted, and the danger of money being diverted to religious uses was quite real. The distinction between textbooks and other materials was meaningful, because textbooks on secular subjects could only be used for those subjects, whereas equipment like film projectors and computers could be used for many purposes, including sectarian ones.[192]

Noting that a Catholic had submitted a brief to the Court opposing the aid program on the grounds that it enticed Catholic schools to compromise their principles, Souter denied that anti-Catholicism had anything to do with the separationist position. The nature of Catholic education was under discussion because Catholic schools were the principal recipients of the disputed aid.[193]

In 2002 the Court further loosened its restrictions on aid to religious schools when it approved in principle a landmark "voucher" program by which Cleveland parents were issued certificates for payment of tuition either in private schools or in public schools other than their own.[194] Rehnquist wrote the majority opinion. The Cleveland public schools showed a history of poor achievement, he found, and private schools offered parents and students a viable alternative. Schools eligible for vouchers promised not to discriminate against any category of student.[195]

Rehnquist built on the *Mueller*, *Witters*, and *Zobrest* precedents, which he said showed that the Establishment Clause was not violated in the case of programs that were religiously neutral and chosen by the parents themselves. Any "incidental advancement" of religion was due to the actions of the citizens themselves, not the government, religion aided solely as the result of "innumerable decisions of private individuals."[196]

The program made available a wide range of schools to parents and children, and it was not relevant, Rehnquist found, that the majority of participating private schools were religious in nature. It was merely incidental that 96 percent of those receiving vouchers chose to attend religious schools, a figure that in any case obscured the actual range of choices that students enjoyed.[197] Rehnquist found unproven the claim that the program was divisive, and the claim was also circular, in that the only demonstrated divisiveness was the fact that a suit had been filed against it.[198]

O'Connor concurred, pointing out that if the full range of alternative schools available to students was taken into account, only 16.5 percent of the voucher recipients chose religious schools, and the amount of money spent on religious education was minor compared with the huge amounts spent on public education.[199]

O'Connor believed that in the *Agostini* decision, the Court had in effect incorporated the "entanglement" clause of the Lemon Test into the "secular purpose" clause, so that a program that had a legitimate secular purpose escaped the suspicion of entanglement. She charged that a concern for "neutrality" was inconsistent with the *Agostini* decision, which had found that there was an obligation to aid both religious and nonreligious programs.[200]

Thomas also concurred, characterizing the voucher program as one that "gives hope to the poor" and going on to argue that the Fourteenth

Amendment, in guaranteeing the rights of all citizens, virtually required protection of the benefits of private education. The Amendment, he asserted, ought to advance liberty, not contain it. But separationists had robbed the Establishment Clause of its task of protecting liberty and, in a "tragic irony," had converted it into a restriction on liberty.[201]

Without education, citizens could not exercise the rights guaranteed by the Fourteenth Amendment, Thomas reasoned, and the poor would suffer most. Separationsts offered formalistic arguments concerning the Establishment Clause while ignoring the real issues of freedom implied by the Fourteenth Amendment.[202] He disparaged the "romanticized ideal of universal public education which resonates with the cognoscenti."[203]

Stevens dissented, charging that vouchers would pay for the "indoctrination of thousands of grammar school children in particular religious faiths," because the availability of vouchers might entice some parents to send their children to religious schools who would not otherwise do so.[204]

Souter also dissented. There was no excuse for dispensing with constitutional restrictions on public aid, he insisted, and the voucher program in effect subsidized the teaching of various religions. Statements of purpose by participating schools showed that religion dominated their curricula.[205] Souter lamented that after a period of strict interpretation of the Establishment Clause from 1947 to 1968, the Court had begun to compromise its position. From 1968 to 1983 it had sought to prohibit any form of aid that might be diverted to religious uses, but since then it had abandoned even that vigilance. The seminal *Everson* decision had permitted only purely secular aid, in the form of bus fares.[206]

The current decision did not achieve neutrality but favored religious education at the expense of public education, since there was a disproportionate amount of money given to religious schools in contrast to the amount set aside, for example, for special tutorials in public schools.[207] Souter wondered how much genuine choice was available to parents and asked whether various public school options, such as "magnet schools," were really satisfactory.[208] That the program in question was an enticement to religious education was manifested, he thought, in the fact that two-thirds of parents choosing religious schools for their children stated that they had not chosen them for religious reasons but merely sought a better secular education for their children.[209]

The voucher program also violated the Free-Exercise Clause, Souter argued, in that the state imposed certain restrictions on religious schools as conditions for getting money. There was now a realistic prospect that the state would try to regulate private schools.[210]

Justice Breyer also dissented, like Souter, warning that the voucher program would lead to governmental regulation of private schools. What, he asked, of those religions whose beliefs forbade them to accept students of all faiths into their schools?[211]

Conclusion

Prior to 1940 the Supreme Court almost never found an explicit violation of the Free-Exercise Clause. The *Permoli* case (1845) ruled bluntly that the Bill of Rights did not bind the states, thereby barring consideration of most alleged violations of religious liberty, and the Mormon polygamy cases seemed to show that the Court had little solicitude even for religious claims that might fall within its jurisdiction. Only the *Holy Trinity* case (1892) found a violation of religious freedom, although even that decision was limited, in that it did not invalidate a federal law but merely found that Congress had not intended it to apply to churches.

But the Court sometimes advanced such freedom without invoking the Free-Exercise Clause, as in the *Worcester* case (1832), overturning the prosecution of a Methodist minister for violating a Georgia law by working among Indians, and the *Cummings* case (1866), overturning the prosecution of a Catholic priest who refused to take a loyalty oath.

Most important, the nineteenth-century Court laid down an enduring body of principles of great significance for the liberty of organized religious groups, even if not justified explicitly on free-exercise grounds.

- In a long series of decisions stretching from 1815 to 1927, it almost always upheld property claims by churches based on early acquisitions, usually grants made in colonial times.

  The *Terrett* case (1815), the first of these and one of the first religion cases ever to come before the Court, actually reversed part of the disestablishment of religion that had been effected in Virginia at the time of the Revolution, allowing an Episcopal parish to keep its property despite a state law confiscating it. (James Madison had warned against allowing churches to amass property.)

  In some ways the most important case of this kind was *Dartmouth* (1819), where the Court's ruling that the college was a private institution was something of a departure from the previous view that the granting of a charter by a legislature was a public act.[1] The ruling was perhaps the single most important court decision in American history relative to religious education, since it protected private institutions from being taken over by government and allowed the wide proliferation of religiously affiliated colleges and universities that is a unique feature of American higher education.

- In a series of cases stretching from the time of the Civil War until 1914 the Court consistently upheld arrangements whereby persons who joined particular religious groups surrendered their rights to own property. The most interesting of these cases was the last—*Steinhauser* (1914), upholding the validity of a Benedictine monk's vow of poverty. That case went beyond earlier suits on the same subject in that it explicitly raised the issue of whether a vow of poverty violated the constitutional guarantee of personal liberty. (If, as the Declaration of Independence insisted, certain rights were "inalienable," could even their bearers validly alienate them?)[2] The Court, however, chose to ignore this intriguing philosophical question.

- In the *Federal Street Meeting House* case (1861), the Court first explicitly laid down the principle that internal ecclesiastical disputes were to be settled in accordance with the established governing structures of each religious group, a principle that it had articulated as early as the *Mason* case (1824) and that the *Watson* decision (1872)[3] is commonly thought to have established as an abiding principle.

  The principle of ecclesiastical autonomy has for the most part continued in effect to the present and has given religious organizations a degree of independence conceded to no secular group or corporation.

- Although President Madison vetoed an act of Congress incorporating a church, at a time when such incorporation was viewed as a kind of official endorsement, state legislatures throughout the nineteenth century readily granted such charters to churches and many other kinds of groups.[4] The practice was never challenged before the Supreme Court but was tacitly upheld in the *Philadelphia Baptist Association* (1819) and *Kain* (1879) cases, where the Court virtually invited religious groups to incorporate, in order to make themselves eligible to receive legacies.

- Although isolated and eccentric, the *Holy Trinity* decision had crucial importance for the free exercise of religion.[5] It was ironic that the issue was joined by an impeccably American religious institution, the Protestant Episcopal Church, because other denominations at the time—Catholics, Jews, and Lutherans, notably—probably drew a large majority of their clergy from Europe, many of whom were explicitly brought to America to fulfill pastoral responsibilities. Had the decision been different, some churches would have found it impossible to provide clergy for many of their people.

Most of the Court's nineteenth-century decisions in support of organized religion can perhaps be explained as the application of law of contract—those who joined a religious organization agreed to abide by the organization's rules, even as land grants and charters were viewed as contractual in nature. Thus the law of contract was in the nineteenth century perhaps the single most important factor in the recognition of the freedom of organized religious groups, and ensuring such collective freedom was the nineteenth-century Court's major achievement with regard to religious liberty.

The jurisprudence of the nineteenth century was permeated by a general sympathy for religion, which sometimes led to decisions far from the spirit of rigid formalism said to have been characteristic of the era. Thus in the *Wheeler* case (1823), Justice Washington (nephew of the first president) characterized the work of the Society for the Propagation of the Gospel in Foreign Parts as "benevolent and laudable." The most interesting example of this special solicitude was the obscure *Beatty* case (1829), in which Justice Story validated a church's defective title to its cemetery almost solely on the grounds that to do otherwise would affront human and religious sensibilities. In the *Girard* case (1844), he ruled that there was no constitutional right to insult Christianity, and this assertion of the privileged position of Christianity merely expressed the view of Story and others that the common law incorporated Christian moral teachings. In the *Hennington* case (1895) the first Justice Harlan defended the sabbath laws as bringing moral benefits to society.

Whatever else it may have been, the *Holy Trinity* decision was a venturesome way of protecting religious rights then in need of protection, and earlier the Court had shown itself only somewhat less ingenious in its solutions in the *Worcester* and *Cummings* cases.

The Mormon polygamy decisions, although they stand as the single most important restriction on religious freedom in American history, were paradoxically part of the Court's overall solicitude for religion, involving complex constitutional and social questions.

The Mormons, originating in New York State, had been persecuted in Illinois and Missouri, where they found local authorities unwilling or unable to protect them. When the Mormons moved to Utah it was with the assumption that they were protected by the federal Bill of Rights, and, when Utah became a territory in 1850, its legislature guaranteed the rights of polygamists. Also in contrast to other states and territories, it allowed the church to hold an unlimited amount of property.[6]

Because of Utah's dissent from the national moral consensus concerning the nature of marriage, opposition to polygamy became a major issue in the conflict over "states' rights," and polygamy became linked with the issue of slavery as a test of those rights. In 1857 federal troops were dispatched to Utah in an unsuccessful attempt to bring the Mormons under control, and during the presidential campaign of 1860 Abraham Lincoln accused his chief opponent, Stephen A. Douglas, of protecting polygamy by his espousal of states' rights.[7]

Both sides in the dispute appealed to religious principles, Mormons claiming that polygamy was authorized in the Old Testament and that those who opposed it had thus departed from authentic Christianity, while opponents considered Mormonism a blasphemous perversion of Christianity.[8] (The *Girard* decision, which had upheld the blasphemy laws in principle, might have been cited against the Mormons.)

In effect the Mormons appealed to a "higher law," which transcended civil law, and the territory of Utah officially declared that the common law, which banned polygamy, was not applicable in Utah. To their opponents the Mormons thus appeared to be "establishing" Mormonisn in the territory, in violation of the Constitution,[9] an issue that could be raised only so long as Utah remained a territory—once it became a state it could, under the terms of the *Permoli* decision, favor an established religion if it chose to do so.

The federal government's suppression of polygamy was not, however, done in the name of a secular society free of religious authority. On the contrary, as the Court's major polygamy decisions affirmed, the Mormons rejected some of the basic tenets of Christianity, hence were thought to be in violation of the moral foundations of society itself. The religious claim of the Mormons was refuted by an opposing religious claim, and among other things the controversy over polygamy strengthened the belief that the common law had a Christian foundation.[10]

The *Reynolds* case was the first in which the Court undertook to explicate the meaning of the First Amendment, paradoxically using principles developed in state courts, about the nature of marriage, to advance the authority of the federal government during the period prior to the Court's adoption of the theory of "substantive due process" and at the time when states' rights were just beginning to reassert themselves, as the federal government virtually abandoned its commitment to Reconstruction in the lands of the former Confederacy.[11]

Despite its general solicitude for property rights during the post-Reconstruction period, a divided Court upheld the attempt by Congress in effect to destroy the Mormon Church by confiscating its property in the late 1880s, the double attack on polygamy and church property being potentially fatal to the communal nature of Mormonism.[12]

At the time the Fourteenth Amendment (1868) was being debated, some of its supporters expressed outrage that freedom of religion had been violated by the harassment of abolitionist clergy before the Civil War. However, advocates of the Amendment made no explicit claim that it incorporated the Religion Clauses.[13] The Court also did not cite the Fourteenth Amendment in the *Watson* case, although the exact constitutional basis for that decision was unclear.

As Harlan in dissent pointed out with considerable passion, the *Maxwell* (1899) and *Berea* (1908) decisions in effect denied that the Fourteenth Amendment protected religious liberty from infringement by states. Despite his ringing assertion of Christian liberty in the *Holy Trinity* case, Brewer rendered the decision against Berea College's policy of racial integration, and, despite the Court's growing solicitude for property rights, the college's appeal to those rights, along with its timely reminder to the Court that it was a corporation, were also rejected.

The doctrine of "substantive due process," which protected contract and hence property, was a major development of the Court's jurisprudence after the Civil War[14] and was helpful to religious groups in their various disputes about property.

The *Meyer* (1923) and *Pierce* (1925) cases, upholding the rights of private education, marked a transition in the Court's approach to religion, although their exact significance is somewhat murky, because the basis on which they were rendered was not made entirely clear at the time. The two decisions can be seen as based on substantive due process but may also have marked an implicit and tentative move by the Court toward the incorporation theory of the Fourteenth Amendment.[15]

In *Meyer* the appellants explicitly made the argument that the Fourteenth Amendment incorporated the Free-Exercise Clause. Appealing to the theory of substantive due process, they argued that the Nebraska law was analogous to various kinds of state regulation of business that the Court had struck down over the years.[16]

Justice McReynolds's majority opinion was compatible with that argument, but he also made passing reference to religious freedom and in general produced a rather sweeping judgment. (If the Fourteenth Amendment was the basis of his decision, it marked the first time the amendment had been applied on any issue besides race.)[17] Paradoxically, the decision said almost nothing about religious liberty, although it has been understood as the first step in the Court's modern expansion of personal liberties, because it was not decided on narrow grounds.

Holmes dissented in the case, somewhat belying his later reputation as a staunch civil libertarian by holding that restrictions imposed by the government merely needed to avoid being irrational or arbitrary. He may have seen the *Meyer* decision as merely another example of the substantive due process doctrine he had rejected in earlier cases.[18]

In the *Pierce* case the state of Oregon attempted to preempt the issue by insisting that the Fourteenth Amendment was procedural only, asserting for good measure that parents had no fundamental rights over the education of their children. On the other side, the plaintiffs avoided an appeal to the Free-Exercise Clause, which their attorneys thought was precluded by *Permoli*, and instead showed that the schools would suffer loss of property if required to close.[19] (This time Holmes joined in the unanimous verdict, without explaining how he thought the decision differed from *Meyer*.)

In the two cases, the Court for the first time seemed to apply substantive due process to personal, as distinct from economic, liberties, but the bases of the two decisions were ambiguous.[20] Perhaps the Court regarded substantive due process as less sweeping in its application, hence as preferable to the explicit incorporation of the Fourteenth Amendment.[21] (Ironically, if the *Meyer* and *Pierce* decisions actually were new and unusual applications of substantive due process, they were the only precedents to survive the demise of that theory.)[22]

However, this apparent expansion of personal liberties in the mid-1920s was not extended a few years later to the claims of pacifists, that the Court treated as mere privileges that the government could grant or withhold on its own terms. In the *Schwimmer* case (1929), the positions of the justices were almost the reverse of what they had been in *Meyer*, with a majority ruling against the appellant but Holmes now arguing strongly that she should be granted citizenship despite her pacifism, a position that suggests that his view of liberty had evolved substantially in four years.[23]

In the *Hamilton* case (1934), Justice Cardozo, citing *Meyer* and *Pierce*, became the first member of the Court since Harlan to claim that the Fourteenth Amendment incorporated the Free-Exercise Clause, an announcement that none of his brethren contradicted.

Justice Stone's famous footnote in the *Carolene* case (1937), urging that the Court show special solicitude for the rights of "discrete and insular minorities," is conventionally seen as the charter of the modern jurisprudence of personal liberty. In his footnote Stone cited both *Meyer* and *Pierce* as precedents and treated as fact the incorporation theory of the Fourteenth Amendment.[24] His exhortation has been understood to mark a shift from a "negative" to a "positive" or "fundamental" concept of liberty[25]—from merely forbidding its abridgement to being solicitous of opportunities to maximize it, guarding even against "prejudices" that might threaten those rights.[26]

This new solicitude for personal liberties was the result of a gradual development by which the Court assumed the duty of protecting against the misuse of legislative authority, especially through the Due Process Clause, while newer philosophies of law recognized the importance of the personal beliefs, possibly the pejudices, of judges. These changes began around 1920 and were already developing by the beginning of the New Deal in 1933.[27]

But through the power of appointment, President Franklin D. Roosevelt at least accelerated these changes in the philosophy of the Court. Stung by decisions that struck down some of the economic legislation of the New Deal, Roosevelt, after first unsuccessfully trying to enlarge the Court, chose justices inclined to approach the Constitution in a "broad" and "flexible" spirit, as a document offering general principles capable of meeting changing social needs. A Court chosen to embody this philosophy with regard to economic legislation inevitably espoused it in other ways as well, and an unforeseen result of Roosevelt's transformation of the Court was its sudden expansion of the meaning of religious freedom.[28]

The Roosevelt Revolution solidified that transformation, but Stone, the architect of it, had been appointed to the Court by Calvin Coolidge, and there is little evidence that Roosevelt himself gave any thought to religious issues in his judicial appointments. (Relative to the Establishment Clause, in his public speeches he invoked God more frequently than most of his predecessors in the White House.)[29]

The *Irvington* decision of 1939, upholding the Jehovah's Witnesses' right to proselytize, may have been the first application of the *Carolene* principle to religious liberty. But the Court's seemingly inconsistent decisions in the *Cantwell* and *Gobitis* cases in 1940—the first expanding the liberty of the Witnesses, the second restricting it—demonstrates that, except for Justice Frankfurter, the earliest Roosevelt appointees to the Court had no developed theory of the Free-Exercise Clause, with Justices Black, Douglas, and Murphy—soon to be stalwart advocates of personal liberties—surprised by Stone's dissent in the *Gobitis* case, then converted by his argument.[30]

But Justices Jackson and Rutledge were on record as disapproving of the *Gobitis* decision when they were named to the Court,[31] and Roosevelt's solicitor general, Francis Biddle, also disapproved of the decision. The Witnesses themselves regarded Roosevelt as sympathetic to their plight.[32]

Under the new jurisprudence, the Court showed itself willing to protect believers even against laws of general validity that created difficulties for religious practice. The distinction between belief and action, first made in the *Reynolds* case, was now significantly modified. (The distinction had in effect rendered the Free-Exercise Clause irrelevant, since freedom of belief was already protected by freedom of speech and press.)[33]

But the Court did not abandon the principle that religion, while it was to be tolerated as widely as possible, could nonetheless be restricted when it produced socially harmful results. Thus the expansion of religious liberty would always depend on the question as to whether it was compatible with the good of society. (If the heightened patriotism of the Second World War contributed greatly to the harassment of Witnesses who refused to salute the flag, the war may also have contributed to their vindication, on the grounds that the nation was precisely fighting to protect personal freedom.)

The *Cantwell* case marked the first time the Court ever responded favorably to the claim of a religious group that its beliefs caused it to be the victim of discrimination, and, by validating religious exemptions from laws binding equally on everyone, the decision set the direction that most religious-freedom cases would follow for the next half century.

Equally important as the flag-salute decision was the Court's expansion of the rights of proselytization and of conscientious objection to war, along with the principle laid down in the *Ballard* case (1944)—that courts should not inquire into the sincerity of religious beliefs.

But the abandonment of the belief-action distinction was not absolute, because of the ambiguity of the foundations on which the decisions rested. Especially in the *Barnette* case and in the numerous cases involving public proselytizing, the Court sometimes seemed to invoke freedom of speech and press as much as religion.[34] Insofar as saluting the flag and proselytizing were viewed as forms of expression, they enjoyed almost unlimited freedom. But viewed as actions, they were subject to restrictions, as in the *Prince* case, which found proselytizing by a minor to violate the child-labor laws. Thus the *Barnette* decision did not reject Frankfurter's claim that the state could require things essential to national unity but merely held that saluting the flag was not essential. So also at the end of World War II the Court in *Cleveland* and several other cases once more found that polygamy violated the standards of civilized society.

The foundations of the modern jurisprudence of the Religion Clauses were laid between 1940 and 1948, and after that, the Court, perhaps preoccupied with racial issues, for some years paid relatively little attention to religion.

The Roosevelt Court was succeeded by the Warren Court, for whom the quest for equality (or "fairness") was perhaps the driving principle. If forged in connection with racial issues, this concern had relevance to religion as well.[35] (One of the Witnesses cases, *Opeleika* [1943], involved blacks arrested for proselytizing, although the plaintiffs did not consider their activities a harbinger of the civil rights movement.)[36]

The most important of the free-exercise cases decided by the Warren Court had to do with the rights of persons who were not religious believers in any conventional sense.

The *Burstyn* case (1955) was significant as the first decision in support of the rights of nonbelievers, holding that insults to religion were protected as free expression, thereby overturning Story's affirmation of the blasphemy laws in the *Girard* case and formally negating the old claim that Christianity held a privileged place in the common law. In 1961 the *Torcaso* decision logically applied Article VI of the Constitution by ruling that atheists could not be denied the right to hold public office.

The most important area of expansion in the 1960s was conscientious objection, which the Court now began to treat almost as a right, to be extended fairly to all claimants. But the Court here faced a dilemma, in that the Selective Service Act specified that exemptions from military service could be given only to those who affirmed belief in "a Supreme

Being." However, if nonbelievers had rights equal to believers, this requirement was a violation of both the Religion Clauses.

In *Torcaso*, Black sought to broaden the definition of religion beyond theism and cited "Secular Humanism" as an example. In the *Seeger* case (1965), the plaintiff explicitly disclaimed belief in a Supreme Being, and Justice Clark took the opportunity to broaden the definition even further. Putting aside the phrase "Supreme Being," which had been derived from Hughes's dictum in the *Hamilton* case, Clark noted a variety of possible understandings of religion and finally seemed to favor the formulation of the liberal Protestant theologian Paul Tillich—religion as "ultimate concern," as a search for "the ground of being"—a definition under which the plaintiff qualified.

This expansion was ratified in the *Welsh* case (1970), where, in the midst of a war that seemed to be tearing the country apart, the Court was faced with the obligation of declaring the Selective Service Act's conscientious-objection provisions unconstitutional, because they discriminated against nontheists. Instead, as Harlan bluntly observed, the Court chose to "lobotomize" the statute by interpreting it in a way quite contrary to what Congress had intended. (The 1967 draft law omitted the phrase "Supreme Being" but specified that "religious training and belief does not include essentially political, sociological, or philosophical views, or a merely personal moral code,"[37] a provision that Black in *Welsh* urged the Court "not to take too literally.")

In the *Sherbert* case (1963), the Court opened an important new area of religious freedom by finding in favor of a plaintiff who had been denied unemployment benefits after refusing, for religious reasons, to work on Saturday. After 1963, however, the employment issue remained dormant for another fourteen years, until the Burger Court expanded the *Sherbert* principle in several cases, requiring that private employers also respect employees' religious rights.

The most interesting of the Burger Court's free-exercise cases was *Yoder* (1971), permitting Amish parents to refrain from enrolling their children in high school, which they thought would undermine their traditional way of life. The decision seemed to go against the jurisprudence of *Seeger* and *Welsh*, in that Burger ruled that the exemption could be granted only for "religious" reasons, explicitly excluding any claim made on merely philosophical grounds.

The case was the first in which the Court granted a religious exemption from a criminal law—failing to send children to school[38]—including an exemption from the child-labor laws,[39] something that the 1944 *Prince* decision had refused to the Witnesses.

The Burger Court showed limited signs of retreating from the *Watson* principle. In the *Serbian Orthodox* case (1976), Justice Rehnquist insisted that the Court could not be bound by every ecclesiastical document purporting to be definitive, and, acting as a circuit justice in the *Methodist Homes* case (1978), he was accused of misconstruing Methodist polity. In *Jones v. Wolff*, a Presbyterian property dispute the following year, the Court examined only the secular, as distinct from the ecclesiastical, documents relevant to the case.[40]

One of the potentially most far-reaching of the Court's decisions concerning religious liberty was the *Bob Jones* case (1983), where the official national commitment to racial equality was found to override the beliefs and practices of a particular religious group. However, the constitutional implications of the decision remained unclear, because the issue was tax exemptions, something the courts have always treated not as a right but as a concession by the government.

In the *Dayton Christian School* case (1986), the Court avoided the even more crucial question of whether civil rights laws require religious groups to modify their teachings and practices merely in order to exist, since the plaintiff demanded that the school continue her employment even though she had acted contrary to the religious group's stated beliefs concerning the role of women. The decision did not reach that fundamental question but did require that the school answer the queries of a public agency, the Court refusing to rule that such an inquiry was itself a violation of religious freedom. (The case was apparently settled without further litigation.)

The *Goldman* decision (1986), upholding an Air Force regulation that prohibited a Jewish officer from wearing a ritual head covering, was the first modern case in which the Court found that a merely "legitimate" state interest could justify such restrictions, rather than the "compelling" state interest that had been the criterion since the *Barnette* decision.

The Rehnquist Court after 1990, often sharply divided and with several unpredictable "swing" votes, continued to depart from modern free-exercise precedents in certain ways.

The most controversial of these were the *Smith* (1990) and *Lyng* cases, the former refusing to recognize a right to use an illegal drug in an American Indian ceremony, the second denying an Indian plea to enjoin the building of a public road through land that the Indians regarded as sacred. In the first case, Scalia, writing for the the majority, invoked once again the government's claim to a merely "legitimate" interest rather a "compelling" one.

In the *Boerne* case (1997), the Court swept away the congressional efforts to reverse these two decisions, taking the rare step of invalidating an act of Congress, by holding that the Religious Freedom Restoration Act infringed the Court's own constitutional jurisdiction.

In doing so the Court appeared to hold that infringements of religious liberty can occur only if they are intentional, and the Court cited the 1940

Gobitis decision (which had been overturned in 1943) justifying burdens placed on religious believers by general laws.[41]

Thus by the beginning of the twenty-first century a slim majority of the Court seemed to take a more restrictive view of religious liberty than had prevailed over the previous more than sixty years, a consistant interpretation of the Free-Exercise Clause likely to depend on justices named to the Court sometime in the future.

ESTABLISHMENT

The Court showed little interest in the Establishment Clause prior to 1947, as it consistently rebuffed challenges to the sabbath laws, for example, or permitted tax support of religious institutions deemed to serve the public good. (In the *Speer* case [1905] the Court ruled that no organization was to be considered "sectarian" so long as it served such a purpose.)

The Mormon polygamy issue implicitly involved both the Religion Clauses, since Utah was in effect accused of establishing the Mormon religion, while polygamy was condemned by the federal government in accordance with the belief that Christian moral teachings underlay the civil law and the good order of society.

Although churches lost every tax case that they brought before the Court, the justices, while giving local governments discretion in granting religious exemptions, in each instance also implicitly upheld the constitutionality of doing so.

The law of contract also played a role in establishment issues, so that in the two *Lowery* cases (1907, 1910), the Court held that the state of Hawaii was required to teach Protestant doctrine in a state school, because of an agreement made with a Protestant missionary organization.

The Court enshrined the accommodationist position in a series of cases around the beginning of the twentieth century—*Bradfield* (1899), *Speer* (1905), *Quick Bear* (1907), and *Lowery* (1907, 1910)—and reaffirmed it as late as the *Cochran* case (1930).

But, having effected during World War II a revolution in the understanding of the Free-Exercise Clause, the Court turned its attention to the Establishment Clause immediately afterward, in *Everson* (1947) and *McCollum* (1948). Its espousal of the separationist position at that time is usually explained on the grounds that those two cases marked the first time the Court recognized the Fourteenth Amendment as applying the Establishment Clause to the states, thus requiring the justices to face entirely new questions.

Everson allowed minimal public assistance to children enrolled in religious schools, even as it set forth the theoretical argument as to why such aid was unconstitutional. *McCollum* forbade public schools to cooperate in making religious instruction available to their students, a position from which the *Zorach* decision (1952) seemed partly to retreat. After that the Court paid no attention to the Establishment Clause for almost a decade.

When it resumed dealing with the issue in 1961, *Everson-McCollum* triumphed over *Zorach*, and the majority generally adopted a stance of suspicion toward the public recognition of religion, following a parallel whereby expanded religious liberty seemed necessarily to require stringent separation between government and religion.

The first of the new issues involved the sabbath laws, the only religion cases in which Chief Justice Warren himself wrote the decisions. Here the majority seemed actually to be accommodationist, as the Court upheld laws forbidding commerce on Sundays and rejected appeals from those who were not Christians. However, these rulings proved to be compatible with separationism, in that Warren found that the sabbath laws no longer had any religious significance.

Subsequently, however, the Court showed the extent of its separationist commitment in first forbidding authorized prayer in the public schools (*Engel* [1962]), then forbidding authorized Bible reading (*Schempp* [1963]).

In the *Epperson* case (1968), the Court overturned an Arkansas law prohibiting the teaching of evolution in the public schools, the Court's vigilance against establishment manifested in the fact that, although the law did not explicitly mention religion, Justice Fortas in his majority opinion postulated that it had been so inspired,[42] treating religion as a suspect motive in public life. (Black reminded his brethren that they had previously held that the motives of legislators were irrelevant in determining constitutionality.)

In 1968 also the Court heard the first (*Allen*) in a continuing series of cases concerning public support of religious education, with the Court over time interpreting the Establishment Clause as forbidding most forms of public aid to religious elementary and secondary schools but permitting it for colleges and universities.

Despite Republican complaints about the previous direction of the Court, applications of the Establishment Clause did not change substantially under the Burger Court, as Burger himself for a time proved to be liberal, and Justice Blackmun, another Nixon appointee, even more liberal, while one of the accommodationists was Justice White, a Kennedy appointee. Two nominees of President Ford—Justices Stevens and Powell—were also separationists. (The Burger Court has been described as moving away from the principles of the Warren Court without fully repudiating them.)[43]

Under Burger the most significant development with regard to establishment occurred in the *Lemon* case (1971), invalidating various kinds of assistance to religious schools. Burger's Lemon Test decreed that laws or government policies had to have a "secular purpose" and could not lead to "excessive entanglement" between government and religion. The "entanglement" criterion proved to be a trap from which there was almost no escape, in that the attempt to ensure the conformity of religious schools to federal regulations was itself deemed to constitute entanglement. But the Test was less frequently invoked as time went on.

The Court reached accommodationist conclusions in the *Walz* (1970) and *Marsh* (1983) cases, the former upholding tax exemptions for religious organizations, the latter the practice of paid legislative chaplains. In each case, Burger relied heavily on the weight of history, arguing that long practice to some extent justified arrangements that might otherwise be considered dubious.

The *Stone* case (1980) prohibited the state of Kentucky from posting the Ten Commandments in public school classrooms, the separationist stance now so firmly entrenched that the decision was issued per curiam, without even the necessity of formal argument.

The common theory that the Religion Clauses work together, in that the Establishment Clause serves primarily to protect religious liberty, can flounder in situations where the two clauses appear to be in conflict with each other, and in a series of cases—*Widmar* (1981), *Mergens* (1984), *Lamb's Chapel* (1993), *Rosenberger* (1995), and *Good News* (2001)— the Court found that denying student religious groups the same access to facilities given to other groups in public schools was a violation of the Free-Exercise Clause, while granting access was not a violation of the Establishment Clause.

The meaning of the Establishment Clause was left in some doubt by two cases involving religious Christmas symbols on public property. In the *Lynch* case (1983), the Court allowed the custom, then forbade it in the *Allegheny* case six years later. The *Lynch* decision was in one sense not a departure from separationism, in that one of Burger's arguments, like Warren's concerning the sabbath, was that the symbolism of Christmas had ceased to be religious in nature. In *Allegheny*, Justice O'Connor, President Reagan's first appointee to the Court, proposed a new test of constitutionality—whether a particular arrangement seemed to imply an official "endorsement" of religion.

In *Edwards* (1987), the Court invalidated a state law requiring that "creation science" be taught in public schools along with the theory of evolution.

The strictest separationist principles were applied in the *Jaffree* decision (1985), overturning a state law authorizing an official moment of silence each day in the public schools.

Ronald Reagan, like other Republican presidents, promised to turn the Court in a more conservative direction, but the most tangible progress toward that goal occurred during the administration of the first President George Bush in the 1990s, with Rehnquist as chief justice, and two ardent conservatives—Justices Scalia and Thomas—joining him on the Court. Bush, however, also appointed the liberal Justice Souter and the "moderate" Kennedy.

The majority of the Rehnquist Court, not including the chief justice himself, continued to be separationist with respect to the public schools, invalidating school prayer in the *Weisman* (1992) and *Santa Fe* (2000) cases. However, in the *Capitol Square* case (1995), the Court allowed the erection of a cross in a public square that was traditionally open to displays by all kinds of groups.

As early as the *Witters* case (1986), the majority showed itself cautiously accepting of public aid to religious schools, a trend that continued in the *Zobrest* (1993), *Agostini* (1997), and *Mitchell* (2000) decisions, *Agostini* in effect overturning the findings of *Aguilar* twelve years before.

In *Mitchell* the principal debate was between two sides of the accommodationist majority, with O'Connor finding that there was no proof that Catholic schools misused public aid, while Scalia and Thomas insisted that the issue of possible misuse was itself improper and unnecessary. In the *Zelman* decision (2002), the Court took a major step toward an accommodationist position relative to religious schools, when it approved a "voucher" progam.

During the Rehnquist era the Court's decisions, often made on a 5-4 basis, revealed the uncertainty of its understanding of the Establishment Clause. As with free exercise, the future understanding of establishment seemed to depend almost entirely on the kind of justices who might subsequently be appointed to the Court.

NOTES

Notes to Chapter One

1. Full title *Terrett and Others v. Taylor and Others* (9 *Cranch* 42).
2. Ibid., at 42–45.
3. Ibid., at 46–53.
4. *Town of Pawlet v. Daniel Clark and Others* (9 *Cranch* 291).
5. Ibid., at 292, 306, 308.
6. Ibid., at 293–98.
7. Ibid., at 297.
8. Ibid., at 300–12.
9. Ibid., at 318–20.
10. Ibid., at 321–23.
11. Ibid., at 323–24.
12. Ibid., at 323–26.
13. Ibid., at 332–34.
14. Ibid., at 334.
15. Ibid., at 337.
16. *Society for the Propagation of the Gospel in Foreign Parts v. Town of New Haven and William Wheeler* (8 *Wheaton* 465).
17. Ibid., at 475. The Statute of Mortmain (1279) forbade alienation of land to religious bodies without royal permission. The name "mortmain," meaning "dead hand," referred to property held by an impersonal and enduring institution (Sandra Raban, *Mortmain Legislation and the English Church, 1279–1500* [New York, 1982]).
18. 8 *Wheaton* 465, at 480–89.
19. *John Mason, Appellant, v. John Muncaster, Survivior of George Deneale and John Muncaster, Church-Wardens of Christ's Church, Fairfax Parish, Alexandria, and Said John Muncaster and Edmund J. Lee, Present Church-Wardens of the Said Church, and Other Respondents* (9 *Wheaton* 445).
20. Ibid., at 445–49.
21. Ibid., at 456–67.
22. *Missionary Society v. Dalles* (107 *US* 336). Two related cases were decided at the same time—*Missionary Society v. Kelly* and *Missionary Society v. Wait*.
23. *Catholic Bishop of Nesqually v. Gibbon* (158 *US* 155).
24. *Municipality of Ponce v. Roman Catholic Apostolic Church in Puerto Rico* (210 *US* 296), at 319–23.
25. *The Trustees of the Philadelphia Baptist Association et al. v. Hart's Executors* (4 *Wheaton* 1).
26. *Stanley v. Colt* (5 *Wall* 119).
27. *Christian Union v. Yount* (101 *US* 352).
28. *Gilmer v. Stone* (120 *US* 586).
29. Ibid., at 588–89.

30. Ibid., at 591–93.

31. *Kain v. Gibborey* (101 *US* 362).

32. Ibid., at 364–65.

33. Ibid., at 365.

34. Ibid., at 365–67.

35. *John G. Goesele and Others, Appellants, v. John M. Bimeler and Others* (14 *Howard* 589).

36. Ibid., at 605–609.

37. Karl J. R. Arndt, *George Rapp's Years of Glory: Economy on the Ohio, 1834–1847* (New York, 1987); *George Rapp's Harmony Society, 1785–1847* (Rutherford, N.J., 1972); *George Rapp's Successors and Material Heirs* (Rutherford, N.J., 1971); *The Harmony Society of Economy, Penn'a, Founded by George Rapp,* A.D. *1805* (New York, 1971).

38. *Romelius L. Baker and Jacob Henrici, Trustees of the Harmony Society of Beaver County, Pennsylvania, and Others, Appellants, v. Joshua Nachtrieb* (19 *Howard* 126).

39. *Speidel v. Henrici* (120 *US* 377).

40. Ibid., at 385–90.

41. *Schwartz v. Duss* (18 *US* 8).

42. Ibid., at 21–26.

43. Ibid., at 28–34.

44. Ibid., at 35–38.

45. Ibid., at 39–40.

46. *Order of St. Benedict of New Jersey v. Steinhauser, Individually and As Administrator of Wirth* (239 *US* 640).

47. Ibid., at 644–51.

48. *William S. Smith and Others v. Leroy Swormstedt and Others* (19 *Howard* 283).

49. Ibid., at 288–97.

50. Ibid., at 302–308.

51. *Insurance Company v. Chase* (5 *Wall.* 509).

52. Ibid., at 509–10.

53. Ibid., at 511–12.

54. Ibid., at 514–16.

55. *Attorney General v. Federal Street Meeting House* (1 *Black* 262).

56. 13 *Wall.* 679. For the background of the case see Charles Fairman, *Reconstruction and Reunion, 1864–88* (New York, 1971), I, 895–918.

57. 13 *Wall.* 679, at 713–27.

58. Ibid., at 728.

59. Ibid., at 735.

60. Ibid., at 733.

61. *Boudin v. Alexander* (82 *US* 131).

62. *Helm v. Zarecour* (222 *US* 32).

63. *Sharpe v. Bonham* (224 *US* 241).

64. *Shephard et al. v. Barkley, Moderator of the General Assembly and Chairman of the Executive Commission of the General Assembly of the Presbyterian Church in the U.S.A. et al.* (247 *US* 1).

65. *Santos v. Holy Roman Catholic and Apostolic Church, Parish of Tamboborg* (216 US 463).

66. *Gonzalez v. Roman Catholic Archbishop of Manila* (280 US 1).

67. Ibid., at 15–19.

68. *Kedroff v. St. Nicholas Cathedral* (344 US 94). For the background of the case, see Philip Kurland, *Religion and the Law of Church and State and the Supreme Court* (Chicago, 1962), 91–92.

69. 344 *US* 94, at 95–121.

70. Ibid., at 121–25.

71. Ibid., at 127–31.

72. *Kreskik et al. v. St. Nicholas Cathedral of the Russian Orthodox Church in North America* (363 US 190 [1960]).

73. *Presbyterian Church in the US v. Mary Elizabeth Blue Hull Memorial Presbyterian Church* (393 US 440).

74. *Maryland and Virginia Eldership of the Churches of God, et al. v. Church of God at Sharpsburg, Inc., et al.* (396 US 367).

75. *Serbian Eastern Orthodox Diocese of the US and Canada v. Milivojevich* (426 US 696).

76. Ibid., at 698.

77. Ibid., at 699–708.

78. Ibid., at 708–24.

79. Ibid., at 725.

80. Ibid., at 726–27.

81. Ibid., at 728–35.

82. *Jones v. Wolff* (443 US 595).

83. Ibid., at 596–606.

84. Ibid., at 607–10.

85. Ibid., at 610–21.

86. *General Council on Finance and Administration, United Methodist Church v. California Superior Court, San Diego County (Baker et al., Real Parties in Interest)* (439 US 1369).

87. Ibid., at 1369–70.

88. Ibid., at 1372. Individual justices are designated as "circuit justices" with responsibility for particular districts of the United States. Among other things, they rule on motions that are claimed to be emergencies and decide whether such motions require immediate action by the Supreme Court.

NOTES TO CHAPTER TWO

1. 4 *Wheaton* 518.

2. Francis N. Stites, *Private Interest and Public Gain: The Dartmouth College Case, 1819* (Amherst, Mass., 1972), 12–22; Maurice G. Baxter, *Daniel Webster and the Supreme Court* (Amherst, Mass., 1966), 67–108. Webster, Dartmouth's most celebrated alumnus, pleaded the case of the ousted trustees before the Court. For a general account of the case, see Charles Haines, *The Role of the Supreme Court in American Government and Politics* (Berkeley, Calif., 1944) I, 379–419.

3. Stites, *Private*, 12, 18; Lynn W. Turner, *William Plumer of New Hampshire, 1759–1850* (Williamsburg, Va., 1962), 234–35.

4. Stites, *Private*, 23–38; Baxter, *Webster*, 69–72.

5. Turner, *Plumer*, 6–10, 72, 339; Morton Borden, *Jews, Turks, and Infidels* (Chapel Hill, N.C., 1984), 32–36.

6. Turner, *Plumer*, 234–35, 302.

7. Ibid., 302–303.

8. 4 *Wheaton* 518, at 519–630.

9. Ibid., at 631, 634.

10. Ibid., at 666–713.

11. Ibid., at 664.

12. Ibid., at 713.

13. *Charles A. Beatty and John T. Ritchie, Appellants, v. Daniel Kurtz and Others, Trustees of the German Lutheran Church of Georgetown, Appellees* (2 *Peters* 566).

14. Ibid., 567–71.

15. Ibid., 581–83.

16. Ibid., 584.

17. Ibid.

18. Full title *Samuel A. Worcester, Plaintiff in Error, v. State of Georgia* (6 *Peters* 515).

19. For accounts of the case, see William G. McLoughlin, *Cherokees and Missionaries, 1789–1839* (New Haven, Conn., 1984), 241–64, and R. Pierce Beaver, *Church, State, and the American Indian* (St. Louis, 1966), 97–113.

20. Full title *Bernard Permoli, Plaintiff in Error, v. Municipality No. 1 of the City of New Orleans, Defendant in Error* (3 *Howard* 589).

21. Michael S. Ariens and Robert A. Destro (eds.), *Religious Liberty in a Pluralistic Society* (Durham, N.C., 1996), 143–44.

22. 3 *Howard* 589, at 591–97.

23. Ibid., at 601–606.

24. Ibid., at 609–10.

25. 14 *Wall* 277.

26. Ibid., at 283.

27. Ibid., at 284–87. The Constitution (Article I, Section 9), without defining them, specified that "No bill of attainder or ex post facto law shall be passed."

28. Ibid., at 293–95.

29. Ibid., at 303–304.

30. Ibid., at 296–302.

31. Ibid., at 303.

32. Ibid., at 305–306.

33. Ibid., at 307–12.

34. Ibid., at 313.

35. Ibid., at 316–18.

36. Ibid., at 318–28.

37. Ibid., at 382–90. The dissent was published in connection with a companion case, *Ex Parte Garland*, which did not involve a religious issue.

38. Ibid., at 310–13.

39. Ibid., at 392, 397.

40. Ibid., at 398.

41. 98 *US* 145.

42. Richard S. Van Wagoner, *Mormon Polygamy* (Salt Lake City, 1982), 111; B. Carmon Hardy, *Solemn Covenant: The Mormon Polygamous Passage* (Urbana, Ill., 1992), 44; Edwin Brown Firmage and Richard Collin Mangrum, *Zion in the Courts: A Legal History of the Church of Jesus Christ of Latter Day Saints, 1830–1900* (Urbana, Ill., 1988), 128–59; Sarah Barringer Gordon, *The Mormon Question* (Chapel Hill, N.C., 2002), 111–43; Bruce A. Van Orden, *Prisoner for Conscience: The Life of George Reynolds* (Salt Lake City, 1992).

43. 90 *US* 145, at 164–67.

44. *The Late Corporation of the Church of Jesus Christ of Latter Day Saints v. the United States* (136 *US* 1). See Firmage, *Zion*, 161–97, 253–58; Gordon, *Mormon Question*, 180–220.

45. 136 *US* 1, at 48.

46. Ibid., at 50, 51. Suttee (*sati*) was a practice in India whereby a widow was required to throw herself alive, on her husband's funeral pyre, to be consumed by the flames. It was suppressed by the British during the nineteenth century (John Stratton Hawley [ed.], *Sati, the Blessing and the Curse* [New York, 1994]).

47. 136 *US* 1, at 66.

48. *Davis v. Beeson* (133 *US* 333).

49. Ibid., at 342–48.

50. *Young v. Godbe* (82 *US* 562).

51. Gordon, *Mormon Question*, 26, 70, 81.

52. *Miles v. US* (103 *US* 304).

53. Ibid., at 310–11.

54. Gordon, *Mormon Question*, 83, 156–60.

55. 103 *US* 304, at 313.

56. Gordon, *Mormon Question*, 115.

57. 103 *US*, 304 at 315–16.

58. *Murphy v. Ramsey and Others* (114 *US* 15). Also on appeal were: *Pratt v. Ramsey; Randall v. Ramsey; Clawson v. Ramsey;* and *Barlow v. Ramsey.* See also *Clawson v. US* (114 *US* 477).

59. 114 *US* 15, at 37–44, 47.

60. Ibid., at 45.

61. *Cannon v. US* (116 *US* 55).

62. *In Re Snow* (120 *US* 274).

63. *Hans Neilsen, Petitioner* (131 *US* 176).

64. *Barrett v. US* (137 *US* 496).

65. Hardy, *Solemn Covenant*, 127–66; Van Wagoner, *Mormon Polygamy*, 139–44; Edward L. Lyman, *Political Deliverance: The Mormon Quest for Statehood* (Urbana, Ill. 1994); Firmage, *Zion*, 365–70; Gordon, *Mormon Question*, 220.

66. 143 *US* 457.

67. Ibid., at 465–72.

68. *Maxwell v. Dow* (176 *US* 581).

69. Ibid., at 587.

70. Ibid., at 615–16.

71. *Berea College v. Commonwealth of Kentucky* (211 US 45) (1908).

72. Ibid., at 47–49. The case cited was *Lochner v. People of New York* (198 US 45).

73. 211 US 45, at 54.

74. Ibid., at 67–68.

75. Ibid., at 61–62.

76. Ibid., at 70.

77. 262 US 390. For the background of the case, see Orville H. Zabel, *God and Caesar in Nebraska: A Study of the Legal Relationship of Church and State, 1854–1954* (Lincoln, Nebr., 1955), 145–48, and William G. Ross, *Forging New Freedoms: Nativism, Education, and the Constitution, 1917–1927* (Lincoln, Nebr., 1994), 30–133.

78. *Bartels v. State of Iowa; Bohring v. State of Ohio; Pohl v. State of Ohio; Nebraska District of of the Evangelical Lutheran Synod of Missouri, Ohio, and Other States, et al., v. McKelvie et al.* (All 262 US 404). Bartels taught in a Lutheran school, Bohring and Pohl in a Congregationalist school.

79. Ross, *Forging*, 89–93.

80. 262 US 390, at 412–13.

81. Full title *Pierce v. Society of Sisters of the Holy Names of Jesus and Mary* (268 US 510). For the background of the case, see Ross, *Forging*, 148–73, and David B. Tyack, *Law and the Shaping of Public Education, 1785–1954* (Madison, Wis., 1987), 177–92.

82. 268 US 510, at 535.

83. *U.S. v. Schwimmer* (1929) (279 US 644.)

84. *U.S. v. MacIntosh* (1931) (283 US 605).

85. *US v. Bland* (283 US 442).

86. *Hamilton v. Regents of the University of California* (1934) (293 US 245).

87. 279 US 644, at 646–55.

88. 283 US 605, at 621–25.

89. Ibid., at 630–33.

90. 283 US 442.

91. 293 US 245, at 263–64.

92. Ibid., at 265.

93. Ibid., at 266–68.

NOTES TO CHAPTER THREE

1. Full title *Francois Fenelon Vidal, John F. Girard et al., . . . and Henry Stump v. the Mayor, Aldermen, and Citizens of Philadelphia, the Executors of Stephen Girard et al.* (2 Howard 125). For the background of the case, see Wilfred B. Wolcott, *Background of the Educational Provisions of the Will of Stephen Girard* (Philadelphia, 1949).

2. 2 *Howard* 125, at 141, 144, 151.

3. Ibid., at 154, 167.

4. Ibid., at 172, 174. Webster's speech is in *The Writings and Speeches of Daniel Webster*, ed. Charles M. Wiltse (Hanover, N.H., 1987), XI, 137–82.

5. *2 Howard* 125, 144–46, 155–56.

6. Ibid., 176.

7. Ibid., 197–98.

8. *Robertson v. Baldwin* (125 *US* 275, at 281.) The decision was written by Justice Horace Brown.

9. Baxter, *Webster*, 168.

10. 143 *US* 457, at 465, 471.

11. *9 Cranch* 43.

12. *William R. Hallett and Robert L. Walker, Executors of Joshua Kennedy, Deceased, John G. Aiken and Clarissa His Wife, John H. Hastie, and His Wife Secluda, Augustus R. Meslier and His Wife Mary Augusta Kennedy, Joshua Kennedy, James Inerarity, Samuel Kitchen, William Kitchen, James Campbell, and the Branch Bank of the State of Alabama at Mobile, Appellants, v. Sidney E. Collins* (51 *How.* 174).

13. Ibid., at 180–82.

14. For the background of the case, see Elizabeth Urban Alexander, *Notorious Woman: The Celebrated Case of Myra Clark Gaines* (Baton Rouge, La., 2002). Gaines's dispute was the issue in sixteen cases brought before the Court between 1837 and 1891.

15. *Patterson v. Gaines* (6 *Howard* 550).

16. *Myra Clark Gaines v. Richard Relf and Beverly New, Executors, et al.* (12 *Howard* 472).

17. *Myra Clark Gaines, Appellant, v. Duncan N. Herren* (24 *Howard* 553).

18. Ibid., at 580–81, 587.

19. Ibid., at 582–87.

20. *The Rector, Church Wardens, and Vestrymen of Christ Church, in the City of Philadelphia, in Trust for Christ Church Hospital, Plaintiffs in Error, in the County of Philadelphia* (24 *How.* 300).

21. *Gibbons v. District of Columbia* (116 *US* 404).

22. *Chicago Theological Seminary v. Illinois* (186 *US* 662).

23. Ibid., at 674.

24. Ibid., at 678–80.

25. *Montana Catholic Mission v. Missoula County* (200 *US* 118).

26. Ibid., at 120–21.

27. Ibid., at 122–25.

28. Ibid., at 126–29.

29. *Board of Education of the Kentucky Annual Conference of the Methodist Episcopal Church v. Illinois* (203 *US* 553).

30. *Charles Richardson and Others, Claimants of the Barque Tangier, Appellants, v. Daniel Goddard and Others* (24 *How.* 28).

31. Ibid., at 30–37.

32. Ibid., at 39–44.

33. *The Philadelphia, Wilmington, and Baltimore Railroad Company, Appellants, v. the Philadelphia and Havre de Grace Steam Towboat Co.* (24 *How.* 209).

34. Ibid., at 218–19.

35. *Bucher v. Cheshire Railroad Company* (125 *US* 275).
36. Ibid., at 577–81.
37. Ibid., at 585.
38. *Soon Hing v. Crowley* (113 *US* 703).
39. Ibid., at 710–11.
40. *Hennington v. Georgia* (163 *US* 299).
41. Ibid., at 304–307.
42. Ibid., at 318.
43. *Stone v. US* (167 *US* 178). Harlan wrote the decision.
44. *Petit v. Minnesota* (177 *US* 164).
45. 175 *US* 290.
46. Ibid., at 297–98.
47. *Speer v. Colbert* (200 *US* 130).
48. Ibid., at 135–39, 141.
49. Ibid., at 142–47.
50. *Colbert v. Speer, Mosher v. Whitney, Speer v. Whitney* (24 *App. D.C.* 187).
51. 200 *US* 130, at 147.
52. Ibid., at 142.
53. *Reuben Quick Bear v. Leupp, Commissioner of Indian Affairs* (210 *US* 50.) For the background of the case, see Paul F. Prucha, *The Churches and the Indian Schools, 1888–1912* (Lincoln, Nebr., 1979), 88–116.
54. 210 *US* 50, at 80–82.
55. *Lowrey v. Hawaii* (206 *US* 206).
56. Ibid., at 206.
57. Ibid., at 206, 217.
58. Ibid., at 219–24.
59. *Lowrey v. Territory of Hawaii* (215 *US* 554).
60. Ibid., at 564–80.
61. *Selective Draft Law Cases* (245 *US* 366), at 389–90.
62. 283 *US* 605, at 624.
63. *Hygrade Provision Company, Inc., et al., v. Sherman, As Attorney General of the State of New York, et al.* (266 *US* 497). Decided at the same time were *Lewis and Fox Company v. Sherman, As Attorney General of the State of New York* and *Satz v. Sherman, Attorney General of the State of New York.*
64. Ibid., at 501–503.
65. *Cochran v. Louisiana State Board of Education* (281 *US* 370).
66. Ibid., at 373.
67. Ibid., at 374.
68. Ibid., at 374–75.

Notes to Chapter Four

1. 301 *US* 144, at 153.
2. Anthony A. Hoekema, *Jehovah's Witnesses* (Grand Rapids, Mich., 1963); Herbert Hewitt Stroup, *The Jehovah's Witnesses* (New York, 1945).

3. David Manwaring, *Render to Caesar: The Flag Salute Controversy* (Chicago, 1962); Michael Kent Curtis (ed.), *The Flag Salute Cases* (New York, 1998); Shawn F. Peters, *Judging Jehovah's Witnesses: Religious Persecution and the Dawn of the Rights Revolution* (Lawrence, Kans., 2000), 1–8.

4. *Minersville School District v. Gobitis* (1940) (310 US 586). Apparently the family name was "Gobitas" but was consistently misspelled in official documents (Richard Danzig in Curtis, *Constitution and Flag*, 242; Peters, *Judging*, 19). For the background of the case, see Peters, 19–28, 36–71.

5. 310 US 586, at 595–98.

6. Ibid., at 597–600.

7. Ibid., at 594.

8. Schwartz, *Main Currents*, 501.

9. 30 US 586, at 602–606.

10. 319 US 624.

11. Ibid., at 630–35.

12. Ibid., at 635–42.

13. Ibid., at 643–44.

14. Ibid., at 645–46.

15. Ibid., at 647–70.

16. Ibid., at 642–43.

17. *Taylor v. Mississippi* (319 US 583). Decided at the same time were *Benoit v. Mississippi* and *Cummings v. Mississippi*. For the background of the *Taylor* case, see Peters, *Judging*, 189–98.

18. *Lovell v. City of Griffin* (303 US 444).

19. *Schneider v. State (Town of Irvington)* (308 US 147). Heard at the same time were three similar cases, all involving solicitation for secular purposes. The decision was unanimous except for Justice McReynolds, who did not write a dissenting opinion.

20. *Cantwell v. Connecticut* (310 US 296). For the background of the case, see Peters, *Judging*, 178–86.

21. 310 US 296, at 303–11.

22. *Cox v. New Hampshire* (312 US 569).

23. *Jones v. Opeleika, Bowden v. Fort Smith, Jobin v. Arizona* (316 US 584). For the background of the case, see Merlin O. Newton, *Armed with the Constitution: Jehovah's Witnesses in Alabama and the U.S. Supreme Court* (Tuscaloosa, Ala., 1995) and Peters, *Judging*, 230–36.

24. 310 US 584, at 593–600.

25. Ibid., at 600–11.

26. Ibid., at 612–23.

27. Ibid., at 623–24.

28. *Largent v. Texas* (318 US 418). See also *Busey et al. v. District of Columbia* (319 US 579).

29. *Hussock v. New York* (312 US 359); *Leiby v. Manchester* (313 US 562); *Bevins v. Prindable* (314 US 573); *Trent v. Hunt* (314 US 573); *Hannan v. City of Haverhill* (314 US 641); *Pascoe v. Massachusetts* (314 US 641).

30. *Martin v. City of Struthers* (319 US 141).

31. *Murdock v. Pennsylvania* (319 US 105).

32. Ibid., at 108–16.

33. Ibid., at 118–33.

34. Ibid., at 134–40.

35. *Follett v. Town of McCormick* (321 US 573).

36. Ibid., at 576–77.

37. Ibid., at 579–81.

38. Ibid., at 581–83.

39. Ibid., at 579.

40. *Jamison v. Texas* (318 US 413).

41. *Douglas et al. v. City of Jeannette et al.* (319 US 157).

42. Ibid., at 164–66.

43. Ibid., at 166–82.

44. *Prince v. Massachussets* (321 US 158). For the background of the case, see Peters, *Judging*, 198–201.

45. 321 US 158, at 165–71.

46. Ibid., at 172–76.

47. Ibid., at 176–78.

48. *Chaplinksy v. New Hampshire* (315 US 568). For the background of the case, arguing strenuously that the decision was an injustice, see Peters, *Judging*, 203–39.

49. *Tucker v. Texas* (1945) (326 US 517).

50. *Marsh v. Alabama* (326 US 501). See Newton, *Armed*, and Peters, *Judging*, 285–90.

51. 326 US 501, at at 505–508.

52. Ibid., At 510.

53. Ibid., at 512–16.

54. *Saia v. New York* (334 US 558).

55. Ibid., at 560–62.

56. Ibid., at 563.

57. Ibid., at 566–67.

58. Ibid., at 569–70.

59. Ibid., at 570.

60. *Niemotko v. Maryland* (340 US 268).

61. *Fowler v. Rhode Island* (345 US 67).

62. Ibid., at 271–73.

63. Ibid., at 274–88.

64. *Kunz v. New York* (340 US 290).

65. Ibid., at 293–94.

66. Ibid., at 295–314. He referred to *McCollum v. Board of Education* (333 US 203 [1948]). See chapter 6.

67. *Poulos v. New Hampshire* (345 US 395).

68. Ibid., at 405–14.

69. Ibid., at 414–18.

70. Ibid., at 421–22.

71. Ibid., at 423.

72. Ibid., at 423–26.

73. *Watchtower Bible and Tract Society of New York, Inc., et al., Petitioners, v. Village of Stratton, et al.* (536 US 150).

74. Ibid., at 161–69.

75. Ibid., at 171.

76. Ibid., at 172–80.

77. Mulford Q. Sibley and Philip E. Jacob, *The American State and the Conscientious Objectors, 1940–1947* (Ithaca, N.Y., 1952); Julian Cornell, *The Conscientious Objector and the Law* (New York, 1943). The writ of habeas corpus ("if you have the body . . .") is an order by a court directing an individual, often a government official, to answer the claim that he is detaining someone unlawfully.

78. *Falbo v. US* (320 US 549).

79. Ibid., at 554.

80. Ibid., at 555.

81. Ibid., at 556–57.

82. Ibid., at 557–58.

83. Ibid., at 560.

84. Ibid., at 561.

85. *Estep v. US* and *Smith v. US* (327 US 114).

86. Ibid., at 120–25.

87. Ibid., at 125–29.

88. Ibid., at 129–30.

89. Ibid., at 131–32.

90. Ibid., at 133.

91. Ibid., at 134–42.

92. Ibid., at 144–45.

93. Ibid., at 145.

94. *Gibson v. US* and *Dodey v. US* (329 US 338).

95. Ibid., at 345–51.

96. Ibid., at 357–61.

97. *Cox v. US, Thompson v. US, Roisum v. US* (332 US 442).

98. Ibid., at 448–52.

99. Ibid., at 455–56.

100. Ibid., at 457–59.

101. *In Re Summers* (325 US 561) (1944). The phrase "In Re" ("in the matter of") was used because the Illinois Supreme Court treated the issue not as a formal law suit but as an administrative matter having to do with the licensing of attorneys as "officers of the court."

102. Ibid., at 570–73.

103. Ibid., at 574–75.

104. Ibid., at 293.

105. Ibid., at 576–77.

106. *Girouard v. US* (1946) (328 US 61).

107. *Eagles, Post Commanding Officer, v. US ex Rel. Samuels* (329 US 304). The term "ex rel" means "ex relatione," or "as related (told) by . . ." It was used here because the government was conducting a process of *habeas corpus* based on Samuels's claim, which named the army-base commander as detaining the appellant unlawfully.

108. Ibid., at 312–14.
109. Ibid., at 315–17.
110. *Eagles, Post Commanding Officer, v. US ex Rel. Horowitz* (329 US 317).
111. *Dickinson v. US* (346 US 389).
112. Ibid., at 395–98.
113. Ibid., at 398–400.
114. *US v. Nugent* and *US v. Packer* (346 US 1).
115. *Witmer v. US* (348 US 375).
116. *Summers v. US* (348 US 397).
117. *Gonzales v. US* (348 US 407).
118. Ibid., at 413–18.
119. *Sicurella v. US* (748 US 385).

NOTES TO CHAPTER FIVE

1. 322 *US* 78. For the I Am Movement, see *The Encyclopedia of American Religions*, ed. J. Gordon Melton (Tarrytown, N.Y., 1991), III, 90.
2. 322 *US* 28, at 82.
3. Ibid., at 81–82.
4. Ibid., at 84–87.
5. Ibid., at 92.
6. Ibid., at 89–91.
7. Ibid., at 192–95.
8. *Ballard et al. v. US* (329 US 187).
9. Ibid., at 193–95.
10. Ibid., at 196.
11. Ibid., at 197–202.
12. Ibid., at 203–207.
13. *Chatwin v. US* (326 US 455).
14. Ibid., at 459–62.
15. *Cleveland v. US* (1946) (329 US 14).
16. Van Wagoner, *Mormon Polygamy*, 196–97.
17. 329 *US* 14, at 18–23.
18. *Wisconsin v. Yoder* (406 US 205), at 247.
19. 329 *US* 14, at 25–29.
20. *Messer at al. v. Utah* (333 US 95).
21. Ibid., at 97–98.
22. Ibid., at 99–103.
23. 367 *US* 488.
24. 380 *US* 163.
25. *US v. Jakobsen.*
26. *Pewter v. US.*
27. 380 *US* 163, at 184.
28. Ibid., at 184–85.
29. Ibid., at 188–93.

30. *Oestereich v. Selective Service System Local Board No. 11, Cheyenne, Wyo., et al.* (393 US 233).

31. Ibid., at 237–49.

32. 398 US 333.

33. Ibid., at 341–44.

34. Ibid., at 345–67. In deliberations prior to the *Seeger* decision, Harlan argued that Congress had in effect violated the Constitution in its formulation of the conscientious-objector provision (Del Dickson [ed.], *The Supreme Court in Conference* [New York, 2001], 435).

35. 398 US 333, at 367–69.

36. Ibid., at 369–74.

37. *Mulloy v. US* (398 US 410).

38. *Ehlert v. US* (402 US 99).

39. Ibid., at 106–108.

40. Ibid., at 108–11.

41. *Clay, AKA Ali, v. US* (403 US 697). One of Ali's attorneys was Hayden Covington, a Jehovah's Witness who had been the Witnesses's principal attorney during their seminal cases of the 1940s (Peters, *Judging*, 296.)

42. 403 US 697, at 703–704. "Per curiam" ("through the Court") is a phrase used when the issue seems so obvious to most of the justices that they do not find it necessary to present sustained opinions. The decision is then issued in the name of the Court collectively.

43. *Gillette v. US* (401 US 437) (1971).

44. Ibid., at 463–69.

45. *Negre v. Larsen*, at Ibid.

46. 401 US 437, at 470–75.

47. *Johnson, Administrator of Veterans' Affairs, et al v. Robinson* (415 US 369).

48. Ibid., at 369–85.

49. Ibid., at 386–90.

50. *Hernandez et al. v. Veterans' Administration et al.* (415 US 391).

51. 374 US 398.

52. Ibid., at 403–13.

53. Ibid., at 413–18.

54. Ibid., at 418–19.

55. 374 US 398, at 418–23.

56. *Trans World Airlines v. Hardison* and *International Association of Machinist v. Hardison* (432 US 63).

57. Ibid., at 76–85.

58. Ibid., at 85–97.

59. *Pacific Union, Conference of Seventh-Day Adventists, et al. v. Marshall et al.* (434 US 1305), at 1305–1306.

60. Ibid., at 1306–1309.

61. *Thomas v. Review Board* (450 US 707).

62. Ibid., at 718–19.

63. Ibid., at 721–27.

64. *Estate of Thornton et al. v. Caldor Inc.* (472 US 703).

65. *Tony and Susan Alamo Foundation et al. v. Secretary of Labor* (471 US 290).

66. *Ohio Civil Rights Commission v. Dayton Christian School* (477 US 619), at 629.

67. *Ansonia Board of Education et al. v. Philbrook et al.* (479 US 60).

68. Ibid., at 66, 70.

69. Ibid., at 68–71.

70. *Ibid.*, at 72–75.

71. Ibid., at 76.

72. Ibid., at 77–81.

73. *Church of Jesus Christ of Latter Day Saints v. Amos* (483 US 327).

74. Ibid., at 335–39.

75. *Hobbie v. Unemployment Appeals Commission of Florida* (480 US 136).

76. *Frazee v. Illinois Board of Employment Security* (489 US 829).

77. *Equal Economic Opportunity Commission v. Arabian American Oil Co., et al.* (499 US 244), at 247.

78. Ibid., at 248–53.

79. Ibid., at 261–66.

80. *Walker at al. v. City of Birmingham* (388 US 307).

81. Ibid., at 316–18.

82. Ibid., at 324–27.

83. Ibid., at 338–41, 349.

84. *Shuttlesworth v. City of Birmingham* (394 US 147).

85. 406 US 205.

86. Ibid., at 210–36.

87. Ibid., at 237.

88. Ibid., at 238–41.

89. Ibid., at 241–48.

90. *Wooley, Chief of Police of Lebanon, et al., v. Maynard* (430 US 705).

91. Ibid., at 714–16.

92. Ibid., at 718.

93. Ibid., at 720–22.

94. *Heffron v. International Society of Krishna Consciousness* (452 US 640). For an account of the movement, see J. Stillson Judah, *Hare Krishna and the Counter-Culture* (New York, 1974).

95. 452 US 640, at 650–56.

96. Ibid., at 656–63.

97. *Goldman v. Weinberger* (475 US 503).

98. Ibid., at 509–10.

99. Ibid., at 511–12.

100. Ibid., at 516–24.

101. Ibid., at 526–27.

102. Ibid., at 526–33.

103. *Bowen v. Roy* (476 US 693).

104. Ibid., at 699–712.

105. Ibid., at 713–15.

106. Ibid., at 717–23.

107. Ibid., at 726–32.

108. *Board of Airport Commissioners of the City of Los Angeles et al. v. Jews for Jesus, Inc., et al.* (482 US 569).

109. Full title *Employment Division, Dept. of Human Resources of Oregon, v. Smith* (494 US 872). For the background of the case, see Carolyn N. Long, *Religious Freedom and Indian Rights: The Case of Oregon v. Smith* (Lawrence, Kans., 2000), and Garrett Epps, *To an Unknown God: Religious Freedom on Trial* (New York, 2001).

110. 494 US 474 at 878–88.

111. Ibid., at 893–95.

112. Ibid., at 907–20.

113. *Church of Lukumi Babalu Aye, Inc., and Ernesto Pichardo v. City of Hialeah* (508 US 520).

114. Ibid., at 533–47.

115. Dick J. Reavis, *The Flames of Waco* (New York, 1995).

116. *Jaime Castillo, et al., Petitioners, v. US.* (530 US 120).

117. *Cruz v. Beto, Corrections Director* (405 US 319).

118. Ibid., at 323.

119. Ibid., at 324–26.

120. *O'Lone v. Estate of Shabbaz* (482 US 342).

121. Ibid., at 351–52.

122. Ibid., at 356–58.

123. *National Labor Relations Board v. Bishop of Chicago* (440 US 490).

124. Ibid., at 495–507.

125. Ibid., at 509–18.

126. *Widmar v. Vincent* (454 US 263).

127. Ibid., at 265–76. Stevens applied the so-called Lemon Test, based on the majority opinion in *Lemon v. Kurtzman* (1971) (chapter 7).

128. 454 US 263, at 277–81.

129. Ibid., at 282–84.

130. Ibid., at 284–89.

131. *Bender v. Williamsport Area School District* (475 US 534).

132. Ibid., at 543–49.

133. Ibid., at 549–50.

134. Ibid., at 551–54.

135. Ibid., at 554–56.

136. 496 US 226. Full Title *Board of Education of the Westport Community Schools (District 66) et al. v. Mergens by and through Their Next Friends, Mergens et al.* The term "next friends" is used in cases where the plaintiffs are not of legal age or are otherwise defined as incompetent to pursue litigation on their own behalf. For the background of the case, see Kenneth W. Starr, *First among Equals: The Supreme Court in American Life* (New York, 2002), 89, 102–103.

137. 496 US 226, at 239–53.

138. Ibid., at 261.

139. Ibid., at 263–70.

140. Ibid., at 271–89.

141. *Lamb's Chapel and John Steigenwald v. Center Moriches Union Free School District et al.* (508 US 384).

142. Full title *Rosenberger v. Rector and Visitors of the University of Virginia et al.* (515 US 819).

143. Ibid., at 822–45.

144. Ibid., at 846–52.

145. Ibid., at 852–63.

146. Ibid., at 863–99.

147. *Good News Club, et al., v. Milford Central School* (533 US 98).

148. Ibid., at 107–20.

149. Ibid., at 120–24.

150. Ibid., at 129.

151. Ibid., at 131–33.

152. Ibid., at 138–43.

153. *First Unitarian Church of Los Angeles v. County of Los Angeles et al.* (357 US 545).

154. Ibid., at 547.

155. Ibid., at 548.

156. Ibid., at 548.

157. *US v. Christian Echoes National Ministry, Inc.* (404 US 561).

158. *US v. American Friends Service Committee et al.* (419 US 7).

159. Ibid., at 13–16.

160. *St. Martin's Evangelical Lutheran Church et al. v. South Dakota* (451 US 772).

161. *California et al. v. Grace Brethren Church et al.* (457 US 393).

162. Ibid., at 405–13.

163. Ibid., at 415–17.

164. Ibid., at 420.

165. *US v. Lee* (455 US 252).

166. See David G. Bromley and Anson D. Shupe Jr., *"Moonies" in America* (Beverly Hills, Calif., 1979).

167. *Larsen v. Valente* (456 US 228.)

168. Ibid., at 244–58.

169. Ibid., at 259–63.

170. Ibid., at 264–72.

171. 461 US 574.

172. *Goldsboro Christian Schools Inc. v. US.* (461 US 574).

173. 461 US 574, at 595–605.

174. Ibid., at 606–12.

175. Ibid., at 612–23.

176. For the church's own account of its teachings, see Jack Horner, *Dianology* (Westwood Vilage, Calif., 1970).

177. *Hernandez v. Commissioner of Internal Revenue* and *Graham v. Commisioner of Internal Revenue* (490 US 680), at 684–99.

178. Ibid. at 705–709.

179. *Jimmy Swaggart Ministries v. Board of Equalization of California* (493 US 378).

180. *Davis v. Lee* (110 US 2014).

181. *McDaniel v. Paty* (435 US 618).

182. Ibid., at 626–29.

183. Ibid., at 630–42.

184. Ibid., at 642–43.

185. Ibid., at 643–46.

186. *Lyng, Secretary of Agriculture, et al., v. Northwest Indian Cemetery Protective Association, et al.* (485 US 439).

187. Ibid., at 451–58.

188. Ibid., at 460–75.

189. *Shaare Tefila Congregation et al. v. Cobb et al.* (481 US 615).

190. *United States Catholic Conference et al. v. Abortion Rights Mobilization, Inc., et al.* (487 US 72).

191. Ibid., at 76–80.

192. Ibid., at 80.

193. Washington *Post*, March 13, 1997, B1.

194. Full title *City of Boerne, Petitioner, v. P. F. Flores, Archbishop of San Antonio, and United States* (521 US 507). For the background of the case, see Long, *Religious Freedom*, 253–59, and John T. Noonan Jr., *Narrowing the Nation's Power: The Supreme Court Sides with the States* (Berkeley, Calif., 2002), 15–40.

195. For the background of the R.F.R.A., see Long, *Religious Freedom*, 203–40.

196. 521 US 507, at 513–14.

197. Ibid., at 515.

198. Ibid., at 517–19.

199. Ibid., at 524.

200. Ibid., at 530–32.

201. Ibid., at 534.

202. Ibid., at 535.

203. Ibid., at 535–36.

204. Ibid., at 537.

205. Ibid., at 537–44.

206. Ibid., at 544–45.

207. Ibid., at 546–47.

208. Ibid., at 549–64.

209. Ibid., at 564.

210. Ibid., at 565–66.

211. Ibid., at 566.

212. *Boy Scouts of America and Monmouth Council et al. v. Petitioners and James Dale* (530 US 640).

213. Ibid., at 670–71.

214. *Watchtower Bible and Tract Society* (122 S.Ct. 2080).

NOTES TO CHAPTER SIX

1. Frank Sorauf, The *Wall of Separation* (Minneapolis, 1975); Ivers, *Build a Wall*, 25–26.

2. Full title *Everson v. Board of Education of Ewing Township* (330 US 1). For the background of the case, see Theodore Powell, *The School Bus Law, a Case Study in Education, Religion, and Politics* (Middletown, Conn., 1960), and Jo Renee Formicola and Hubert Morken (eds.), *Everson Revisited: Education and Law at the Crossroads* (Lanham, Md., 1997).

3. 330 *US* l, at 3–18.

4. Ibid., at 18.

5. Ibid., at 19.

6. Ibid., at 20–28.

7. Ibid., at 29–33.

8. Ibid., at 34–46.

9. Ibid., at 58–60.

10. 333 *US* 303. For the sucessful plaintiff's account of the case, see Vashti McCollum, *One Woman's Fight* (Boston, 1961).

11. 330 *US* 203, at 205–12.

12. Ibid., at 212–32.

13. Ibid., at 232–38.

14. Ibid., at 238–52.

15. Ibid., at 253–54.

16. 343 *US* 306.

17. Ibid., at 308–15.

18. Ibid., at 316–20.

19. Ibid., at 319–23.

20. Ibid., at 323–25.

21. For examples, see Manwaring, *Render to Caesar,* 245.

22. *Joseph Burstyn Inc. v. Wilson, Commissioner of Education of New York, et al.* (343 US 495). For the background of the case, see Alan F. Westin, *The Supreme Court and the Movies: The Miracle Case* (Tuscaloosa, Ala., 1961).

23. 343 *US* 495, at 501–505.

24. Ibid., at 519–29.

25. Ibid., at 531–37.

26. 367 *US* 488.

27. 366 *US* 420.

28. Ibid., at 425–30.

29. Ibid., at 431–53.

30. Ibid., at 459–60.

31. Ibid., at 491–98.

32. *Braunfeld v. Braun* (366 US 599).

33. Ibid., at 603–609.

34. Ibid., at 610–15.

35. *Gallagher, Chief of Police of Springfield, Massachusetts, et al. v. Crown Kosher Super Markets of Massachusetts, Inc., et al.* (366 US 617).

36. *Two Guys from Harrison-Allentown Inc. v. McGinley, District Attorney, Lehigh County, Pa., et al.* (366 US 582).

37. *Arlen's Department Store of Louisville, Inc., et al. v. Kentucky* (364 US 218).

38. Ibid., at 219–20.

39. *Estate of Thornton v. Caldor* (472 US 703).

40. 370 US 421.

41. Ibid., at 424–36.

42. Ibid., at 437–39.

43. Ibid., at 439–43.

44. Ibid., at 443–44.

45. Ibid., at 445–50.

46. *Chamberlain et al. v. Dade County Board of Public Instruction et al.* (377 US 402).

47. Ibid., at 402–403.

48. *Sherbert* (374 US 398), at 413–15.

49. *Doremus et al. v. Board of Education of the Borough of Hawthorne et al.* (342 US 429).

50. Ibid., at 432–35.

51. Ibid., at 435.

52. 374 US 203, at 236–37.

53. *Murray v. Curlett* (372 US 901).

54. 374 US 203, at 206–209.

55. See O'Hair, *Freedom under Siege: The Impact of Organized Religion on Your Liberty and Your Pocketbook* (Los Angeles, 1974). Her son later converted to Christianity and became an evangelist. See William Murray, *Let Us Pray, a Plea for Prayer in Our Schools* (New York, 1995) and *My Life without God* (Nashville, 1982).

56. 274 US 203, at 210–11.

57. Ibid., at 213–23.

58. Ibid., at 224–26.

59. Ibid., at 227–30.

60. Ibid., at 230–42.

61. Ibid., at 278–82.

62. Ibid., at 283–94.

63. Ibid., at 294–304.

64. Ibid., at 305–308.

65. Ibid., at 308–309.

66. Ibid., at 309–12.

67. Ibid., at 312–20.

68. *Stone v. Graham* (449 US 39).

69. Ibid., at 40–42.

70. Ibid., at 43–47.

71. Ibid., at 43.

72. 508 US 384, at 397–401.

73. *Wallace v. Jaffree* (472 US 38). For a record of the case, see Robert Sikorski (ed.), *Prayer in the Public Schools and the Constitution, 1961–1992* (New York, 1993), II.

74. 472 US 38, at 48–61.

75. Ibid., at 62–66.

76. Ibid., at 67.

77. Ibid., at 68–70.

78. Ibid., at 71–76.
79. Ibid., at 77–78.
80. Ibid., at 79–82.
81. Ibid., at 83–84.
82. Ibid., at 84–85.
83. Ibid., at 85–90.
84. Ibid., at 90–91.
85. Ibid., at 92–113.
86. *Lee v. Weisman* (505 US 577).
87. Ibid., at 586–90.
88. Ibid., at 591–92.
89. Ibid., at 593–96.
90. Ibid., at 597–98.
91. Ibid., at 599–608.
92. Ibid., at 609–31.
93. Ibid., at 631–38.
94. Ibid., at 639–46.
95. *Santa Fe Independant School District, Petitioners, v. Jane Doe, Individually and As Next Friend for Her Minor Children, John and Jane Doe, et al.* (530 US 290).
96. Ibid., at 294.
97. Ibid., at 296.
98. Ibid., at 301.
99. Ibid., at 306–308.
100. Ibid., at 309.
101. Ibid.
102. Ibid., at 309–10.
103. Ibid., at 318.
104. Ibid., at 318–19.
105. Ibid., at 320.
106. Ibid., at 321.
107. *Epperson v. Arkansas* (393 US 97). For the background of the case, see Marcel C. LaFollette (ed.), *Creationism, Science, and the Law: The Arkansas Case* (Cambridge, Mass., 1983), and Edward J. Larson, *Trial and Error: The American Controversy over Creation and Evolution* (New York, 1985), 98–119.
108. 393 US 97, at 104–109.
109. Ibid., at 109–11.
110. Ibid., at 112–14.
111. Ibid., at 115.
112. Ibid., at 116.
113. *Edwards, Governor of Louisiana, et al., v. Aguillard et al.* (482 US 578). For the background of the case, see Larson, *Trial,* 163–67.
114. 482 US 578, at 583–92.
115. Ibid., at 599–604.
116. Ibid., at 608.
117. Ibid., at 611.
118. Ibid., at 611–15.

119. Ibid., at 619–25.
120. Ibid., at 629–30.
121. Ibid., at 630–34.
122. Ibid., at 640.
123. *Tangipahoa Parish Board of Education v. Herb Freiler, et al.* (530 US 1251).
124. Ibid., at 1251.
125. Ibid., at 1253–54.
126. 463 *US* 783.
127. Ibid., at 787–92.
128. Ibid., at 792.
129. Ibid., at 793–95.
130. Ibid., at 796–97.
131. Ibid., at 797–800.
132. Ibid., at 803–13.
133. Ibid., at 814–17.
134. Ibid., at 818.
135. Ibid., at 823–24.
136. 465 *US* 668. For the background of the case, see Wayne R. Swanson, *The Christ Child Goes to Court* (Philadelphia, 1990).
137. 465 *US* 668, at 672–80.
138. Ibid., at 681–83.
139. Ibid., at 684–87.
140. Ibid., at 687–94.
141. Ibid., at 694–700.
142. Ibid., at 701–704.
143. Ibid., at 705–12.
144. Ibid., at 714.
145. Ibid., at 715–26.
146. Ibid., at 726–27.
147. *County of Allegheny v. American Civil Liberties Union, Greater Pittsburgh Chapter.* Heard at the same time were *Chabod v. American Civil Liberties Union* and *City of Pittsburgh v. American Civil Liberties Union, Greater Pittsburgh Chapter* (492 US 573). See Swanson, *Christ Child.*
148. 492 *US* 573, at 594.
149. Ibid., at 574–90.
150. Ibid., at 598–601.
151. Ibid., at 610–13.
152. Ibid., at 614–17.
153. Ibid., at 626–29.
154. Ibid., at 633–35.
155. Ibid., at 638–45.
156. Ibid., at 650–54.
157. Ibid., at 657–58.
158. Ibid., at 661–66.
159. Ibid., at 667–74.
160. Ibid., at 674–78.

161. Complete title *Capitol Square Review and Advisory Board et al. v. Pinnette et al.* (515 US 756).
162. Ibid., at 757–59.
163. Ibid., at 760.
164. Ibid., at 760.
165. Ibid., at 761.
166. Ibid., at 762–65.
167. Ibid., at 765, 768.
168. Ibid., at 767.
169. Ibid., at 768.
170. Ibid., at 769.
171. Ibid., at 770.
172. Ibid., at 771–72.
173. Ibid., at 772–76.
174. Ibid., at 776–77.
175. Ibid., at 777, 779.
176. Ibid., at 780–81.
177. Ibid., at 787–88.
178. Ibid., at 791–92.
179. Ibid., at 792–94.
180. Ibid., at 798, 800.
181. Ibid., at 802–807.
182. Ibid., at 797–98, 806–809.
183. Ibid., at 811–12.
184. Ibid., at 818.
185. *City of Edmund v. Robinson* (517 US 1201).
186. *City of Elkhart v. William A. Boos, et al.* (532 US 1058).
187. Ibid., at 1059–61.
188. Ibid., at 1058–59.
189. *Larkin v. Grendel's Den* (459 US 116).
190. Ibid., at 121–27.
191. Ibid., at 135.
192. *Roe v. Wade* (410 US 113).
193. *Harris, Secretary of Health and Human Services, v. McRae, et al.* (1979) (448 US 297).
194. Ibid., at 320–21.
195. Ibid., at 329–57.
196. *Catholic League v. Women's Health Center* (469 US 1303).
197. *Bowen, Secretary of Health and Human Services, v. Kendrick, et al.* (487 US 589).
198. Ibid., at 617–23.
199. Ibid., at 624–38.
200. Ibid., at 639–42.
201. *Thornburgh, Governor of Pennsylvania, et al., v. American College of Obstetricians and Gynecologists, et al.* (476 US 747).
202. Ibid., at 778.
203. Ibid., at 781.

204. Ibid., at 795.
205. *Bowers, Attorney General of Georgia, v. Hardwick et al.* (478 US 186).
206. Ibid., at 210–12.
207. *Roy Romer, Governor of Colorado, et al., Petitioners, v. Richard Evans, at al.* (517 US 620).
208. Ibid., at 626–27, 633–35.
209. Ibid., at 636–37, 648.
210. *Diffenderfer et al. v. Central Baptist Church of Miami, Fla., Inc., et al.* (404 US 412).
211. Ibid., at 413–14.
212. Ibid., at 415–17.
213. 397 *US* 664.
214. Ibid., at 668–71.
215. Ibid., at 672–73.
216. Ibid., at 674–75.
217. Ibid., at 676–79.
218. Ibid., at 680–87.
219. Ibid., at 687.
220. Ibid., at 688–89.
221. Ibid., at 690–91.
222. Ibid., at 692.
223. Ibid., at 693.
224. Ibid., at 694.
225. Ibid., at 700–701.
226. Ibid., at 703.
227. Ibid., at 704–706.
228. Ibid., at 707–16.
229. *Texas Monthly Inc. v. Bullock, Comptroller of Public Accounts of State of Texas, et al.* (489 US 1).
230. Ibid., at 29–45.

Notes to Chapter Seven

1. 392 *US* 236, at 243–44.
2. Ibid., at 245–48.
3. Ibid., at 249.
4. Ibid., at 251.
5. Ibid., at 252–54.
6. Ibid., at 254–56.
7. Ibid., at 257–65.
8. Ibid., at 266.
9. Ibid., at 270–72.
10. 392 *US* 83.
11. Ibid., at 85–106.
12. Ibid., at 107–14.
13. Ibid., at 114.

14. Ibid., at 115–16.
15. Ibid., at 117–19.
16. Ibid., at 120–24.
17. Ibid., at 125–30.
18. Ibid., at 131–33.
19. 403 *US* 602. The Rhode Island case heard at the same time was *Earley v. DiCenso.*
20. Ibid., at 612–13.
21. Ibid., at 613–14.
22. Ibid., at 615–19.
23. Ibid., at 620–23.
24. Ibid., at 623–24.
25. Ibid., at 625.
26. Ibid., at 627–30.
27. Ibid., at 630–31.
28. Ibid., at 632–35.
29. Ibid., at 635–42.
30. Ibid., at 650–52.
31. Ibid., at 652–61.
32. Ibid., at 662–67.
33. Ibid., at 668–70.
34. *Lemon et al. v. Kurtzman, Superintendant of Public Instruction of Pennsylvania, et al.* (411 *US* 192).
35. Ibid., at 197–207.
36. Ibid., 209–12.
37. 403 *US* 672.
38. Ibid., at 676–78.
39. Ibid., at 678–79.
40. Ibid., at 679–82.
41. Ibid., at 682–83.
42. Ibid., at 683–87.
43. Ibid., at 687–88.
44. Ibid., at 688–89.
45. Ibid., at 692–93.
46. Ibid., at 693.
47. Ibid., at 694.
48. Ibid., at 695. The Presbyterian leader quoted was Eugene Carson Blake.
49. Complete title *Committee for Public Education and Religious Liberty v. Nyquist* (413 *US* 756).
50. Ibid., at 772–80.
51. Ibid., at 781–88.
52. Ibid., at 789–798.
53. Ibid., at 799–801.
54. Ibid., at 802–805.
55. Ibid., at 807–12.
56. Ibid., at 801–805.
57. Ibid., at 814–24.

58. *Hunt v. McNair, Governor of South Carolina, et al.* (413 *US* 734).
59. *Sloan, Treasurer of Pennsylvania, et al. v. Lemon et al.* (413 *US* 825).
60. Ibid., at 830–34.
61. Ibid., at 834.
62. *Levitt, Comptroller of New York, et al., v. Committee for Public Education and Religious Liberty, et al.* (413 *US* 472).
63. *Norwood et al. v. Harrison et al.* (413 *US* 455).
64. Ibid., at 457–60.
65. 413 *US* 455, at 465.
66. Ibid., at 463–64.
67. Ibid., at 465–70.
68. *Luetkemeier et al. v. Kaufmann et al.* (419 *US* 888). "Summary judgment" is handed down by the Court when most of its members think the lower-court decision under appeal has so obviously been decided correctly that no formal hearing of the appeal is necessary.
69. Ibid., at 888–90. The *Everson* case was 330 *US* 1.
70. *Wheeler et al. v. Barrera et al.* (417 *US* 402).
71. Ibid., at 402–28.
72. Ibid., at 429.
73. Ibid., at 430–32.
74. 421 *US* 349.
75. Ibid., at 360–66.
76. Ibid., at 367–73.
77. Ibid., at 374–78.
78. Ibid., at 381.
79. Ibid., at 385–87.
80. Ibid., at 389–90.
81. Ibid., at 391–94.
82. Ibid., at 395–96.
83. *Roemer v. Board of Public Works of Maryland* (426 *US* 736).
84. Ibid., at 746–47.
85. Ibid., at 755–58.
86. Ibid., at 758–61.
87. Ibid., at 762–66.
88. Ibid., at 768–70.
89. Ibid., at 770–73.
90. Ibid., at 773–75.
91. Ibid., at 775.
92. 433 *US* 229.
93. Ibid., at 237–54.
94. Ibid., at 255.
95. Ibid., at 256.
96. Ibid., at 257–60.
97. Ibid., at 261–62.
98. Ibid., at 262.
99. Ibid., at 263.
100. Ibid., at 264.

101. Ibid., at 265–66.

102. *New York v. Cathedral Academy* (434 US 125).

103. Ibid., at 134.

104. *Committee for Public Education and Religious Liberty v. Regan* (444 US 646).

105. Ibid., at 654–62.

106. Ibid., at 663–64. Court divisions on the previous cases cited by Blackmun were often complicated, with justices voting to uphold parts of statutes while rejecting others. Blackmun's charge of "defection" was presumably directed at Burger and Stewart, both of whom had on occasion voted to invalidate particular school aid programs, while supporting others.

107. Ibid., at 664–71.

108. Ibid., at 671.

109. *Valley Forge Christian College v. Americans United for Separation of Church and State* (454 US 464).

110. Ibid., at 471–90.

111. Ibid., at 490–500.

112. Ibid., at 501–13.

113. Ibid., at 513–15.

114. 463 US 388.

115. Ibid., at 394–98.

116. Ibid., at 399–403.

117. Ibid., at 404–406.

118. Ibid., at 406–17.

119. 475 US 402.

120. Ibid., at 409–14.

121. Ibid., at 415–17.

122. Ibid., at 419–20.

123. Ibid., at 420–21.

124. Ibid., at 423–24.

125. Ibid., at 425.

126. Ibid., at 425–26.

127. Ibid., at 427–31.

128. Complete title *School District of the City of Grand Rapids v. Ball* (473 US 373).

129. Ibid., at 382–87.

130. Ibid., at 387–92.

131. Ibid., at 395–98.

132. Ibid., at 398–400.

133. Ibid., at 400.

134. Ibid., at 400–401.

135. Complete title *Witters v. Washington Department of Services for the Blind* (474 US 481).

136. Ibid., at 485–90.

137. Ibid., at 490.

138. Ibid., at 490–92.

139. Ibid., at 493.

140. Michael McConnell, in Stephen V. Monsma and J. Christopher Soper (eds.), *Equal Treatment of Religion in a Pluralist Society* (Grand Rapids, Mich., 1998), 45.

141. Complete title *Larry Zobrest et Ux., et al., Petitioners, v. Catalina Foothills School District* (509 US 1).

142. Ibid., at 8–14.

143. Ibid., at 14–24.

144. Complete Title *Board of Education of Kiryas Joel Village School District v. Grumet* (512 US 687).

145. Ibid., at 689–98.

146. Ibid., at 699–707.

147. Ibid., at 708–709.

148. Ibid., at 710.

149. Ibid., at 711.

150. Ibid., at 712–19.

151. Ibid., at 722–26.

152. Ibid., at 728–31.

153. Ibid., at 732.

154. Ibid., at 732–33.

155. Ibid., at 734–35.

156. Ibid., at 735–36.

157. Ibid., at 737–38.

158. Ibid., at 739–41.

159. Ibid., at 741–43.

160. Ibid., at 746–49.

161. Ibid., at 750–52.

162. 521 US 203.

163. Ibid., at 209, 216.

164. Ibid., at 225.

165. Ibid., at 226.

166. Ibid., at 227.

167. Ibid., at 228.

168. Ibid., at 230.

169. Ibid., at 232.

170. Ibid., at 234.

171. Ibid., at 235.

172. Ibid., at 243.

173. Ibid., at 245.

174. Ibid., at 249.

175. Ibid., at 250.

176. Ibid., at 251.

177. Ibid., at 254.

178. Ibid., at 255–60.

179. Complete title *Guy Mitchell, et al., Petitioners, v. Mary L. Helms, et al.* (530 US 793).

180. Ibid., at 808.

181. Ibid., at 806, 825.

190 NOTES TO CONCLUSION

182. Ibid., at 815.
183. Ibid., at 816.
184. Ibid., at 826.
185. Ibid., at 828.
186. Ibid., at 837.
187. Ibid., at 849, 852.
188. Ibid., at 855.
189. Ibid., at 855, 866.
190. Ibid., at 871–72.
191. Ibid., at 884.
192. Ibid., at 885–86.
193. Ibid., at 912.
194. *Susan Tave Zelman, Superintendent of Public Instruction of Ohio, et al., Petitioners, v. Doris Simmons-Harris, et al.; Hannah Perkins School, et al.; Senel Taylor, et al., Petitioners, v. Doris Simmons-Harris, et al.* (536 US 639).
195. Ibid., at 643–47.
196. Ibid., at 647–52.
197. Ibid., at 654.
198. Ibid., at 656–57.
199. Ibid., at 664.
200. Ibid., at 664–70.
201. Ibid., at 679–80.
202. Ibid., at 681.
203. Ibid., at 682.
204. Ibid., at 684–85.
205. Ibid., at 686–87.
206. Ibid., at 688.
207. Ibid., at 698–99.
208. Ibid., at 700.
209. Ibid., at 703.
210. Ibid., at 712.
211. Ibid., at 715–29.

Notes to Conclusion

1. Bernard Schwartz, *Main Currents in American Legal Thought* (Durham, N.C., 1993), 121.

2. For example, in an 1890 address, Justice Brewer asserted that the Declaration affirmed that life, liberty, and property were rights "granted by the Almighty to everyone . . . which he may not surrender and of which he may not be deprived" (Charles G. Haines, *The Revival of Natural Law Concepts* [Buffalo, 1978], 201).

3. Although the principle in question has usually been seen as supportive of religious liberty, it has been criticized as giving church authorities "tyrannical" power over church members (Carl J. Zollman, *American Church Law* [St. Paul, Minn., 1933], 65, 285–90).

4. James Hurst, *Law and Social Process in United States History* (Ann Arbor, Mich. 1960), 114.

5. Justice Scalia has been an especially scathing critic of the decision, which he regards as a prime example of the Court's making law (Scalia, *A Matter of Interpretation* [Princeton, N.J., 1997], 18). As has been pointed out, the federal statute exempted "lecturers" from its strictures, a category that could easily have been taken to include clergy (Lawrence Tribe, in ibid., 93). For a liberal defense of the basis on which the decision was made, see Cass Sunstein, *One Case at a Time: Judicial Minimalism on the Supreme Court* (Cambridge, Mass., 1999), 220.

6. Gordon, *Mormon Question*, 4, 8, 26, 107–109.

7. Ibid., 5, 49–62, 110–11.

8. Ibid., 39, 91.

9. Ibid., ll, 22–23, 29, 34, 74, 90–91, 123.

10. Ibid., 34, 38–40, 65–66, 69, 71, 74, 77, 80, 90–91, 135, 138–40, 143, 228.

11. Ibid., 122, 125–26, 132–34.

12. Ibid., 180, 185, 187–88, 196, 207–10, 218, 220, 224.

13. Steven Smith, *Foreordained Failure: The Quest for a Constitutional Principle of Religious Freedom* (New York, 1995), 53; Akhil Reed Amar, *The Bill of Rights* (New Haven, Conn., 1995), 237–39, 254.

14. William Wiecek, *Liberty under Law: The Supreme Court in American Life* (Baltimore, 1988), 123–52; Schwartz, *Main Currents*, 193, 280, 307–14.

15. Philip Bobbitt, *Constitutional Fate: Theory of the Constitution* (New York, 1982), 148–49; John E. Semonche, *Charting the Future: The Supreme Court Responds to a Changing Society, 1890–1920* (Westport, Conn., 1978), 425.

16. Ross, *Forging*, 99, 118–21.

17. Ibid., 186.

18. G. Edward White, *Justice Oliver Wendell Holmes*(New York, 1993), 404, 439–41.

19. Ross, *Forging*, 166–68, 186–87.

20. Ibid., 186–99; Semonche, *Charting*, 425–26; Jefferson Powell, *The Moral Tradition of American Constitutionalism* (Durham, N.C., 1993), 154. The case of *Gitlow v. New York* (268 US 625), involving freedom of speech, explicitly stated that the Fourteenth Amedment protected personal liberties.

21. Ross, *Forging*, 190–93.

22. Wiecek, *Lost*, 163. However, in a 1953 case, Black dissuaded Chief Justice Warren from citing *Meyer* and *Pierce* as precedents in a case involving racial segregation, on the grounds that the decisions were invalidly based on "natural law" (Bernard Schwartz, *The New Right and the Constitution* [Boston, 1990], 54).

23. White, *Holmes*, 448.

24. White, *The Constitution and the New Deal* (Cambridge, Mass., 2000), 163.

25. Wiecek, *Lost*, 10; Edward S. Corwin, *Constitutional Revolution Ltd* (Claremont, Calif., 1941), 79.

26. Robert Bork, *The Tempting of America: The Political Seduction of the Law* (New York, 1990), 60–61. Bork argues that prejudices are not forbidden by the Constitution and that Stone's principle gave the Court the opportunity to enact its own propensities into law. Bork also regards the concept of substantive due

process as "specious" and therefore considers the *Meyer* and *Pierce* cases as having been wrongly decided (Bork in Jack Rakove [ed.], *Interpreting the Constitution: The Debate over Original Intent* [Boston, 1990], 205).

27. White, *Constitution and New Deal*, 173, 191, 194, 205–206, 245–46, 252, 268, 272, 305–309. See also Barry Cushman, *Rethinking the New Deal Court* (New York, 1998).

28. William E. Leuchtenberg, *The Supreme Court Reborn: The Constitutional Revolution in the Age of Roosevelt* (New York, 1995); Corwin, *Constitutional Revolution.*

29. John F. Wilson, *Public Religion in American Culture* (Philadelphia, 1979), 55.

30. Philip J. Cooper, *Battles on the Bench: Conflict inside the Supreme Court* (Upper Saddle River, N.J., 1996), 24.

31. Peters, *Judging*, 238–39.

32. Macmillan, *Jehovah's Witnesses*, 172, 185.

33. Leo Pfeffer, in Robert A. Licht and Robert A. Goldwin (eds.), *The Spirit of the Constitution* (Lanham, Md., 1984), 569.

34. Mark Tushnet, in Martin Marty (ed.), *Modern American Religion* (Chicago, 1986), II, 301; Walter Berns, *The First Amendment and the Future of America* (New York, 1976), 38.

35. Mark Antony DeWolfe Howe, *The Garden and the Wilderness: Religion and Government in American Constitutional History* (Chicago, 1965), 135, 148; Richard Funston, *Constitutional Counter-Revolution?: The Warren Court and the Burger Court* (Cambridge, Mass., 1977), 300; Tushnet (ed.), *The Warren Court* (Charlottesville, Va., 1993), 17. The claim that the Warren Court broke no new ground with respect to religion (John Saxton, in Schwartz, *Warren Court*, 104–105) is erroneous in the light of the conscientious-objector cases.

36. Newton, *Armed*, 29–53.

37. Martin S. Sheffer, *God versus Caesar* (Albany, N.Y., 1999), 62.

38. Berns, *First Amendment*, 38, 195.

39. George Goldberg, *Reconstructing America* (Grand Rapids, Mich., 1984), 77.

40. For a critique of this approach, see Dean M. Kelley, in Paul J. Weber (ed.), *Equal Separation: Understanding the Religion Clause* (New York, 1990), 19–23, and in Goldwin and Art Kaufman (eds.), *How Does the Constitution Work?* (Washington, 1987), 12–18; William Everett, *Religion, Federalism, and the Struggle for Public Life* (New York, 1997), 118–29.

41. Noonan, *Narrowing*, 24.

42. Leonard F. Manning, *The Law of Church-State Relations in a Nutshell* (St. Paul, 1981), 130. In his draft opinion Fortas omitted a published claim by the law's drafters that they were not motivated by religious concerns (Larson, *Trial and Error*, 116).

43. Tushnet, *Warren Court*, 31.

BIBLIOGRAPHY

PRIMARY

Alley Robert S. (ed.), *The Supreme Court on Church and State* (New York, 1988).

Ariens, Michael S., and Robert A. Destro (eds.), *Religious Liberty in a Pluralistic Society* (Durham, N.C., 1996).

Baldwin, Henry, *A General View of the Origins and Nature of the Constitution and Government of the United States* (New York, 1970 [originally 1837]).

Blandford, Linda A., and Patricia Russell Evans (eds.), *Supreme Court of the United States, 1789–1980: An Index to Opinions Arranged according to Justice* (Millwood, N.Y., 1983), two volumes.

Boles, Donald E. (ed.), *The Two Swords: Commentaries and Cases on Religion and Education* (Ames, Iowa, 1967).

Dickson, Del (ed.), *The Supreme Court in Conference (1940–1985)* (New York, 2001).

Doerr, Edd, and Albert J. Menendez (eds.), *Religious Liberty and State Constitutions* (Buffalo, 1993).

Eastland, Terry (ed.), *Religious Liberty in the Supreme Court: The Cases That Defined the Debate over Church and State* (Washington, 1993).

Fellman, David (ed.), *The Supreme Court and Education* (New York, 1969).

Friedman, Leon, and Fred L. Israel (eds.), *The Justices of the United States Supreme Court, 1789–1969: Their Lives and Major Opinions* (New York, 1969), five volumes.

Howe, Mark Antony DeWolfe (ed.), *Cases on Church and State in the United States* (Cambridge, Mass., 1952).

Irons, Peter (ed.), *The Courage of Their Convictions* (New York, 1988).

Jackson, Robert H., *Dispassionate Justice: A Synthesis of the Judicial Opinions of Robert H. Jackson*, ed. Glendon A. Schubert (Indianapolis, 1969).

Kurland, Philip, and Ralph Lerner (eds.), *The Founders' Constitution* (Chicago, 1987), five volumes.

McCollum, Vashti C., *One Woman's Fight* (Boston, 1961).

Miller, Robert T., and Ronald B. Flowers (eds.), *Toward Benevolent Neutrality: Church, State, and the Supreme Court* (Waco, Tex., 1996), two volumes.

Miller, Samuel Freeman, *Lectures on the Constitution of the United States* (Littleton, Colo., 1980 [original edition 1881]).

Murray, William J., *Let Us Pray, a Plea for Prayer in Our Schools* (New York, 1995).

———. *My Life without God* (Nashville, 1982).

Noonan, John T. Jr., and Edward McGlynn Gaffney Jr. (eds.), *Religious Freedom: History, Cases, and Other Materials on the Interaction of Religion and Government* (New York, 2001).

O'Hair, Madalyn Murray, *Freedom under Siege: The Impact of Organized Religion on Your Liberty and Your Pocketbook* (Los Angeles, 1974).

Schwartz, Bernard (ed.), *Roots of the Bill of Rights* (New York, 1980), five volumes.

Tussman, Joseph (ed.), *The Supreme Court on Church and State* (New York, 1962).

United States Reports (Continuing published series of Supreme Court decisions. Until about 1870 these are usually designated by the name of the editor, e.g., *Wheaton, Howard*).

Veit, Helen E., Kenneth R. Bowling, and Charlene Bangs Bickford (eds.), *Creating the Bill of Rights: The Documentary Record from the First Federal Congress* (Baltimore, 1991).

Webster, Daniel, *The Papers of Daniel Webster*, ed. Charles M. Wiltse (Hanover, N.H., 1974–89), fourteen volumes.

Wilson, John F. (ed.), *Church and State in American History* (Boston, 1965).

Worton, Stanley N. (ed.), *Freedom of Religion* (Rochelle Park, N.J., 1975).

SECONDARY

Abraham, Henry J., *Freedom and the Court: Civil Rights and Liberties in the United States* (New York, 1977).

Adams, Arlin M., and Charles J. Emmerich, *A Nation Dedicated to Religious Liberty: The Constitutional Heritage of the Religion Clauses* (Philadelphia, 1990).

Agresto, John, *The Supreme Court and Constitutional Democracy* (Ithaca, N.Y., 1984).

Alexander, Elizabeth Urban, *Notorious Woman: The Celebrated Case of Myra Clark Gaines* (Baton Rouge, La., 2002).

Alexander, Thomas S., *Mormonism in Transition: The History of the Latter-Day Saints, 1890–1930* (Urbana, Ill., 1996).

Alley, Robert S., *School Prayer: The Court, the Congress, and the First Amendment* (Buffalo, 1994).

Anastalpo, George, *The Amendments to the Constitution: A Commentary* (Baltimore, 1995).

———. *The Constitutionalist: Notes on the First Amendment* (Dallas, 1971).

Antieau, Chester J., *The Higher Law Origins of Modern Constitutional Law* (Buffalo, 1994).

———. *The Rights of Our Fathers* (Vienna, Va., 1968).

———. *Commentary on the Constitution of the United States* (Buffalo, 1960).

Antieau, Chester J., Arthur T. Downey, and Edward C. Roberts, *Freedom from Federal Establishment: Formation and Early History of the First Amendment Religion Clauses* (Milwaukee, 1964).

Arndt, Karl J. R., *George Rapp's Years of Glory: Economy on the Ohio, 1834–1847: Okonomie am Ohio* (New York, 1987).

———. *George Rapp's Harmony Society, 1785–1847* (Rutherford, N.J., 1972).

———. *George Rapp's Successors and Material Heirs* (Rutherford, N.J, 1971).

Baxter, Maurice G., *Daniel Webster and the Supreme Court* (Amherst, Mass., 1966).

Beckford, James A., *The Trumpet of Prophecy: A Sociological Study of the Jehovah's Witnesses* (New York, 1975).

Beeman, Richard, Stephen Botein, and Edward Carter II (eds.), *Beyond Confederation: Origins of the Constitution and American National Identity* (Chapel Hill, N.C., 1987).

Berg, Thomas, *The State and Religion in a Nutshell* (St. Paul, Minn., 1998).

Berger, Raoul, *The Fourteenth Amendment and the Bill of Rights* (Norman, Okla., 1989).

———. *Government by Judiciary: The Transformation of the Fourteenth Amendment* (Cambridge, Mass., 1977).

Beth, Loren P., *The American Theory of Church and State* (Gainesville, Fla., 1958).

Blackwell, Victor V., *O'er the Ramparts They Watched* (New York, 1976).

Boles, Donald E., *The Bible, Religion, and the Public Schools* (Ames, Iowa, 1961).

Butts, R. Freeman, *The American Tradition in Religion and Education* (Boston, 1950).

Buzzard, Lynn R. (ed.), *Freedom and Faith: The Impact of Law on Religious Liberty* (Elgin, Ill., 1982).

Buzzard, Lynn R., and Samuel Ericsson, *The Battle for Religious Liberty* (Elgin, Ill., 1982).

Clark, Henry B., II, (ed.), *Freedom of Religion in America: Historical Roots, Philosophical Concepts, and Contemporary Problems* (Los Angeles, 1982).

Cobb, Sanford, *The Rise of Religious Liberty in America* (New York, 1902).

Cortner, Richard C., *The Supreme Court and the Second Bill of Rights: The Fourteenth Amendment and the Nationalization of Civil Liberties* (Madison, Wis., 1981).

Costanzo, Joseph F., *This Nation under God: Church, State, and Schools in America* (New York, 1964).

Currie, David P., *The Constitution in the Supreme Court: The First Hundred Years, 1789–1888* (Chicago, 1985).

Curry, James S., *Public Regulation of the Religious Uses of Land, a Detailed and Critical Analysis of a Hundred Court Cases* (Charlottesville, Va., 1964).

Curtis, Michael Kent (ed.), *The Flag Salute Cases* (New York, 1993).

Cushman, Barry, *Rethinking the New Deal Court: The Structure of a Constitutional Revolution* (New York, 1998).

Dignan, Patrick, *A History of the Legal Incorporation of Catholic Church Property in the United States, 1784–1932* (New York, 1935).

Dolbeare, Kenneth, and Philip E. Hammond, *The School Prayer Decisions: from Court Policy to Local Practice* (Chicago, 1971).

Drakeman, Donald J., *Church-State Constitutional Issues: Making Sense of the Establishment Clause* (New York, 1991).

Dutile, Fernand W., and Edward McGlynn Gaffney, *State and Campus: State Regulation of Religiously Affiliated Higher Education* (Notre Dame, Ind., 1984).

Epstein, Lee, Jeffrey A. Segel, Harold J. Spaeth, and Thomas G. Walker (eds.), *The Supreme Court Compendium: Data, Decisions, and Development* (Washington, 1994).

Esbeck, Carl H., *The Regulation of Religious Organizations As Recipients of Governmental Assistance* (Washington, 1996).

Fairman, Charles, *Reconstruction and Reunion, 1864–88* (New York, 1971), two volumes.

———. *American Constitutional Decisions* (New York, 1948).

Farber, Daniel A., and Suzanna Sherry, *A History of the American Constitution* (St. Paul, Minn., 1990).

Fellman, David, *Religion in American Public Law* (Boston, 1965).

———. *The Limits of Freedom* (New Brunswick, N.J., 1959).

Fenwick, Lynda Beck, *Should the Children Pray?: A Historical, Judicial, and Political Examination of Public School Prayer* (Waco, Tex., 1989).

Firmage, Edwin B., *Zion in the Courts, a Legal History of the Church of Jesus Christ of Latter Day Saints, 1830–1900* (Urbana, Ill., 1988).

Fleming, Donald, and Bernard Bailyn (eds.), *Law in American History* (Boston, 1971).

Flowers, Ronald B., *The Godless Court: Supreme Court Decisions on Church-State Relationships* (Louisville, Ky., 1994).

Formicola, Jo Renee, and Hubert Morken (eds.), *Everson Revisited: Education and Law at the Crossroads* (Lanham, Md., 1997).

Freund, Paul A., and Robert Ulich, *Religion and the Public Schools* (Cambridge, Mass., 1965).

Frommer, Arthur, *The Bible and the Public Schools* (New York, 1963).

Furer, Howard B., *The Fuller Court, 1888–1910* (Port Washington, N.Y., 1986).

Galub, Arthur, *The Burger Court, 1968–1984* (Millwood, N.Y., 1986).

Gelfand, Lavinia, *The Freedom of Religion in America* (Minneapolis, 1969).

Gellhorn, Walter, and R. Kent Greenawalt, *The Sectarian College and the Public Purse: Fordham, a Case Study* (Dobbs Ferry, N.Y., 1970).

Gilman, Howard, *The Constitution Besieged: The Rise and Demise of the Lochner Era Police Powers Jurisprudence* (Durham, N.C., 1993).

Gordon, Sarah Barringer, *The Mormon Question: Polygamy and Constitutional Conflict in Nineteenth-Century America* (Chapel Hill, N.C., 2002).

Griffiths, William E., *Religion, the Court, and the Public Schools: A Century of Litigation* (Cincinatti, 1966).

Gunther, Gerald, *Constitutional Law* (Mineola, N.Y., 1985).

Haines, Charles, *The Role of the Supreme Court in American Government and Politics* (Berkeley, Calif., 1944–57), two volumes.

Hall, Kermit L. (ed.), *The Oxford Guide to United States Supreme Court Decisions* (New York, 1999).

——— (ed.). *The Oxford Companion to the Supreme Court of the United States* (New York, 1992).

——— (ed.), *By and for the People: Constitutional Rights in American History* (Arlington Heights, Ill., 1991).

——— (ed.), *Civil Liberties in American History: Major Historical Interpretations* (New York, 1987).

———— (ed.), *The Judiciary in American Life: Major Historical Interpretations* (New York, 1987).

———— (ed.), *Main Themes in American Constitutional and Legal History: Major Historical Essays* (New York, 1987).

———— (ed.), *The Supreme Court and Judicial Review in American History* (Washington, 1985).

Hall, Kermit L. , James W. Ely Jr., Joel B. Grossman, and William M. Wiecek (eds.), *The Oxford Companion to the Supreme Court of the United States* (New York, 1992).

Hardy, B. Carmon, *The Solemn Covenant: The Mormon Polygamous Passage* (Urbana, Ill., 1992).

Hooker, Clifford P.(ed.), *The Courts and Education* (Chicago, 1978).

Horowitz, Donald L., *The Courts and Social Policy* (Washington, 1977).

Horwitz, Morton J., *The Transformation of American Law, 1780–1860* (Cambridge, Mass., 1977).

House, H. Wayne (ed.), *The Christian and American Law* (Grand Rapids, Mich., 1998).

Huegli, Albert G.(ed.), *Church and State under God* (St. Louis, 1964).

Hyman, Harold M., *Era of the Oath: Northern Loyalty Oaths during the Civil War and Reconstruction* (Philadelphia, 1954).

Hyman, Harold M., and William M. Wiecek, *Equal Justice under Law: Constitutional Development, 1835–1875* (New York, 1982).

Johnson, Alvin W., and Frank H. Yost, *Legal Status of Church-State Relationships: Separation of Church and State in the United States* (Minneapolis, 1948).

Johnson, F. Ernest (ed.), *American Education and Religion: The Problem of Religion in the Schools* (Port Washington, N.Y, 1969).

Johnson, John W., *American Legal Culture, 1908–1940* (Westport, Conn., 1981).

Johnson, Stephen D., and Joseph B. Tamney (eds.), *The Political Role of Religion in the United States* (Boulder, Colo., 1986).

Jorgenson, Lloyd P., *The State and Non-Public Schools, 1825–1925* (Columbia, Mo., 1987).

Kahn, Ronald, *The Supreme Court and Constitutional Theory, 1953–1993* (Lawrence, Kans., 1994).

Katz, Wilbur G., *Religion and American Constitutions* (Evanston, Ill., 1964).

Kauper, Paul G., *Religion and the Constitution* (Baton Rouge, La., 1964).

————. *Uncivil Liberties and the Constitution* (Ann Arbor, Mich., 1962).

Keim, Albert, *Compulsory Education and the Amish: The Right Not to Be Modern* (Boston, 1975).

Kelly, Alfred H., *Foundations of Freedom in the American Constitution* (New York, 1958).

Kelly, Alfred H., and Winfred A. Harbison, *The American Constitution* (New York, 1983).

Keynes, Edward, *The Court v. Congress: Prayer, Busing, and Abortion* (Durham, N.C., 1989).

Kommers, Donald, and Michael J. Wahoske (eds.), *Freedom and Education: Pierce v. Society of Sisters Reconsidered* (Notre Dame, Ind., 1978).

Kraybill, Donald B. (ed.), *The Amish and the State* (Baltimore, 1993).

La Follette, Marcel C. (ed.), *Creationism, Science, and the Law: The Arkansas Case* (Cambridge, Mass., 1983).

LaNoue, George R. (ed.), *Public Funds for Parochial Schools* (New York, 1963).

Larson, Edward J. (ed.), *Trial and Error: The American Controversy over Creation and Evolution* (New York, 1985).

Laubach, John H., *School Prayers: Congress, the Courts, and the Public* (Washington, 1969).

Leuchtenberg, William E., *The Supreme Court Reborn: The Constitutional Revolution in the Age of Roosevelt* (New York, 1995).

Levy, Leonard W. (ed.), *Encyclopedia of the American Constitution* (New York, 1988), four volumes.

Lewis, Frederick P., *The Nationalization of Liberty* (Lanham, Md., 1990).

Long, Carolyn N., *Religious Freedom and Indian Rights: The Case of Oregon v. Smith* (Lawrence, Kans., 2000).

Lyman, Edward L., *Political Deliverance: The Mormon Quest for Utah Statehood* (Urbana, Ill., 1986).

Lynn, Barry, *The Right of Religious Liberty: A Basic ACLU Guide to Religious Rights* (Carbondale, Ill., 1995).

Manning, Leonard F., *The Law of Church-State Relations in a Nutshell* (St. Paul, Minn., 1981).

Manwaring, David, *Render to Caesar: The Flag Salute Controversy* (Chicago, 1962).

Marnell, William H., *The First Amendment: The History of Religious Freedom in the United States* (Garden City, N.Y., 1964).

Mason, Alpheus T., *The Supreme Court from Taft to Burger* (Baton Rouge, La., 1979).

———. *The Supreme Court from Taft to Warren* (New York, 1964).

Mauss, Armand L., *The Angel and the Beehive: The Mormon Struggle with Assimilation* (Urbana, Ill., 1994).

McDonald, Forrest M., with Ellen S. McDonald, *A Constitutional History of the United States* (New York, 1982).

McGarry, Daniel D., *Educational Freedom and the Case of Government Aid to Students in Independent Schools* (Milwaukee, 1966).

McLoughlin, William G., *Cherokees and Missionaries, 1789–1839* (New Haven, Conn., 1984).

McMillen, Richard C., *Religion in the Public Schools, an Introduction* (Macon, Ga., 1984).

——— (ed.), *Education, Religion, and the Supreme Court* (Danville, Va., 1979).

Menendez, Albert J., *The December Wars: Religious Symbols and Ceremonies in the Public Square* (Buffalo, 1993).

———. *School Prayer and Other Religious Issues in American Public Education, a Bibliography* (New York, 1980).

Menendez, Albert J., and Edd Doerr, *Religion and Public Education: Common Sense and the Law* (Long Beach, Calif., 1991).

Michaelson, Robert S., *Piety in the Public Schools: Trends and Issues in the Relationship between Religion and the Public School in the United States* (New York, 1970).

Morgan, Richard E., *The Politics of Religious Conflict: Church and State in America* (Washington, 1980).

———. *The Supreme Court and Religion* (New York, 1972).

Muir, William K., *Prayer in the Public Schools: Law and Attitude Change* (Chicago, 1967).

Murphy, Paul L., *The Shaping of the First Amendment, 1791 to the Present* (New York, 1992).

——— (ed.), *Religious Freedom: Separation and Free Exercise* (New York, 1990), two volumes.

———. *The Constitution in the Twentieth Century* (Washington, 1986).

———. *The Constitution in Crisis Times, 1918–1969* (New York, 1972).

Murphy, Paul L., and James Morton Smith (eds.), *Liberty and Justice* (New York, 1965, 1968), two volumes.

Murphy, Walter F., James E. Fleming, and William F. Harris II, *American Constitutional Interpretation* (Mineola, N.Y., 1986).

Nelson, William E., *The Fourteenth Amendment: From Political Principle to Judicial Doctrine* (Cambridge, Mass., 1988).

Nelson, William E. and Robert C. Palmer, *Liberty and Community: Constitution and Rights in the Early American Republic* (New York, 1987).

Newton, Merlin O., *Armed with the Constitition: Jehovah's Witnesses in Alabama and the U.S. Supreme Court, 1939–1946* (Tuscaloosa, Ala., 1995).

Nieman, Donald G. (ed.), *The Constitution, Law, and American Life: Critical Aspects of the Nineteenth-Century Experience* (Athens, Ga., 1992).

Noll, Mark A.(ed.), *Religion and American Politics from the Colonial Period to the 1980s* (New York, 1990).

Noonan, John T., *The Believers and the Powers That Are: Cases, History, and Other Data Bearing on the Relation of Religion and Government* (New York, 1987).

Norman, Edward R., *The Conscience of the State in North America* (London, 1968).

O'Brien, J. Stephen, and Richard B. Vacca, *The Supreme Court and the Religious-Education Controversy: Tightrope to Entanglement* (Durham, N.C., 1974).

O'Neill, James M., *Religion and Education in the Constitution* (New York, 1949).

Oaks, Dallin, *Trust Doctrine in Church Controversies* (Macon, Ga., 1984).

——— (ed.), *The Wall between Church and State* (Chicago, 1963).

Paul, Arnold M., *Conservative Crisis and the Rule of Law: The Attitude of Bar and Bench, 1887–1895* (Ithaca, N.Y., 1960).

Perry, H. W., *Deciding to Decide: Agenda Setting in the United States Supreme Court* (Cambridge, Mass., 1991).

Perton, M. James, *Apocalypse Delayed: The Story of the Jehovah's Witnesses* (Toronto, 1985).

Peters, Shawn F., *Judging Jehovavh's Witnesses: Religious Persecution and the Dawn of the Rights Revolution* (Lawrence, Kans., 2000).

Powell, Theodore, *The School Bus Law, a Case Study in Education, Religion, and Politics* (Middletown, Conn., 1960).

Power, Edward J., *Religion and the Public Schools in Nineteenth- Century America: The Contribution of Orestes A. Brownson* (New York, 1996).

Pratt, Walter F., *The Supreme Court under Edward Douglass White, 1910–1921* (Columbia, S.C., 1999).

Pritchett, C. Herman, *Constitutional Civil Liberties* (Englewood Cliffs, N.J., 1984).

———. *The American Constitution* (New York, 1968).

———. *The Roosevelt Court: A Study in Constitutional Politics and Values, 1937–1947* (New York, 1948).

Prucha, Francis Paul, *The Church and the Indian Schools, 1898–1912* (Lincoln, Nebr., 1979).

Reid, John Philip, *The Concept of Liberty in the Age of the American Revolution* (Chicago, 1988).

———. *The Constitutional History of the American Revolution* (Madison, Wis., 1986–93), four volumes.

Rice, Arnold S., *The Warren Court, 1953–1969* (Millwood, N.Y., 1987).

Robbins, Thomas, and Roland Robertson (eds.), *Church-State Relations: Tensions and Transitions* (New Brunswick, N.J., 1987).

Robbins, Thomas, William C. Shepherd, and James McBride (eds.), *Cults, Culture, and the Law: Perspectives on the New Religious Movements* (Chico, Calif., 1985).

Ross, William G., *Forging New Freedoms: Nativism, Education, and the Constitution, 1917–1927* (Lincoln, Nebr., 1994).

Rudko, Francis H., *Truman's Court, a Study in Judicial Restraint* (New York, 1988).

Sanders, Thomas G., *The Protestant Concept of Church and State: Historical Background and Approaches for the Future* (New York, 1964).

Sarat, Austin, and Thomas R. Kearns (eds.), *Legal Rights: An Historical and Philosophical Perspective* (Ann Arbor, Mich., 1996).

Schultz, Jeffrey D., John G. West Jr., and Ian McLean (eds.), *Encyclopedia of Religion in American Politics* (Phoenix, 1999).

Schwartz, Bernard (ed.), *The Warren Court, a Retrospective* (New York, 1996).

———. *Main Currents in American Legal Thought* (Durham, N.C., 1993).

———. *The Ascent of Pragmatism: The Burger Court in Action* (Reading, Mass., 1990).

——— (ed.), *Roots of the Bill of Rights* (New York, 1980), five volumes.

———. *A Commentary on the Constitution of the United States* (New York, 1963–68), five volumes.

———. *The Reins of Power, a Constitutional History of the United States* (London, 1963).

Semonche, John E., *Keeping the Faith, a Cultural History of the U.S. Supreme Court* (Lanham, Md., 1998).

———. *Religion and Constitutional Government in the United States, a Historical Overview with Sources* (Carborro, N.C., 1985).

———. *Charting the Future: The Supreme Court Responds to a Changing Society, 1890–1920* (Westport, Conn., 1978).

Sheffer, Martin S., *God Versus Caesar: Belief, Worship, and Proselytization under the First Amendment* (Albany, N.Y., 1999).

Shepherd, William C., *To Secure the Blessings of Liberty: American Constitutional Law and the New Religious Movements* (New York, 1985).

Sibley, Mulford Q., *Conscription of Conscience: The American State and the Conscientious Objector, 1940–1947* (Ithaca, N.Y., 1952).

Siegel, Adrienne, *The Marshall Court, 1801–1835* (Millwood, N.Y., 1987).

Sikorski, Robert (ed.), *Prayer in the Public Schools and the Constitution, 1961–1992* (New York, 1993), three volumes.

Sizer, Theodore R. (ed.), *Religion and Public Education* (Washington, 1982).

Smidt, Corwin E. (ed.), *In God We Trust?: Religion and American Political Life* (Grand Rapids, Mich., 2001).

Smith, Christopher E., *Crucial Judicial Nominations and Political Change: The Impact of Clarence Thomas* (Westport, Conn., 1993).

Smith, Elwyn A., *Religious Liberty in the United States: The Development of Church-State Thought since the Revolutionary Era* (Philadelphia, 1972).

——— (ed.), *The Religion of the Republic* (Philadelphia, 1971).

Smith, Rodney R., *School Prayer and the Constitution, a Case Study in Constitutional Interpretation* (Wilmington, Del., 1987).

Spicer, George W., *The Supreme Court and Fundamental Freedoms* (Chicago, 1970).

Stevens, Leonard A., *Salute!: The Case of the Bible and the Flag* (New York, 1973).

Stites, Francis N., *Private Interest and Public Good: The Dartmouth College Case* (Amherst, Mass., 1972).

Stokes, Anson Phelps, *Church and State in the United States* (New York, 1950), three volumes.

Stokes, Anson Phelps, and Leo Pfeffer, *Church and State in the United States* (New York, 1964).

Stone, Geoffrey, Richard A. Epstein, and Cass R. Sunstein (eds.), *The Bill of Rights and the Modern State* (Chicago, 1992).

Swanson, Wayne R., *The Christ Child Goes to Court* (Philadelphia, 1990).

Swindler, William F., *Court and Constitution in the Twentieth Century* (Indianapolis, 1969–74), three volumes.

Thurow, Sarah B., *Constitutionalism in America* (Lanham, Md., 1988), three volumes.

Tise, Larry E. *The American Counter-Revolution: Retreat from Liberty, 1783–1800* (Mechanicsburgh, Pa., 1998).

Torpey, William G., *Judicial Doctrines of Religious Rights in the United States* (New York, 1948).

Tribe, Laurence H., *American Constitutional Law* (Mineola, N.Y., 1978, 1988).

Turner, Lynn W., *William Plumer of New Hampshire, 1759–1850* (Chapel Hill, N.C., 1962).

Tyack, David B., *Law and the Shaping of Public Education, 1785-1954* (Madison, Wis., 1987).

Urofsky, Melvin I., *Division and Discord: The Supreme Court under Stone and Vinson, 1941–1953* (Columbia, S.C., 1997).

———. *The Continuity of Change: The Supreme Court and Individual Liberties, 1953–1986* (Belmont, Calif., 1991).

Wald, Kenneth D., *Religion and Politics in the United States* (New York, 1987).

Warren, Charles, *The Supreme Court in United States History* (Boston, 1927), two volumes.

Weber, Paul J. (ed.), *Equal Separation: Understanding the Religion Clauses of the First Amendment* (New York, 1990).

Weber, Paul J., and Dennis A. Gilbert, *Private Churches and Public Money: Church-Government Relations* (Westport, Conn., 1981).

Wechsler, Herbert, *The Nationalization of Civil Liberties and Civil Rights* (Austin, Tex., 1969).

Wellington, Harry H., *Interpreting the Constitution: The Supreme Court and the Process of Adjudication* (New Haven, Conn., 1990).

West, Robin, *Progressive Constitutionalism: Reconstructing the Fourteenth Amendment* (Durham, N.C., 1994).

Westin, Alan F., *The Supreme Court and the Movies: The Miracle Case* (Tuscaloosa, Ala., 1961).

White, G. Edward, *The Constitution and the New Deal* (Cambridge, Mass., 2000).

———. *The Marshall Court and Cultural Change, 1815-1835* (New York, 1991).

———. *Patterns of American Legal Thought* (Indianapolis, 1978).

White, Ronald C. Jr., and Albright G. Zimmerman (eds.), *An Unsettled Arena: Religion and the Bill of Rights* (Grand Rapids, Mich., 1990).

Whitehead, K. D., *Catholic Colleges and Federal Funding* (San Franciso, 1988).

Wiecek, William M., *The Lost World of Classical Legal Thought: Law and Ideology in America, 1886–1937* (New York, 1998).

———. *Liberty under Law: The Supreme Court in American Life* (Baltimore, 1988).

Williams, Aaron, *The Harmony Society at Economy, Penn'a, Founded by George Rapp*, A.D. 1805 (New York, 1971).

Wilson, John F., *Public Religion in American Culture* (Philadelphia, 1979).

Wilson, John F. and Donald Drakeman (eds.), *Church and State in American History: The Burden of Religious Pluralism* (Boston, 1987).

Wolcott, Wilfred Bonsieur, *The Background to the Will of Stephen Girard* (Philadelphia, 1948).

Wolf, Donald J., *Toward Consensus: Protestant and Catholic Interpretations of Church and State* (Garden City, N.Y., 1968).

Wood, James E. (ed.), *The First Freedom: Religion and the Bill of Rights* (Waco, Tex., 1993).

——— (ed.), *The Role of Religion in the Making of Public Policy* (Waco, Tex., 1991).

——— (ed.), *Religion and the State: Essays in Honor of Leo Pfeffer* (Waco, Tex., 1985).

——— (ed.), *Religion, the State, and Education* (Waco, Tex., 1984).

——— (ed.), *Ecumenical Perspectives on Church and State: Protestant, Catholic, and Jewish* (Waco, Tex., 1980).

Wood, James E., and Derek Davis (eds.), *The Role of Government in Monitoring and Regulating Religion in Public Life* (Waco, Tex., 1993).

Wright, Benjamin F., *The Growth of American Constitutional Law* (Chicago, 1967).

———. *American Intepretations of Natural Law, a Study in the History of Political Thought* (New York, 1931).

Wright, Stuart A. (ed.), *Armageddon in Waco: Critical Perspectives on the Branch Davidian Conflict* (Chicago, 1995).

Zabel, Orville H., *God and Caesar in Nebraska: A Study of the Legal Relationship of Church and State, 1854–1954* (Lincoln, Nebr., 1955).

Zollman, Carl J., *American Church Law* (St. Paul, Minn., 1933).

INDEX OF JUSTICES

INDEX OF CASES

Jones v. Opeleika, 47–48, 156, 171n.23
Jones v. Wolff, 16, 158, 165n.82

Kain v. Gibborey, 8, 165n.31
Kedroff v. St. Nicholas Cathedral, 14–16, 165n.68
Kiryas Joel School District v. Grumet, 141–144
Kreskik v. St. Nicholas Cathedral, 15, 165n.72
Kunz v. New York, 52, 172n.64

Lamb's Chapel v. School District, 80, 101, 113, 161, 178n.141
Largent v. Texas, 48, 171n.28
Larkin v. Grendel's Den, 116–117, 142, 184n.189
Larsen v. Valente, 83–84, 178n.167
Late Corporation of the Church of Jesus Christ v. U.S., 25, 167n.44
Lee V. Weisman, 103–104, 162, 182n.86
Leiby v. Manchester, 48, 171n.29
Lemon v. Kurtzman, 101, 124–126, 132, 161, 177n.127
Leutkemeier v. Kaufmann, 131, 187n.68
Levitt v. Committee for Public Education, 130, 187n.62
Lochner v. New York, 168n.72
Lovell v. City of Griffin, 46–47, 171n.18
Lowrey v. Hawaii, 40–41, 159, 170n.55
Lynch v. Donnnely, 109–113, 161
Lyng v. Indian Cemetery Association, 85–86, 158, 170n.186

Marsh v. Alabama, 50, 172n.50
Marsh v. Chambers, 108–109, 112, 161
Martin v. City of Struthers, 48, 171n.30
Maryland and Virginia Eldership v. Church of God, 74, 165n.74
Mason v. Muncaster, 6, 12, 150, 164n.19
Maxwell v. Dow, 28, 152, 167n.68
McCollum v. Board of Education, 51–52, 58, 66, 91–92, 96–97, 100–101, 172n.159
McDaniel v. Paty, 85, 179n.181
McGowan v. Maryland, 95, 97
Meek v. Pittenger, 131–133, 136, 139, 146
Messer v. Utah, 62–63, 174n.20
Meyer v. Nebraska, 29, 153–154, 191n.22
Miles v. U.S., 26, 167n.52
Minersville School District v. Gobitis, 44, 90, 92, 155, 158–159, 171n.4
Missionary Society v. Dalles, 6, 164n.22

Missionary Society v. Kelly, 6, 164n.22
Missionary Society v. Wait, 6, 164n.22
Mitchell v. Helms, 145–147, 162
Montana Catholic Mission v. Missoula, 36, 169n.25
Mueller v. Allen, 137, 147
Mulloy v. U.S., 65, 175n.37
Municipality of Ponce v. Roman Catholic Apostolic Church, 7, 164n.24
Murdock v. Pennsylvania, 48–49, l7ln.31
Murphy v. Ramsey, 26, 167n.58
Murray v. Curtlett, 99, 181n.53

National Labor Relations Board v. Bishop of Chicago, 77, 177n.123
Nebraska District of Lutheran Church v. McKelvie, 168n.78
Negre v. Larsen, 66, 175n.45
New York v. Cathedral Academy, 135, 188n.102
Niemotko v. Maryland, 51, 172n.60
Norwood v. Harrison, 130, 187n.63

O'Lone v. Estate of Shabbaz, 7, 177n.120
Oestereich v. Selective Service System, 64, 175n.30
Order of St. Benedict v. Steinhauser, 10–11, 150, 164n.46

Pascoe v. Massachusetts, 48, 171n.29
Patterson v. Gaines, 35, 169n.15
Permoli v. New Orleans, 20–21, 28, 31, 33, 149, 152–153, 166n.20
Petit v. Minnesota, 38–39, 170n.44
Pewter v. U.S., 64, 174n.26
Philadelphia, Wilmington, and Baltimore Railroad v. Philadelphia and Havre de Grace Steamship, 37, 150, 169n.32
Pierce v. Society of Sisters, 29, 122, 129, 153–154, 191n.22
Pohl v. Ohio, 168n.78
Poulos v. New Hampshire, 52, 172n.67
Pratt v. Ramsey, 167n.58
Presbyterian Church v. Hull Memorial, 15, 165n.73
Prince v. Massachusetts, 49–50, 172n.44

Quick Bear v. Leupp, 40, 129, 159, 170n.53

Randall v. Ramsey, 167n.58
Reynolds v. U.S., 24–25, 152, 155
Richardson v. Goddard, 37, 169n.30

GENERAL INDEX

abortion, 86, 117–118
academic freedom, 107, 127, 133
adultery, 27
Africa, 75
agnosticism, 97
Air Force, US, 73–74, 158
Alabama, 50, 102–103
Alexandria (Va.), 3–4, 6
Ali, Muhammed (Cassius Clay), 66
American Association of University Professors (AAUP), 127, 133
American Civil Liberties Union (ACLU), 45, 90
American Jewish Congress (AJC), 90
Amish, 72–73, 83, 157
Anglican Church. See England, Church of
anti-Catholicism, 48, 52, 146–147
anti-Semitism, 45, 52, 86, 115
Arizona, 140–141
Arkansas, 106–107, 160
Armaggedon, 59
Army, US, 6, 136
atheism, 14, 63, 78, 80, 88, 93–94, 99, 156

Ballard, Guy, 60–61
baptism, 118
Baptist Church, 7, 18, 30, 52, 105, 118, 130
bene placitum, 36
Berea College, 152
Berns, Walter, 156, 192n.34
Bible, 20, 60, 84, 97–99, 108, 111, 151; King James version of, 98; in schools, 160
Biddle, Francis, 155
bill of attainder, 21–24, 166n.27
Bill of Rights, incorporation of, 28, 29, 31, 100, 149, 151–154, 159, 191n.20. *See also* Establishment Clause; Free Exercise Clause; press, freedom of; religion, freedom of; speech, freedom of
Bimeler, John M., 9
Birmingham (Ala.), 71–72
bishop, office of, 8, 15–16, 35
Black Muslims. See Nation of Islam

Blake, Eugene Carson, 186n.48
blasphemy, 32–33, 151, 156
Bobbitt, Philip, 153, 191n.15
Bork, Robert, 191n.26
Boston (Mass.), 12, 37
Boy Scouts of America, 89, 120
Branch Davidians, 76
Buddhism, 64, 76–77
buildings, ecclesiastical, 9
buses, school, 90–91, 122–123, 128–129, 131, 134, 148
Bush, George H., 162

California, 17, 82, 84–85
Calvinism, 12, 18, 40
Canada, 30, 56
Canon Law (Catholic), 14, 34–35
Cantwell, Newton, 47
Caribbean Sea, 75
Catholic Church, 7–8, 13–14, 20–21, 29, 34–36, 39, 41–42, 47, 52, 59, 65–67, 77–78, 84, 87–88, 90–91, 105, 110–111, 117, 122–150, 162. *See also* education, religious
cemeteries, 19–21, 85–86, 151, 158
Chanukah, 111–112
chaplains: congressional, 108; legislative, 92, 104, 108–109, 112, 161; military, 28, 92, 100
charities, law of, 7, 32–33, 83–84, 120–121
Chase, William, 12
Cherokee Indians, 20
Chicago (Ill.), 77
child labor laws, 49–50, 157
children, rights of, 73
China, 38
Christianity, legal status of, 20, 28, 32–34, 41, 151–152, 156, 159
Christmas, 109–112, 161
Churches of God, 15
Civil Rights Act, 68, 70–71, 86, 156
Civil Rights Movement, 71–72
Civil War, 21–24, 37, 149, 152–153
Clay, Cassius (Muhammed Ali), 66

NEW FORUM BOOKS

New Forum Books makes available to general readers outstanding original inter-disciplinary scholarship with a special focus on the juncture of culture, law, and politics. New Forum Books is guided by the conviction that law and politics not only reflect culture but help to shape it. Authors include leading political scientists, sociologists, legal scholars, philosophers, theologians, historians, and economists writing for nonspecialist readers and scholars across a range of fields. Looking at questions such as political equality, the concept of rights, the problem of virtue in liberal politics, crime and punishment, population, poverty, economic develop-ment, and the international legal and political order, New Forum Books seeks to explain—not explain away—the difficult issues we face today.